WET HOT AMERICAN SUMMER

CHRISTOPHER HASTINGS • NOAH HAYES • REBECCA NALTY

BOOM!
STUDIOS

BOOM! STUDIOS   CLC

WET HOT AMERICAN SUMMER, November 2018. Published by BOOM! Studios, a division of Boom Entertainment, Inc. WET HOT AMERICAN SUMMER is ™ & © 2018 Enter These Dark Woods Co., LLC. All Rights Reserved. BOOM! Studios™ and the BOOM! Studios logo are trademarks of Boom Entertainment, Inc., registered in various countries and categories. All characters, events, and institutions depicted herein are fictional. Any similarity between any of the names, characters, persons, events, and/or institutions in this publication to actual names, characters, and persons, whether living or dead, events, and/or institutions is unintended and purely coincidental. BOOM! Studios does not read or accept unsolicited submissions of ideas, stories, or artwork.

For information regarding the CPSIA on this printed material, call: (203) 595-3636 and provide reference #RICH - 812280.

BOOM! Studios, 5670 Wilshire Boulevard, Suite 400, Los Angeles, CA 90036-5679. Printed in USA. First Printing.

ISBN: 978-1-68415-214-8, eISBN: 978-1-64144-029-5
Fried Pie Exclusive Edition, ISBN: 978-1-68415-344-2

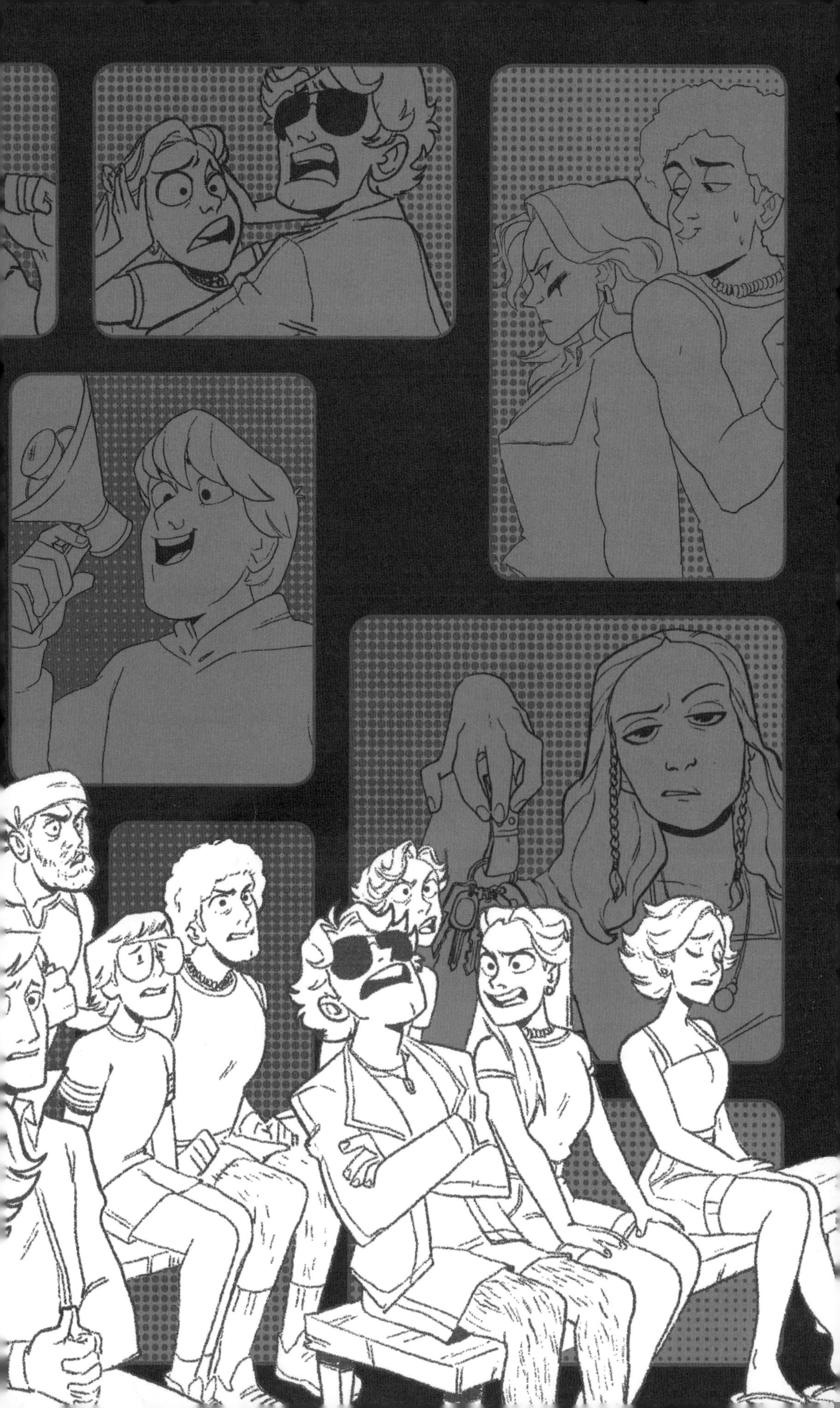

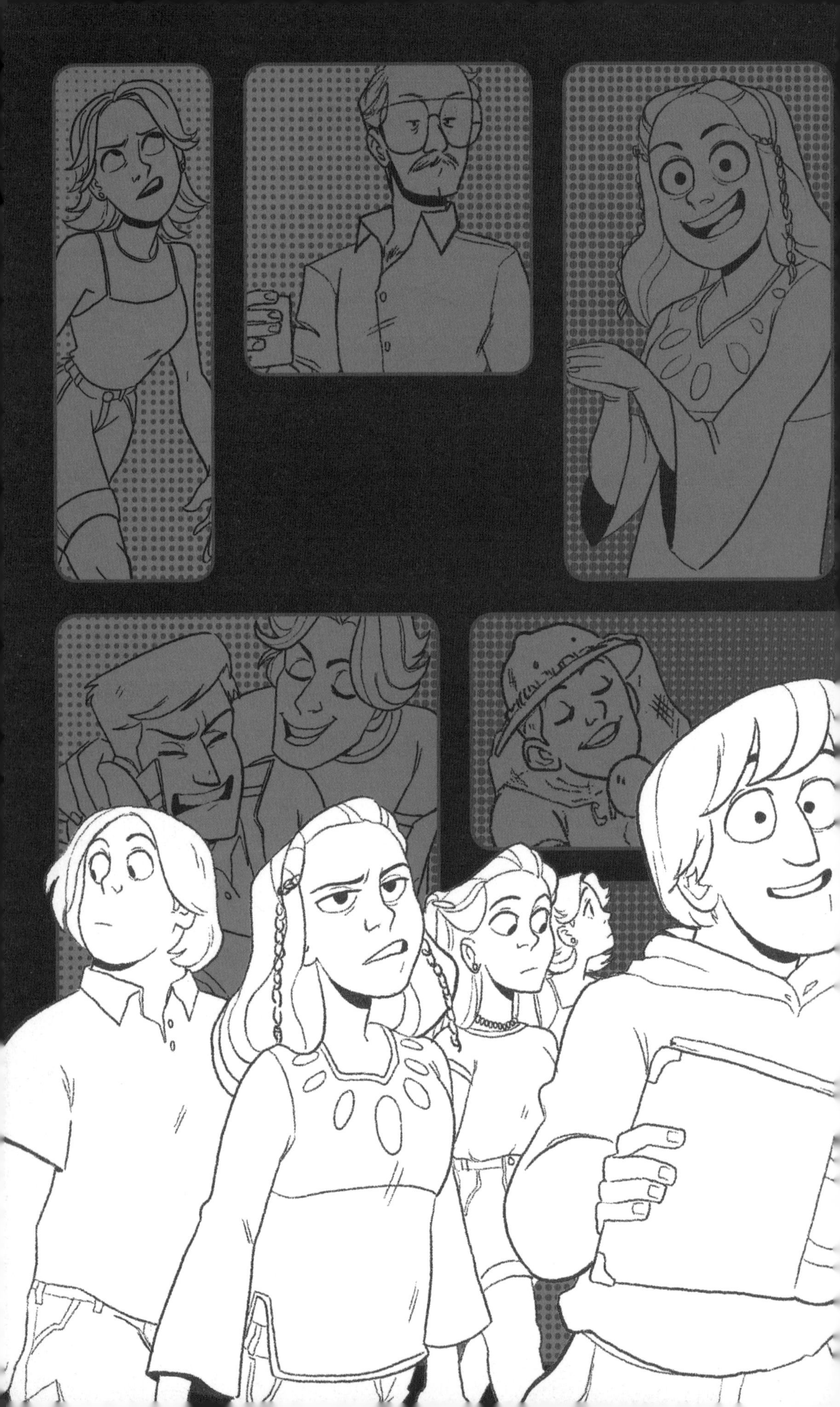

WRITTEN BY
CHRISTOPHER HASTINGS

ILLUSTRATED BY
NOAH HAYES

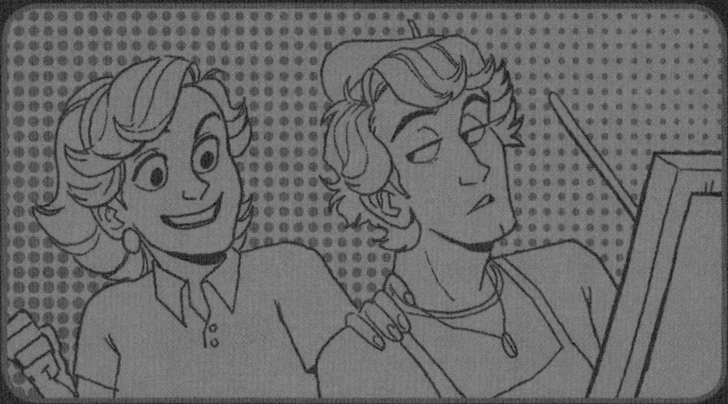

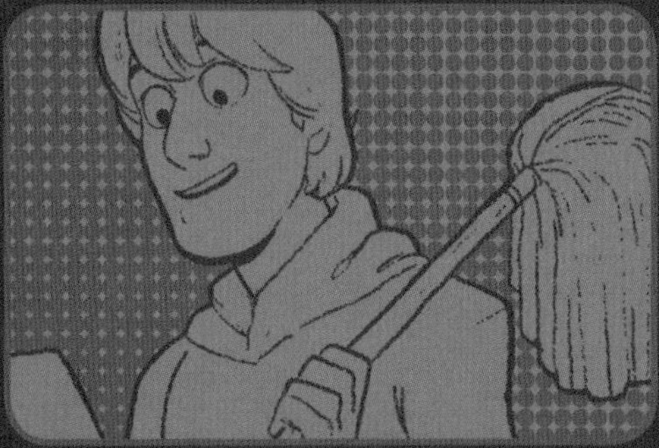

COLORED BY
REBECCA NALTY

LETTERED BY
JIM CAMPBELL

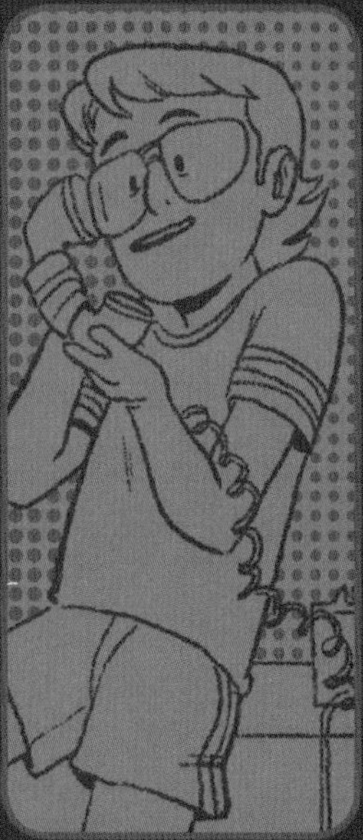

COVER BY
JOE QUINONES

FRIED PIE EXCLUSIVE COVER BY
JOE EISMA

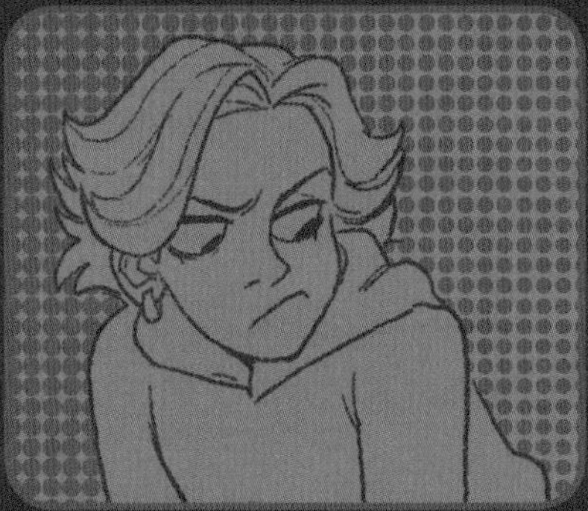

DESIGNER
JILLIAN CRAB

EDITOR
CHRIS ROSA

CREATIVE CONSULTANT
STEPHANIE MARLIS

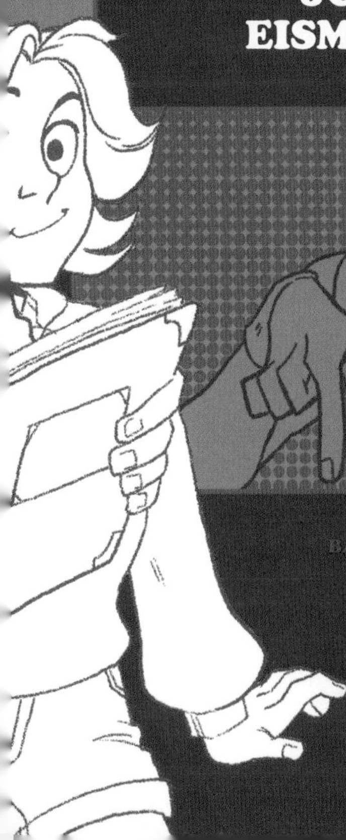

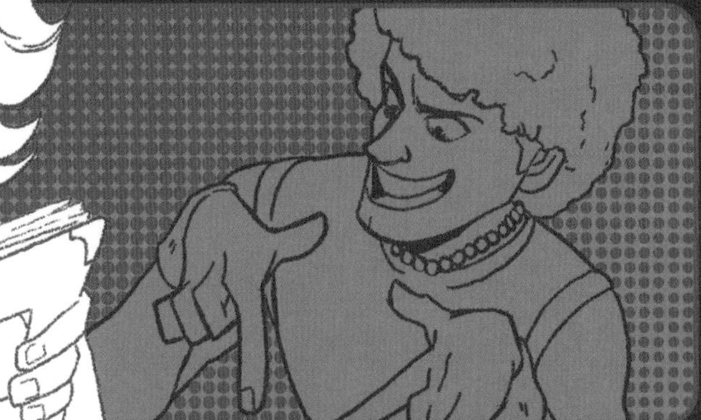

BASED ON CHARACTERS CREATED BY
MICHAEL SHOWALTER & DAVID WAIN

WET HOT AMERICAN SUMMER FILM PRODUCED BY
HOWARD BERNSTEIN

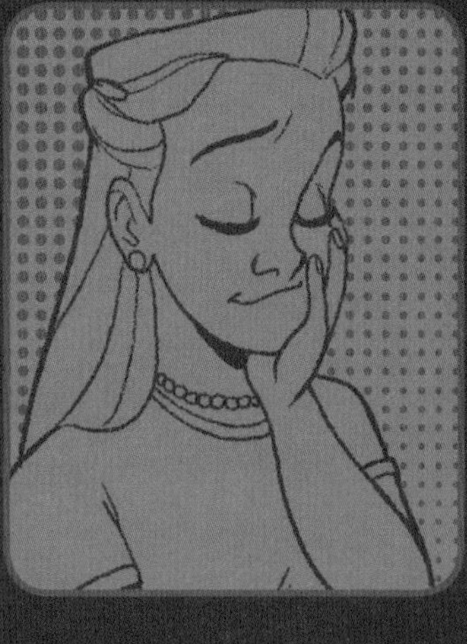

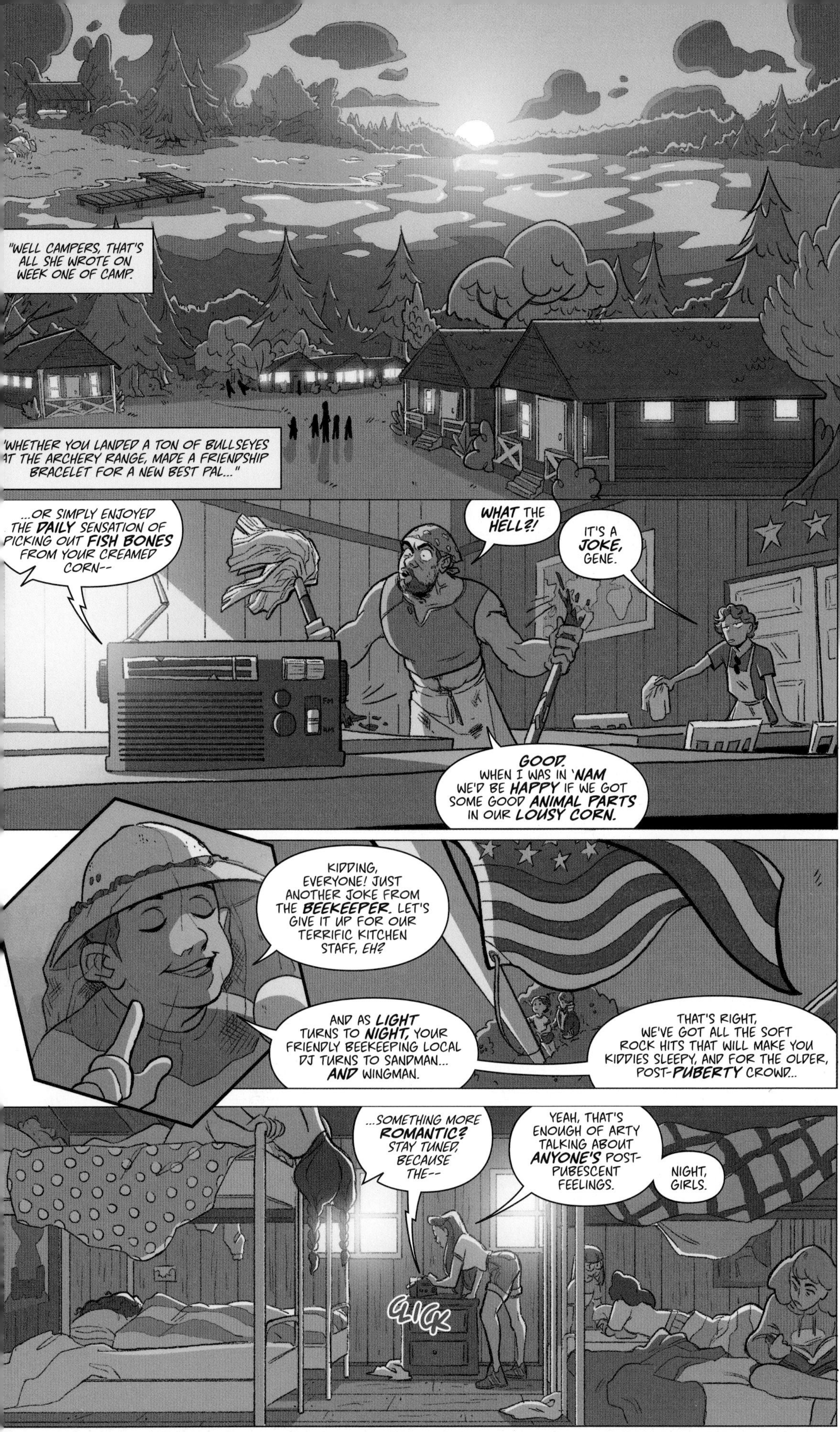
"WELL CAMPERS, THAT'S ALL SHE WROTE ON WEEK ONE OF CAMP.
"WHETHER YOU LANDED A TON OF BULLSEYES AT THE ARCHERY RANGE, MADE A FRIENDSHIP BRACELET FOR A NEW BEST PAL..."
...OR SIMPLY ENJOYED THE DAILY SENSATION OF PICKING OUT FISH BONES FROM YOUR CREAMED CORN--
WHAT THE HELL?!
IT'S A JOKE, GENE.
GOOD. WHEN I WAS IN 'NAM WE'D BE HAPPY IF WE GOT SOME GOOD ANIMAL PARTS IN OUR LOUSY CORN.
KIDDING, EVERYONE! JUST ANOTHER JOKE FROM THE BEEKEEPER. LET'S GIVE IT UP FOR OUR TERRIFIC KITCHEN STAFF, EH?
AND AS LIGHT TURNS TO NIGHT, YOUR FRIENDLY BEEKEEPING LOCAL DJ TURNS TO SANDMAN... AND WINGMAN.
THAT'S RIGHT, WE'VE GOT ALL THE SOFT ROCK HITS THAT WILL MAKE YOU KIDDIES SLEEPY, AND FOR THE OLDER, POST-PUBERTY CROWD...
...SOMETHING MORE ROMANTIC? STAY TUNED, BECAUSE THE--
YEAH, THAT'S ENOUGH OF ARTY TALKING ABOUT ANYONE'S POST-PUBESCENT FEELINGS.
NIGHT, GIRLS.
CLICK

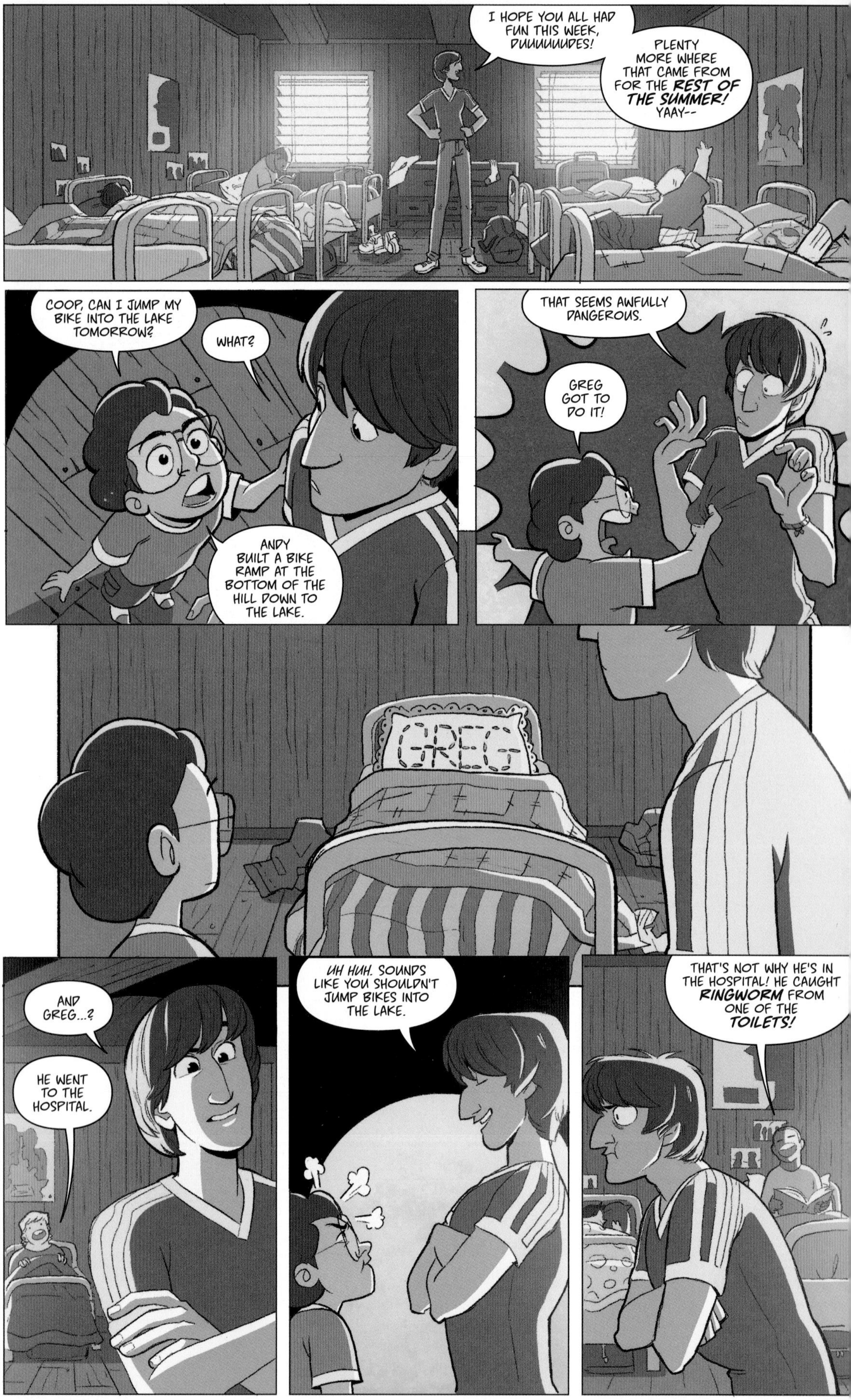
I HOPE YOU ALL HAD FUN THIS WEEK, DUUUUUUDES!
PLENTY MORE WHERE THAT CAME FROM FOR THE **REST OF THE SUMMER!** YAAY--
COOP, CAN I JUMP MY BIKE INTO THE LAKE TOMORROW?
WHAT?
ANDY BUILT A BIKE RAMP AT THE BOTTOM OF THE HILL DOWN TO THE LAKE.
THAT SEEMS AWFULLY DANGEROUS.
GREG GOT TO DO IT!
GREG
AND GREG...?
HE WENT TO THE HOSPITAL.
UH HUH. SOUNDS LIKE YOU SHOULDN'T JUMP BIKES INTO THE LAKE.
THAT'S NOT WHY HE'S IN THE HOSPITAL! HE CAUGHT **RINGWORM** FROM ONE OF THE **TOILETS!**

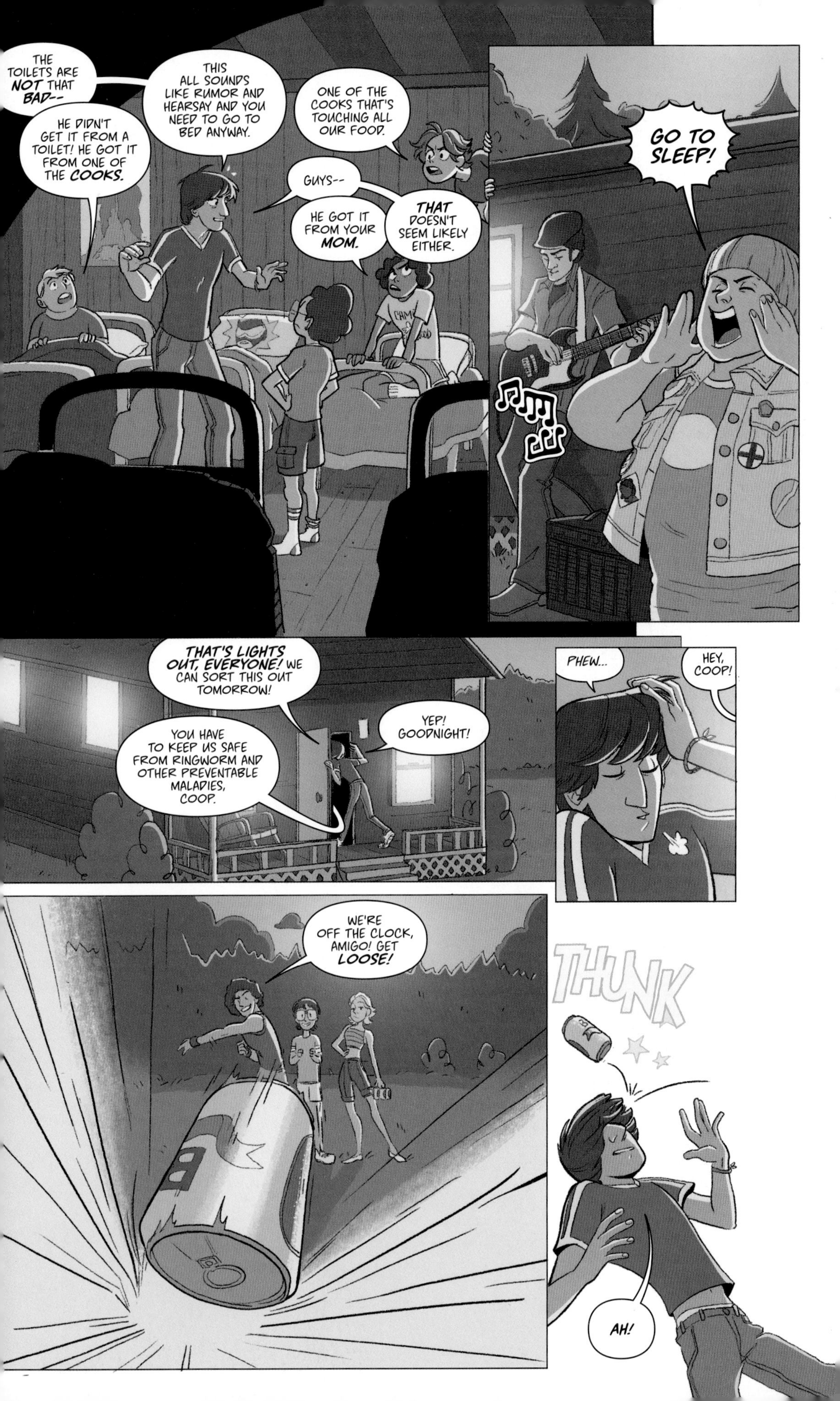
THE TOILETS ARE NOT THAT BAD--
HE DIDN'T GET IT FROM A TOILET! HE GOT IT FROM ONE OF THE COOKS.
THIS ALL SOUNDS LIKE RUMOR AND HEARSAY AND YOU NEED TO GO TO BED ANYWAY.
ONE OF THE COOKS THAT'S TOUCHING ALL OUR FOOD.
GUYS--
HE GOT IT FROM YOUR MOM.
THAT DOESN'T SEEM LIKELY EITHER.
GO TO SLEEP!
THAT'S LIGHTS OUT, EVERYONE! WE CAN SORT THIS OUT TOMORROW!
YOU HAVE TO KEEP US SAFE FROM RINGWORM AND OTHER PREVENTABLE MALADIES, COOP.
YEP! GOODNIGHT!
PHEW...
HEY, COOP!
WE'RE OFF THE CLOCK, AMIGO! GET LOOSE!
THUNK
AH!

9:57 PM

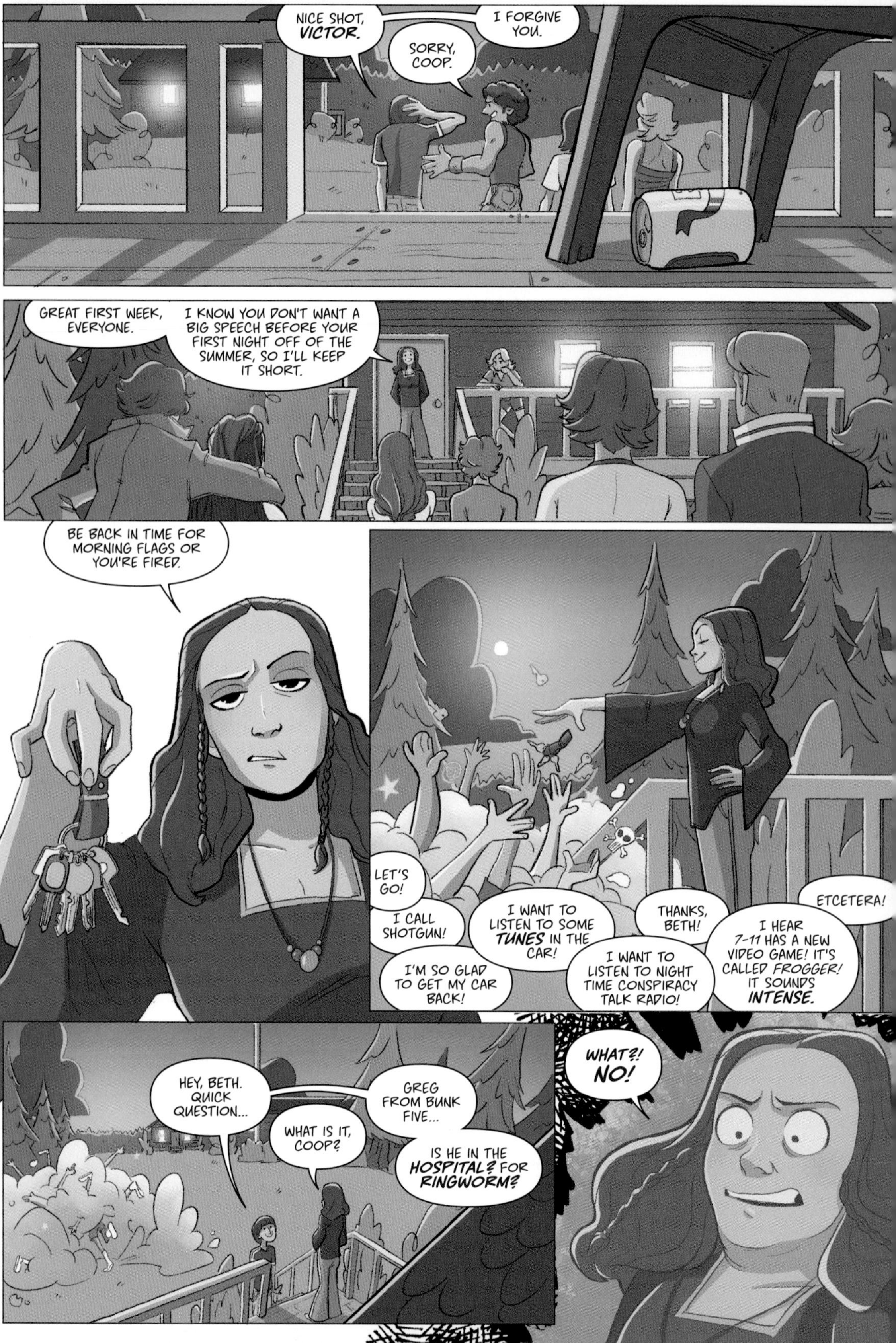

NICE SHOT, VICTOR.
SORRY, COOP.
I FORGIVE YOU.
GREAT FIRST WEEK, EVERYONE.
I KNOW YOU DON'T WANT A BIG SPEECH BEFORE YOUR FIRST NIGHT OFF OF THE SUMMER, SO I'LL KEEP IT SHORT.
BE BACK IN TIME FOR MORNING FLAGS OR YOU'RE FIRED.
LET'S GO!
I CALL SHOTGUN!
I'M SO GLAD TO GET MY CAR BACK!
I WANT TO LISTEN TO SOME TUNES IN THE CAR!
THANKS, BETH!
I WANT TO LISTEN TO NIGHT TIME CONSPIRACY TALK RADIO!
I HEAR 7-11 HAS A NEW VIDEO GAME! IT'S CALLED FROGGER! IT SOUNDS INTENSE.
ETCETERA!
HEY, BETH. QUICK QUESTION...
WHAT IS IT, COOP?
GREG FROM BUNK FIVE...
IS HE IN THE HOSPITAL? FOR RINGWORM?
WHAT?! NO!

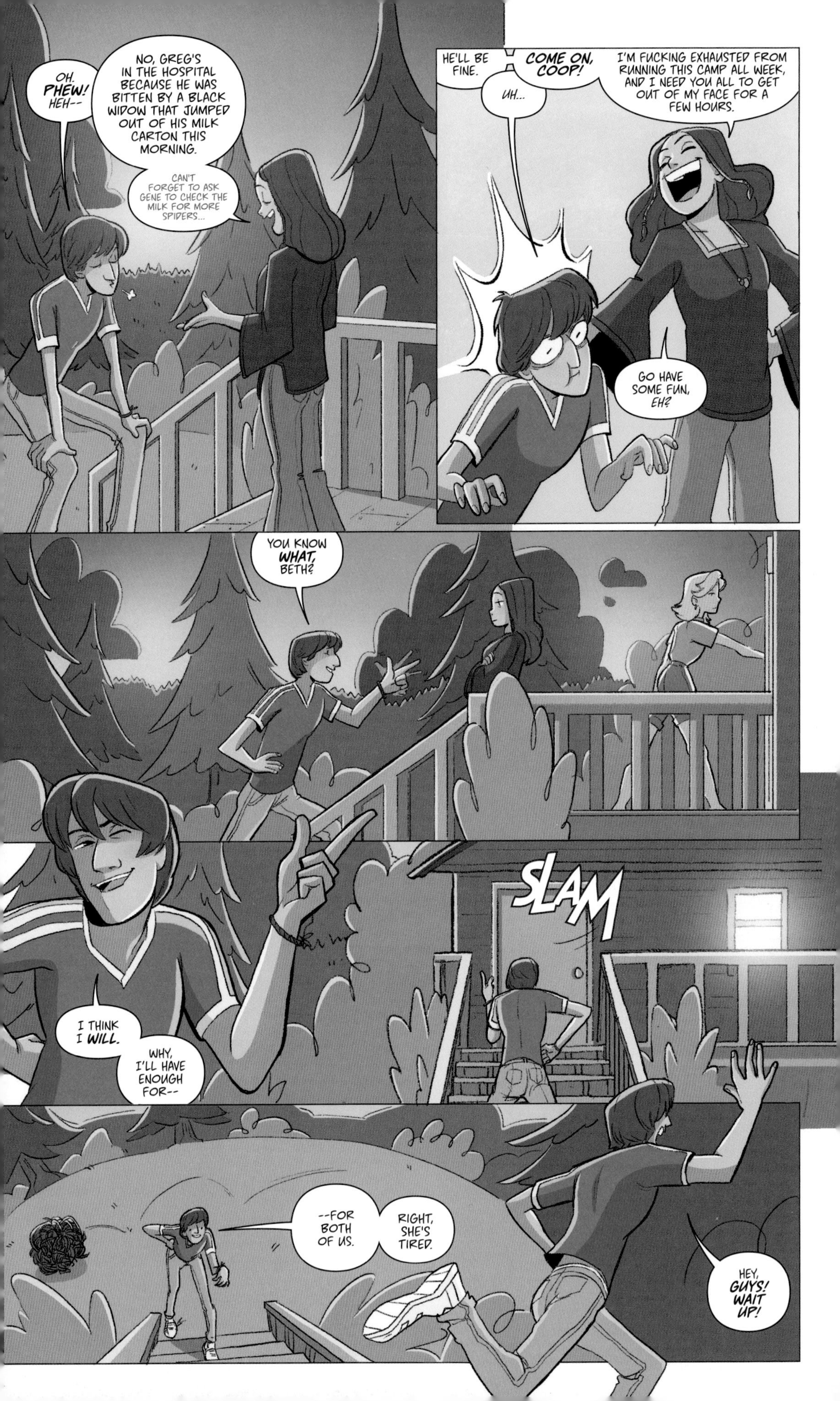

OH. PHEW! HEH--
NO, GREG'S IN THE HOSPITAL BECAUSE HE WAS BITTEN BY A BLACK WIDOW THAT JUMPED OUT OF HIS MILK CARTON THIS MORNING.
CAN'T FORGET TO ASK GENE TO CHECK THE MILK FOR MORE SPIDERS...
HE'LL BE FINE.
UH...
COME ON, COOP!
I'M FUCKING EXHAUSTED FROM RUNNING THIS CAMP ALL WEEK, AND I NEED YOU ALL TO GET OUT OF MY FACE FOR A FEW HOURS.
GO HAVE SOME FUN, EH?
YOU KNOW WHAT, BETH?
I THINK I WILL.
WHY, I'LL HAVE ENOUGH FOR--
SLAM
--FOR BOTH OF US.
RIGHT, SHE'S TIRED.
HEY, GUYS! WAIT UP!

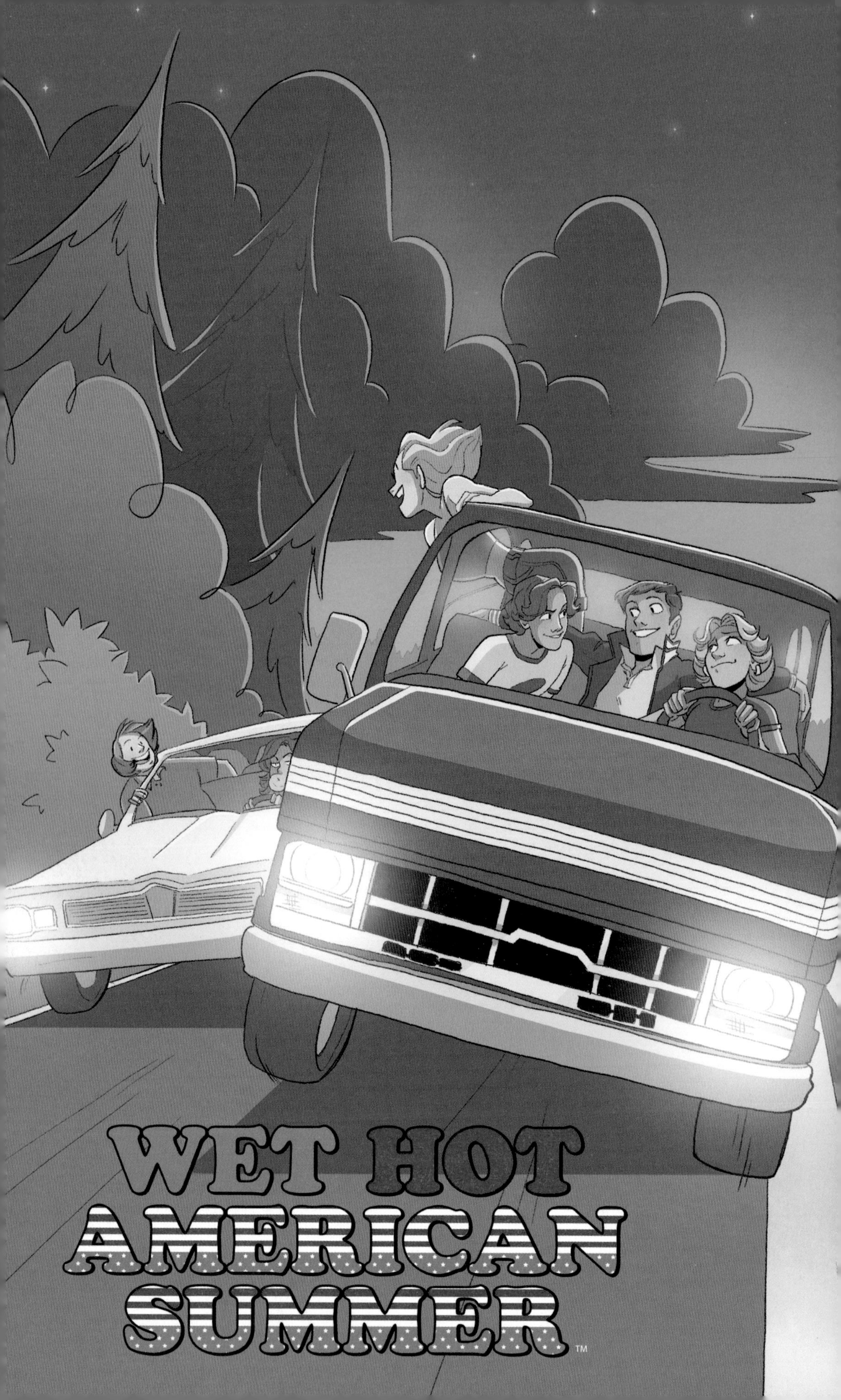

WET HOT
AMERICAN
SUMMER™

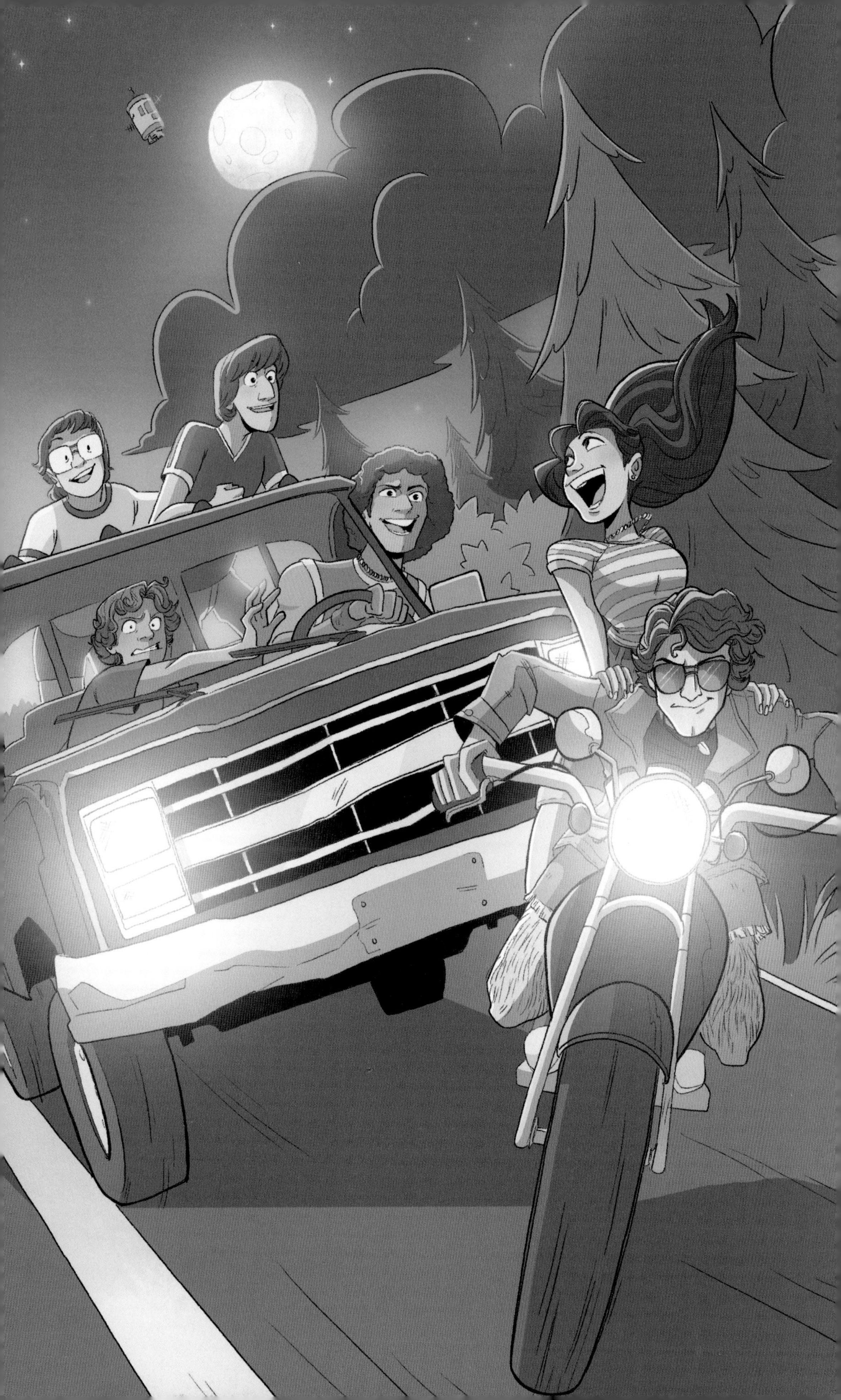

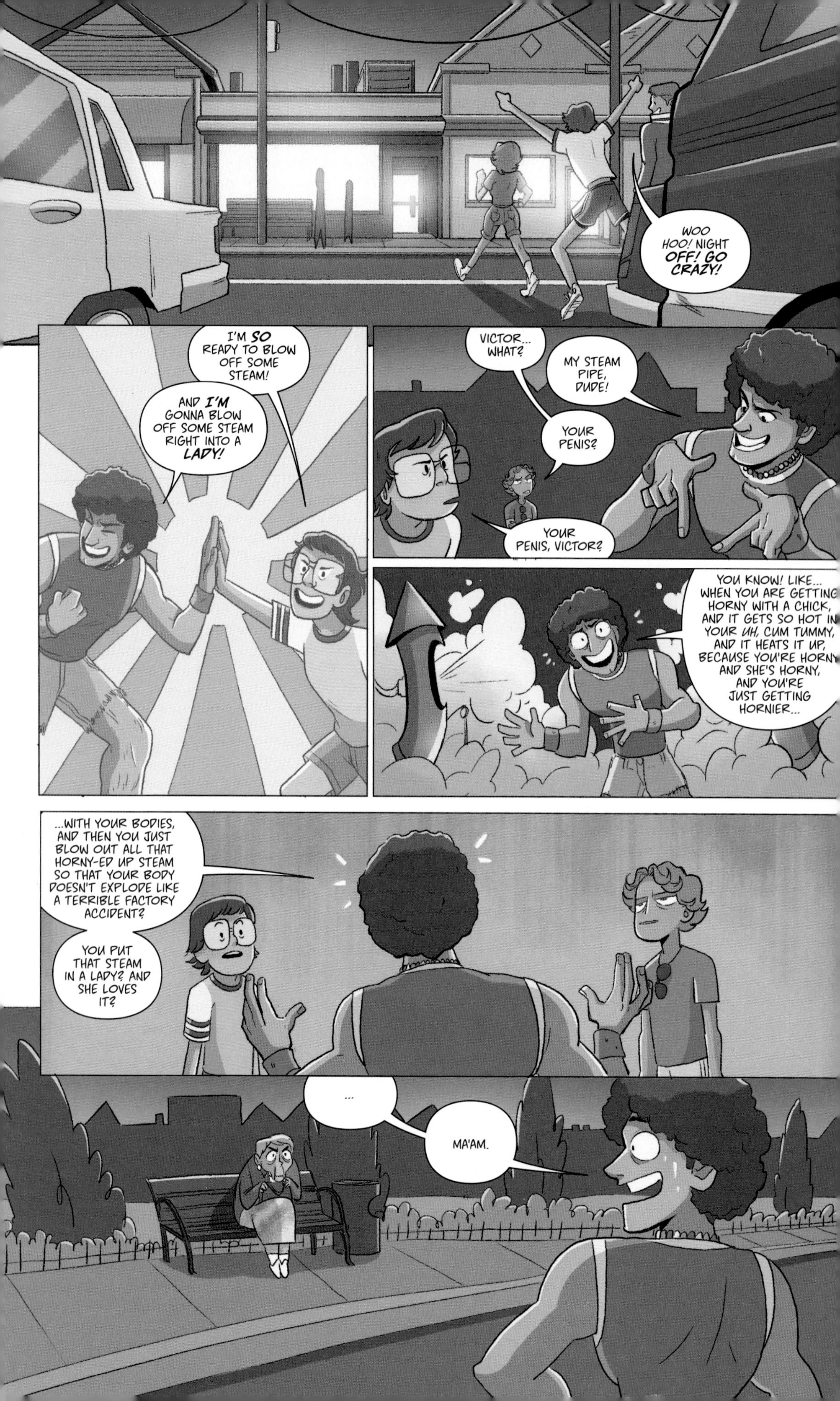
WOO HOO! NIGHT OFF! GO CRAZY!
I'M SO READY TO BLOW OFF SOME STEAM!
AND I'M GONNA BLOW OFF SOME STEAM RIGHT INTO A LADY!
VICTOR... WHAT?
MY STEAM PIPE, DUDE!
YOUR PENIS?
YOUR PENIS, VICTOR?
YOU KNOW! LIKE... WHEN YOU ARE GETTING HORNY WITH A CHICK, AND IT GETS SO HOT IN YOUR UH, CUM TUMMY, AND IT HEATS IT UP, BECAUSE YOU'RE HORNY AND SHE'S HORNY, AND YOU'RE JUST GETTING HORNIER...
...WITH YOUR BODIES, AND THEN YOU JUST BLOW OUT ALL THAT HORNY-ED UP STEAM SO THAT YOUR BODY DOESN'T EXPLODE LIKE A TERRIBLE FACTORY ACCIDENT?
YOU PUT THAT STEAM IN A LADY? AND SHE LOVES IT?
...
MA'AM.

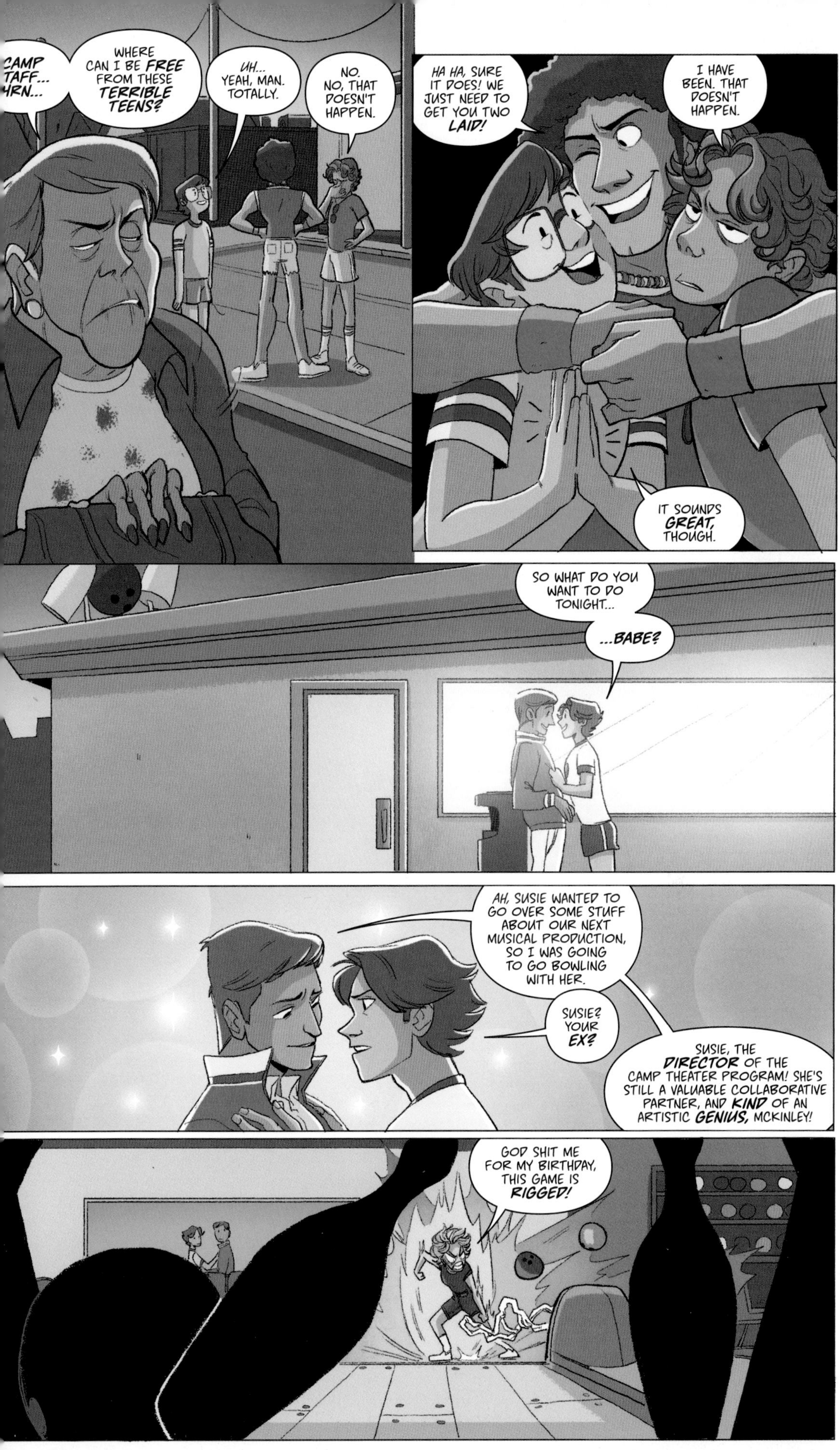
CAMP STAFF... HRN...
WHERE CAN I BE FREE FROM THESE TERRIBLE TEENS?
UH... YEAH, MAN. TOTALLY.
NO. NO, THAT DOESN'T HAPPEN.
HA HA, SURE IT DOES! WE JUST NEED TO GET YOU TWO LAID!
I HAVE BEEN. THAT DOESN'T HAPPEN.
IT SOUNDS GREAT, THOUGH.
SO WHAT DO YOU WANT TO DO TONIGHT...
...BABE?
AH, SUSIE WANTED TO GO OVER SOME STUFF ABOUT OUR NEXT MUSICAL PRODUCTION, SO I WAS GOING TO GO BOWLING WITH HER.
SUSIE? YOUR EX?
SUSIE, THE DIRECTOR OF THE CAMP THEATER PROGRAM! SHE'S STILL A VALUABLE COLLABORATIVE PARTNER, AND KIND OF AN ARTISTIC GENIUS, MCKINLEY!
GOD SHIT ME FOR MY BIRTHDAY, THIS GAME IS RIGGED!

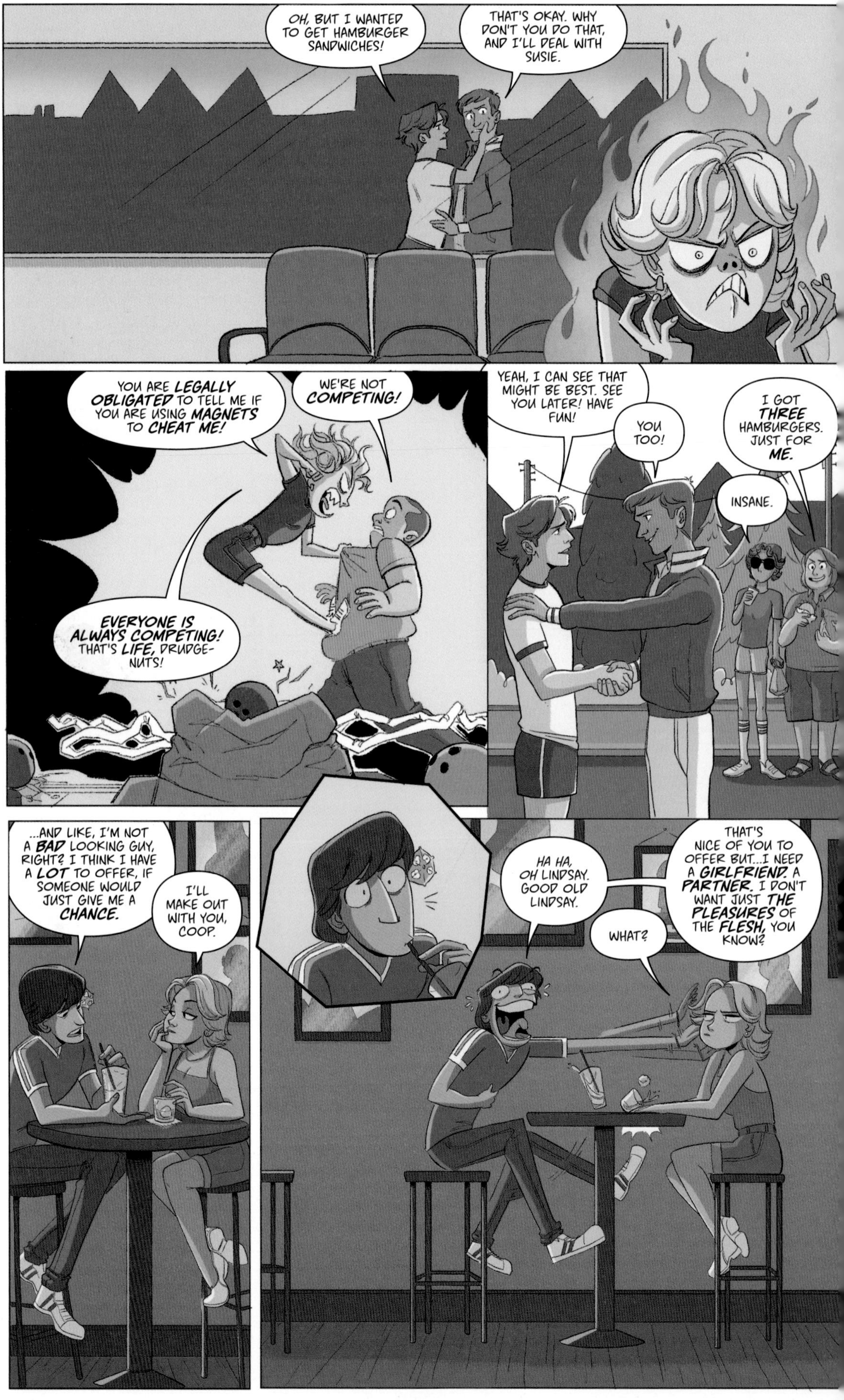
OH, BUT I WANTED TO GET HAMBURGER SANDWICHES!
THAT'S OKAY. WHY DON'T YOU DO THAT, AND I'LL DEAL WITH SUSIE.
YOU ARE LEGALLY OBLIGATED TO TELL ME IF YOU ARE USING MAGNETS TO CHEAT ME!
WE'RE NOT COMPETING!
EVERYONE IS ALWAYS COMPETING! THAT'S LIFE, DRUDGE-NUTS!
YEAH, I CAN SEE THAT MIGHT BE BEST. SEE YOU LATER! HAVE FUN!
YOU TOO!
I GOT THREE HAMBURGERS. JUST FOR ME.
INSANE.
...AND LIKE, I'M NOT A BAD LOOKING GUY, RIGHT? I THINK I HAVE A LOT TO OFFER, IF SOMEONE WOULD JUST GIVE ME A CHANCE.
I'LL MAKE OUT WITH YOU, COOP.
HA HA, OH LINDSAY. GOOD OLD LINDSAY.
THAT'S NICE OF YOU TO OFFER BUT...I NEED A GIRLFRIEND. A PARTNER. I DON'T WANT JUST THE PLEASURES OF THE FLESH, YOU KNOW?
WHAT?

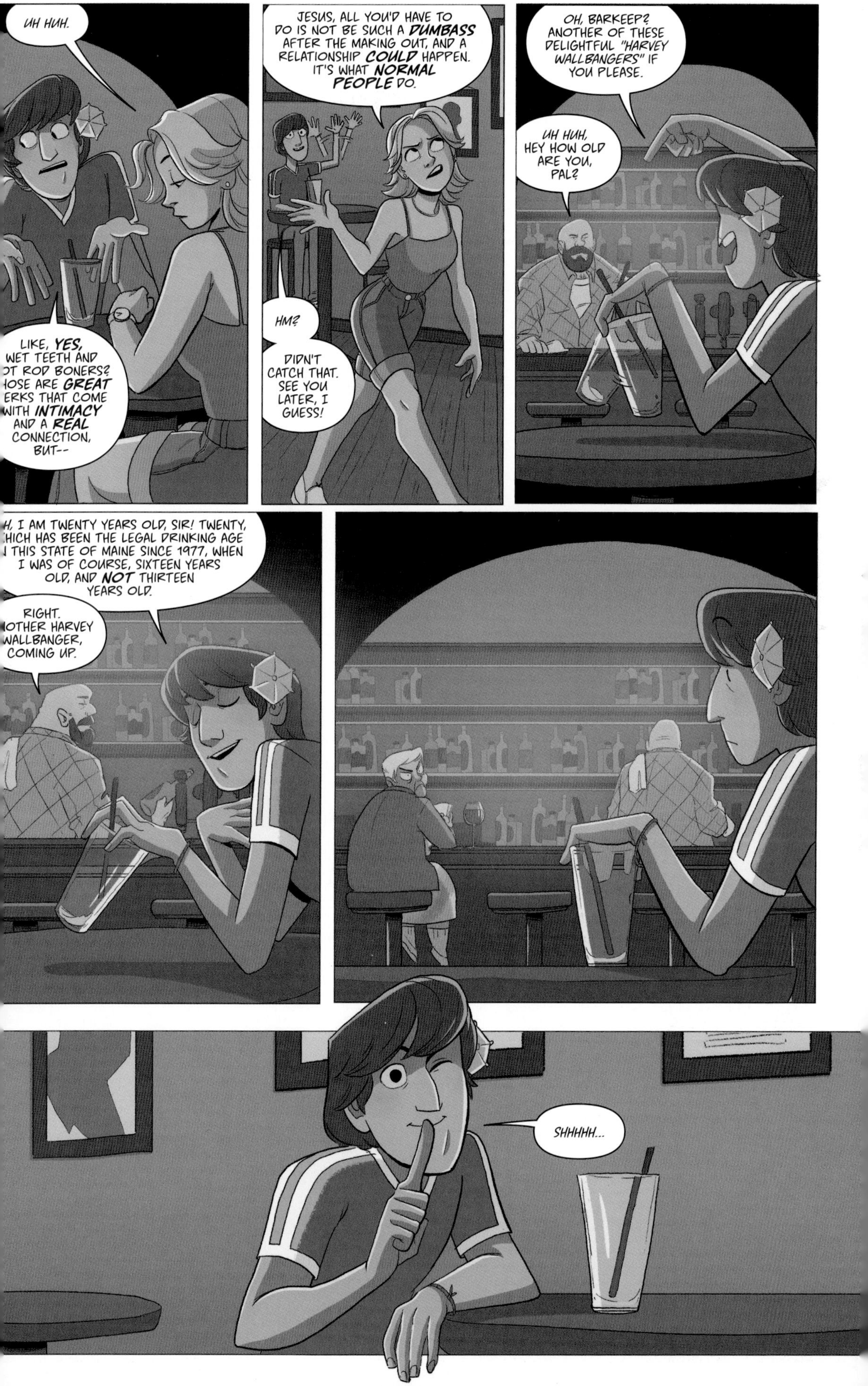
UH HUH.
LIKE, YES, WET TEETH AND OT ROD BONERS? HOSE ARE GREAT ERKS THAT COME WITH INTIMACY AND A REAL CONNECTION, BUT--
JESUS, ALL YOU'D HAVE TO DO IS NOT BE SUCH A DUMBASS AFTER THE MAKING OUT, AND A RELATIONSHIP COULD HAPPEN. IT'S WHAT NORMAL PEOPLE DO.
HM?
DIDN'T CATCH THAT. SEE YOU LATER, I GUESS!
OH, BARKEEP? ANOTHER OF THESE DELIGHTFUL "HARVEY WALLBANGERS" IF YOU PLEASE.
UH HUH, HEY HOW OLD ARE YOU, PAL?
H, I AM TWENTY YEARS OLD, SIR! TWENTY, HICH HAS BEEN THE LEGAL DRINKING AGE N THIS STATE OF MAINE SINCE 1977, WHEN I WAS OF COURSE, SIXTEEN YEARS OLD, AND NOT THIRTEEN YEARS OLD.
RIGHT. NOTHER HARVEY WALLBANGER, COMING UP.
SHHHHH...

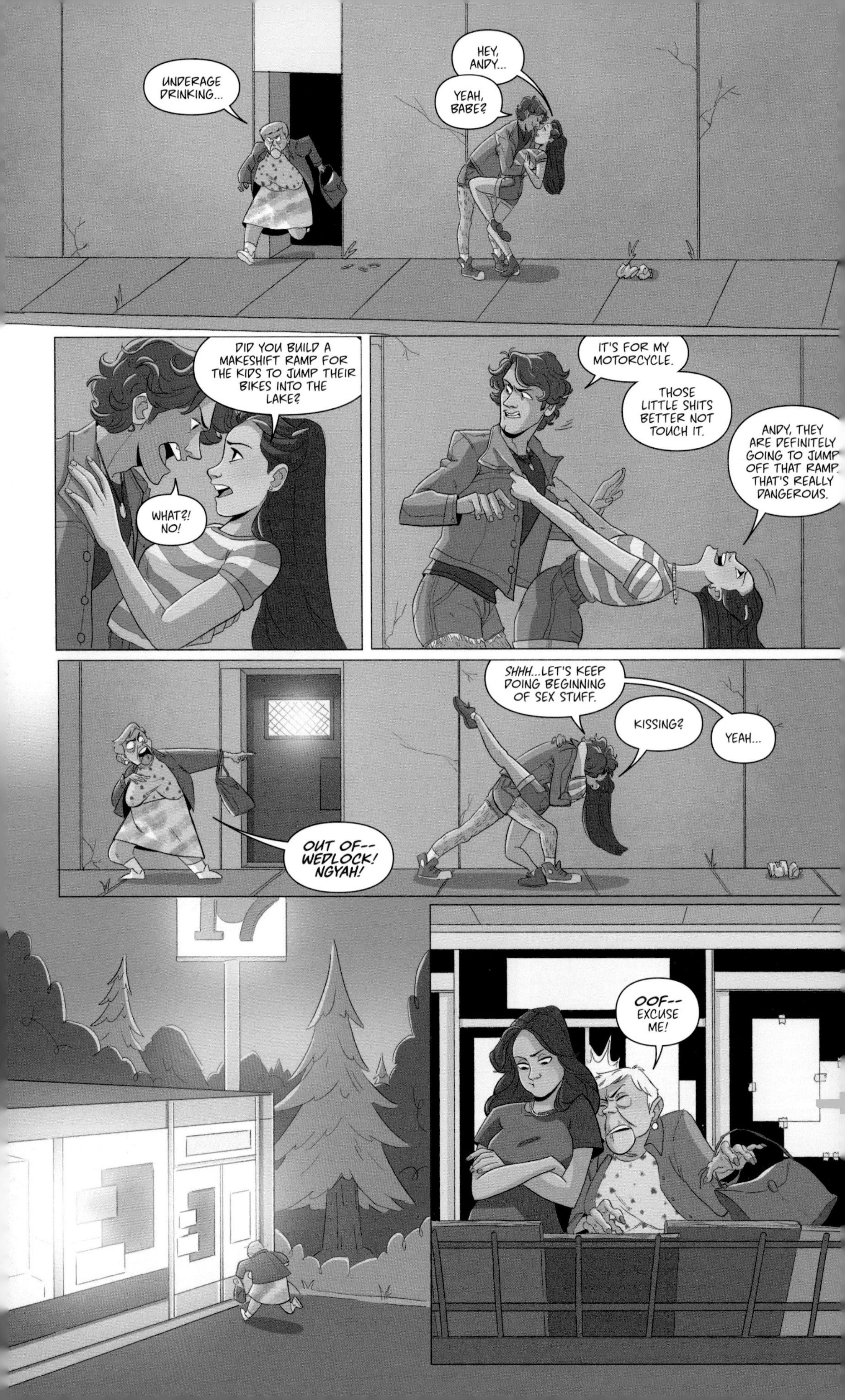
UNDERAGE DRINKING...
HEY, ANDY...
YEAH, BABE?
DID YOU BUILD A MAKESHIFT RAMP FOR THE KIDS TO JUMP THEIR BIKES INTO THE LAKE?
WHAT?! NO!
IT'S FOR MY MOTORCYCLE.
THOSE LITTLE SHITS BETTER NOT TOUCH IT.
ANDY, THEY ARE DEFINITELY GOING TO JUMP OFF THAT RAMP. THAT'S REALLY DANGEROUS.
SHHH...LET'S KEEP DOING BEGINNING OF SEX STUFF.
KISSING?
YEAH...
OUT OF-- WEDLOCK! NGYAH!
OOF-- EXCUSE ME!

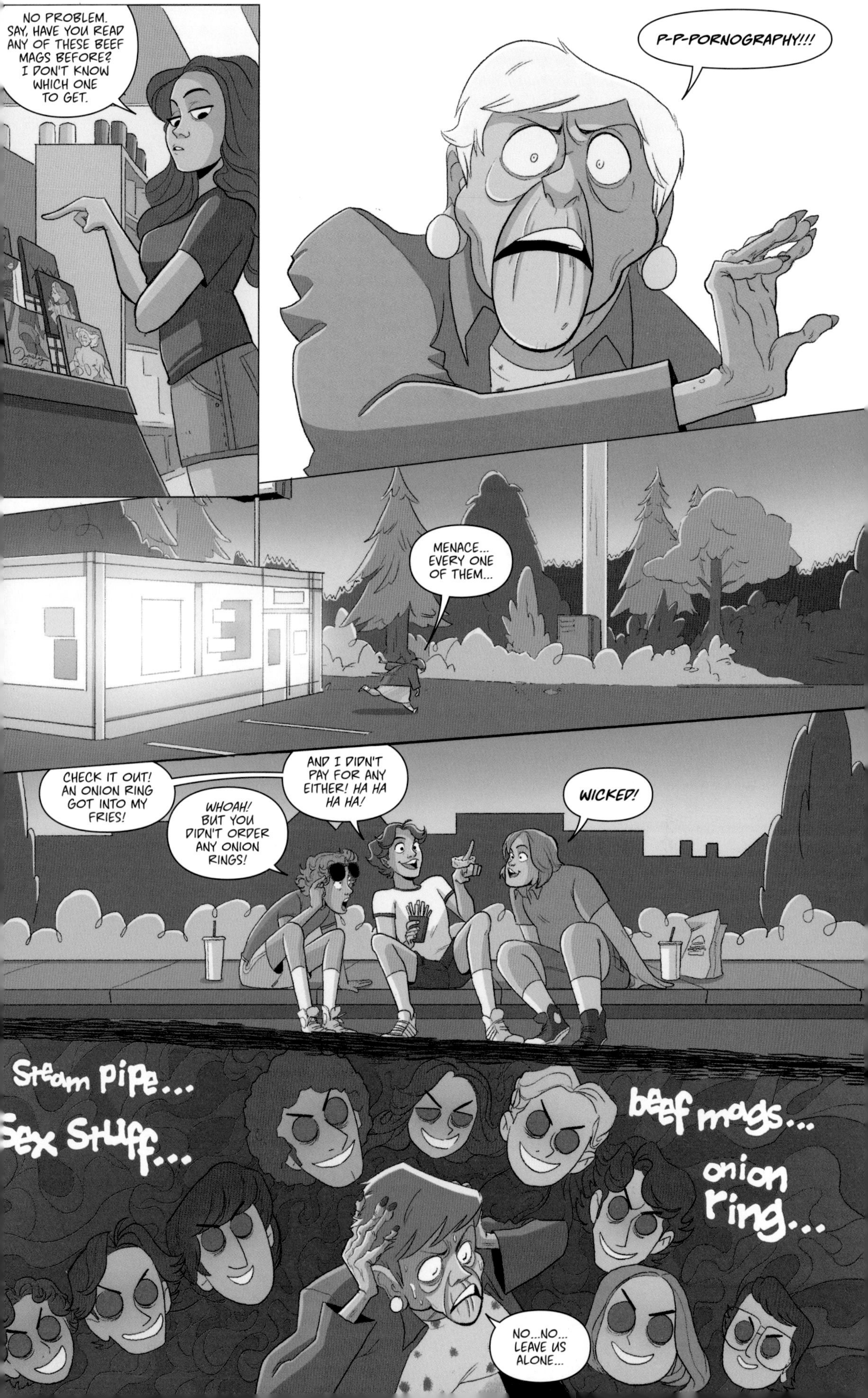
NO PROBLEM. SAY, HAVE YOU READ ANY OF THESE BEEF MAGS BEFORE? I DON'T KNOW WHICH ONE TO GET.
P-P-PORNOGRAPHY!!!
MENACE... EVERY ONE OF THEM...
CHECK IT OUT! AN ONION RING GOT INTO MY FRIES!
WHOAH! BUT YOU DIDN'T ORDER ANY ONION RINGS!
AND I DIDN'T PAY FOR ANY EITHER! HA HA HA HA!
WICKED!
Steam pipe...
Sex Stuff...
beef mags...
onion ring...
NO...NO... LEAVE US ALONE...

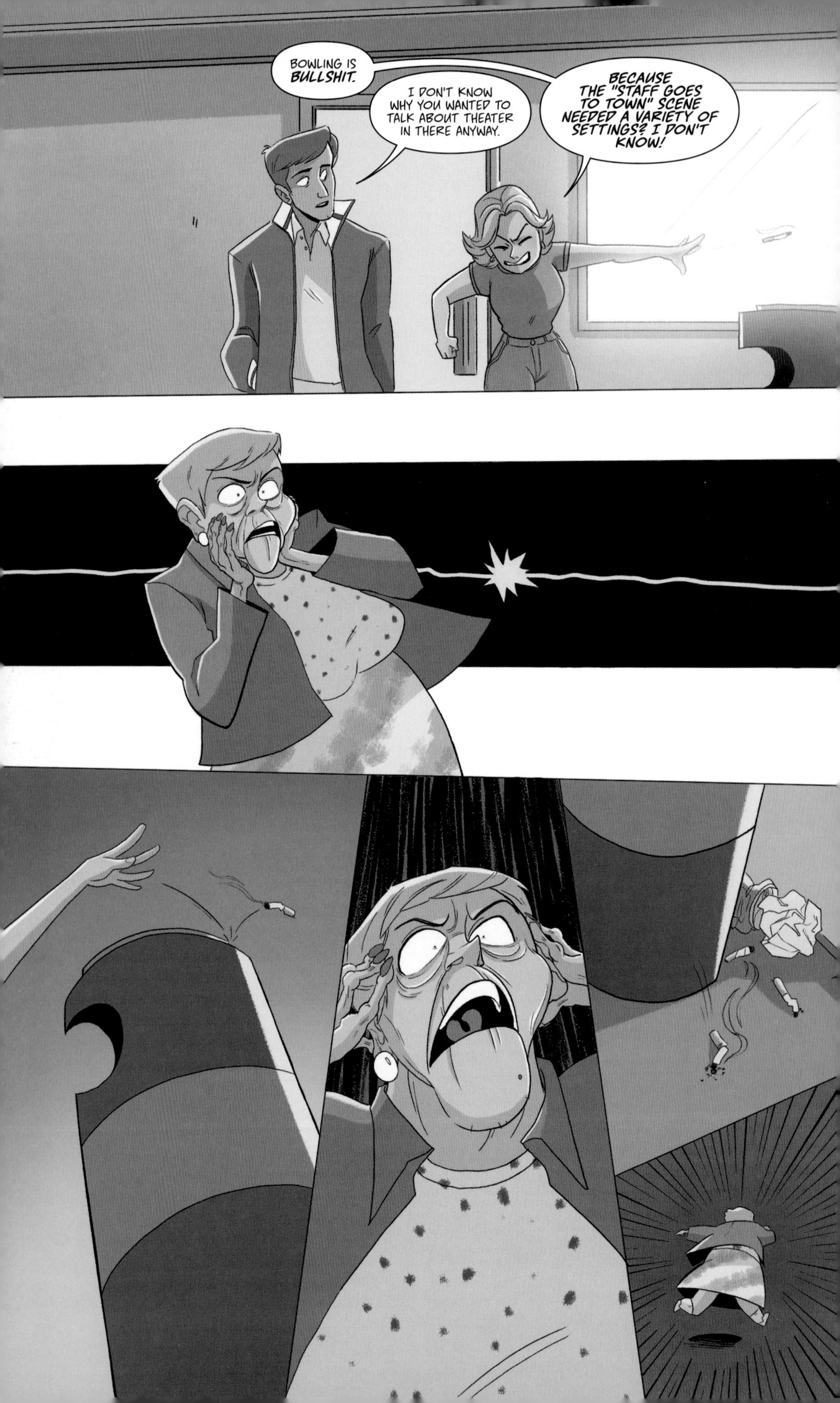

BOWLING IS **BULLSHIT.**
I DON'T KNOW WHY YOU WANTED TO TALK ABOUT THEATER IN THERE ANYWAY.
BECAUSE THE "STAFF GOES TO TOWN" SCENE NEEDED A VARIETY OF SETTINGS? I DON'T KNOW!

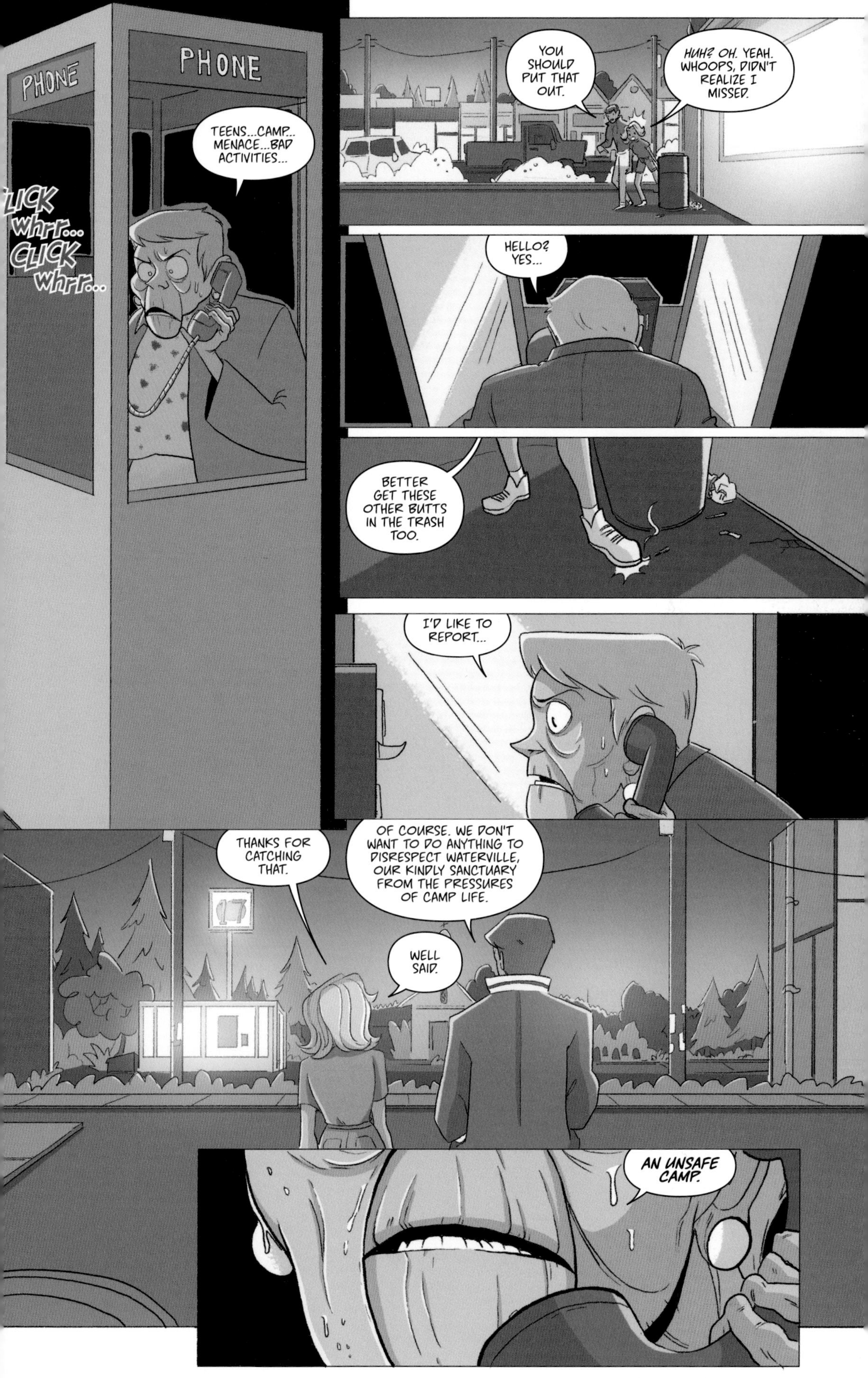
PHONE
PHONE
TEENS...CAMP... MENACE...BAD ACTIVITIES...
LICK whrr... CLICK whrr...
YOU SHOULD PUT THAT OUT.
HUH? OH. YEAH. WHOOPS, DIDN'T REALIZE I MISSED.
HELLO? YES...
BETTER GET THESE OTHER BUTTS IN THE TRASH TOO.
I'D LIKE TO REPORT...
THANKS FOR CATCHING THAT.
OF COURSE. WE DON'T WANT TO DO ANYTHING TO DISRESPECT WATERVILLE, OUR KINDLY SANCTUARY FROM THE PRESSURES OF CAMP LIFE.
WELL SAID.
AN UNSAFE CAMP.

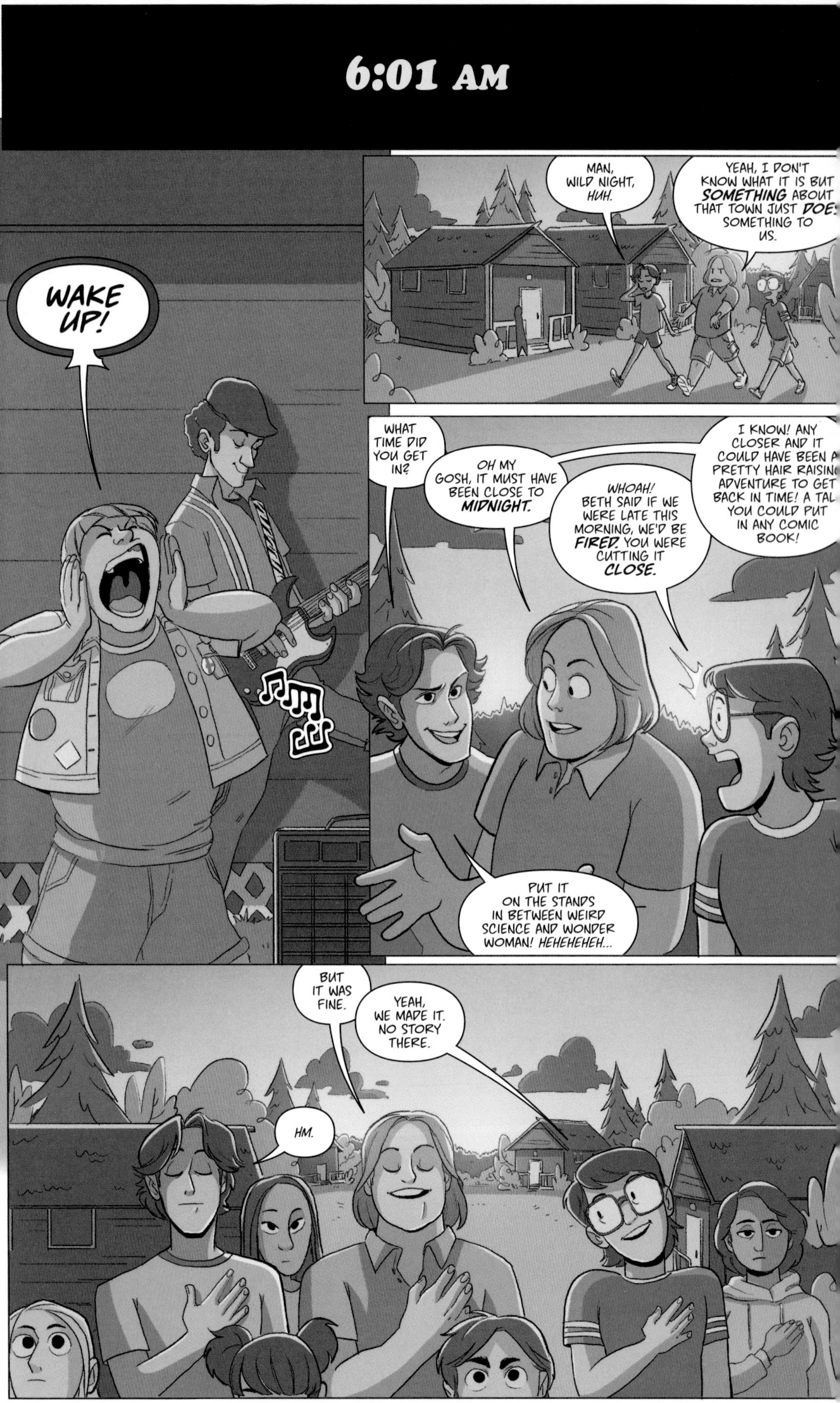
6:01 AM
WAKE UP!
MAN, WILD NIGHT, HUH.
YEAH, I DON'T KNOW WHAT IT IS BUT SOMETHING ABOUT THAT TOWN JUST DOES SOMETHING TO US.
WHAT TIME DID YOU GET IN?
OH MY GOSH, IT MUST HAVE BEEN CLOSE TO MIDNIGHT.
WHOAH! BETH SAID IF WE WERE LATE THIS MORNING, WE'D BE FIRED. YOU WERE CUTTING IT CLOSE.
I KNOW! ANY CLOSER AND IT COULD HAVE BEEN A PRETTY HAIR RAISING ADVENTURE TO GET BACK IN TIME! A TALE YOU COULD PUT IN ANY COMIC BOOK!
PUT IT ON THE STANDS IN BETWEEN WEIRD SCIENCE AND WONDER WOMAN! HEHEHEHEH...
BUT IT WAS FINE.
YEAH, WE MADE IT. NO STORY THERE.
HM.

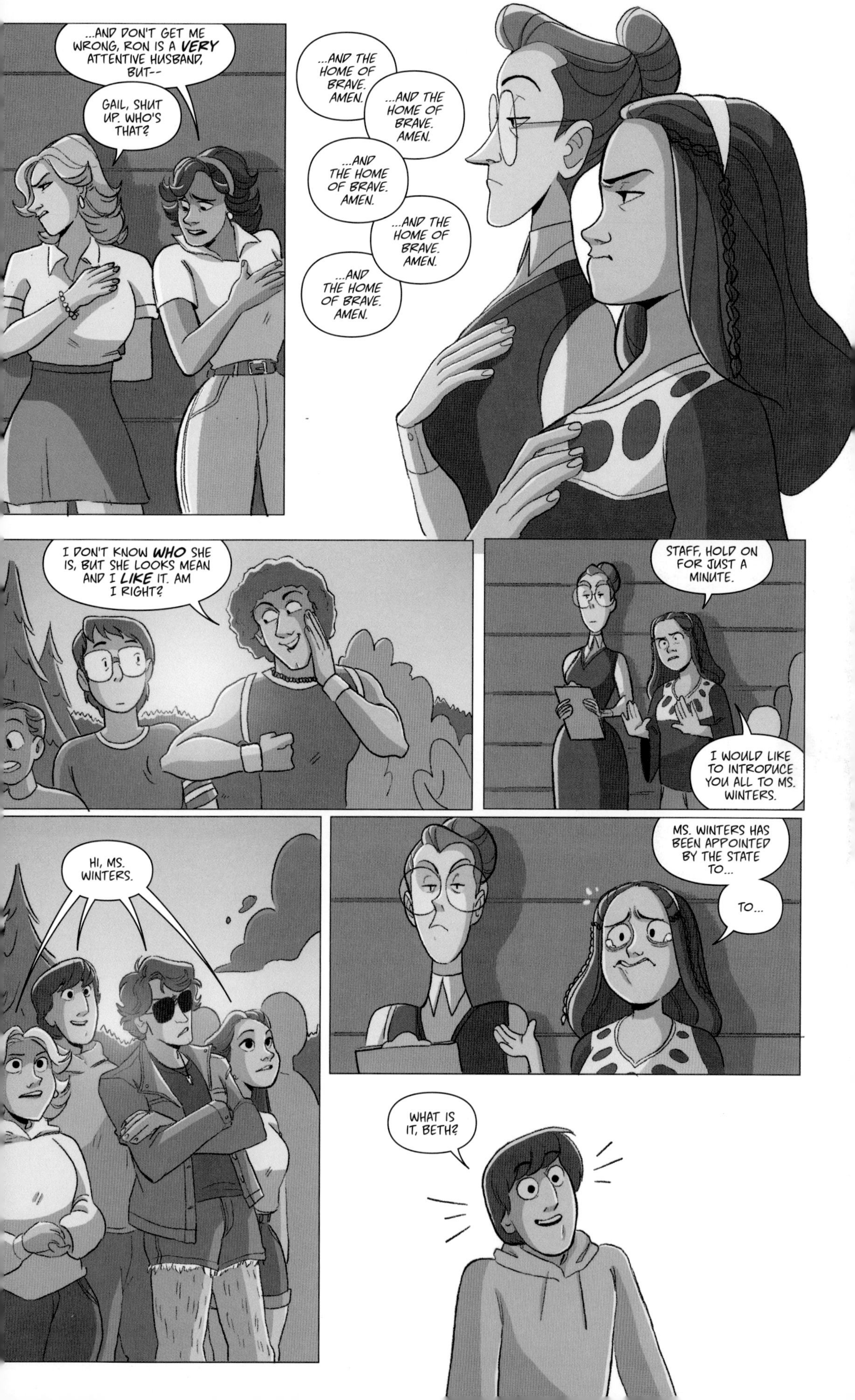
...AND DON'T GET ME WRONG, RON IS A VERY ATTENTIVE HUSBAND, BUT--
GAIL, SHUT UP. WHO'S THAT?
...AND THE HOME OF BRAVE. AMEN.
...AND THE HOME OF BRAVE. AMEN.
...AND THE HOME OF BRAVE. AMEN.
...AND THE HOME OF BRAVE. AMEN.
...AND THE HOME OF BRAVE. AMEN.
I DON'T KNOW WHO SHE IS, BUT SHE LOOKS MEAN AND I LIKE IT. AM I RIGHT?
STAFF, HOLD ON FOR JUST A MINUTE.
I WOULD LIKE TO INTRODUCE YOU ALL TO MS. WINTERS.
HI, MS. WINTERS.
MS. WINTERS HAS BEEN APPOINTED BY THE STATE TO...
TO...
WHAT IS IT, BETH?

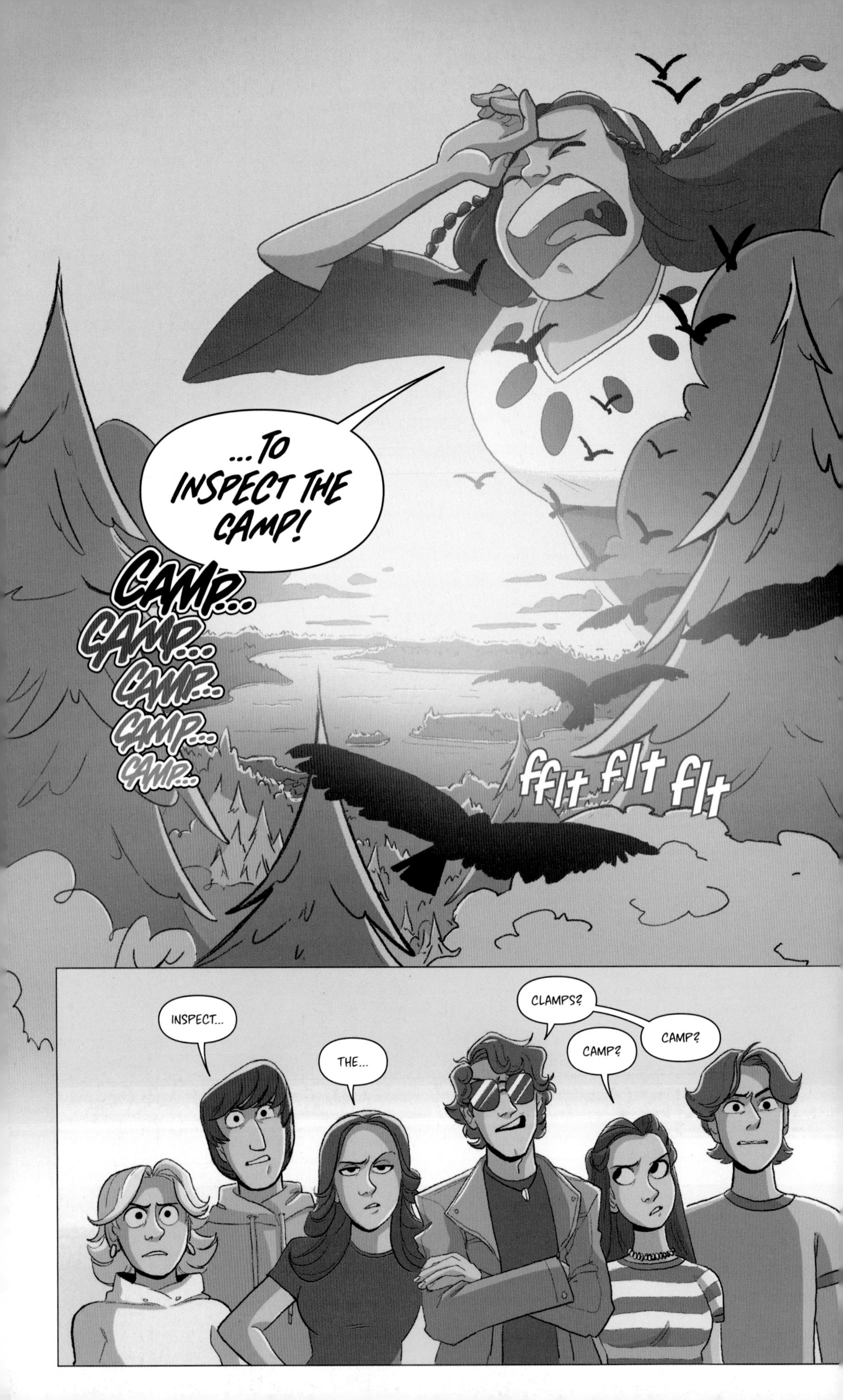
...TO INSPECT THE CAMP!
CAMP...
CAMP...
CAMP...
CAMP...
CAMP...
fflt flt flt
INSPECT...
THE...
CLAMPS?
CAMP?
CAMP?

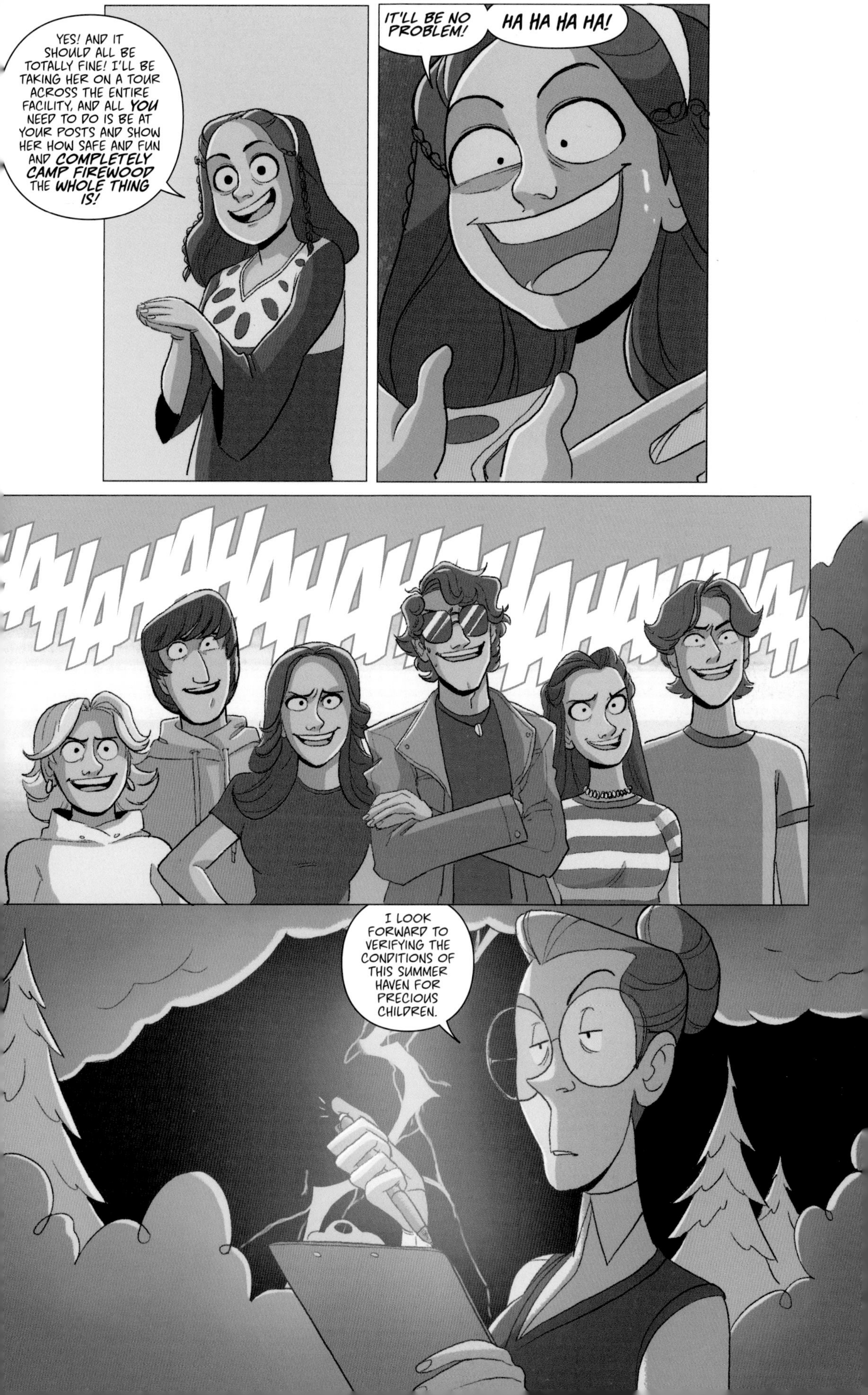

YES! AND IT SHOULD ALL BE TOTALLY FINE! I'LL BE TAKING HER ON A TOUR ACROSS THE ENTIRE FACILITY, AND ALL YOU NEED TO DO IS BE AT YOUR POSTS AND SHOW HER HOW SAFE AND FUN AND COMPLETELY CAMP FIREWOOD THE WHOLE THING IS!
IT'LL BE NO PROBLEM!
HA HA HA HA!
HAHAHAHAHAHAHAHAHA
I LOOK FORWARD TO VERIFYING THE CONDITIONS OF THIS SUMMER HAVEN FOR PRECIOUS CHILDREN.

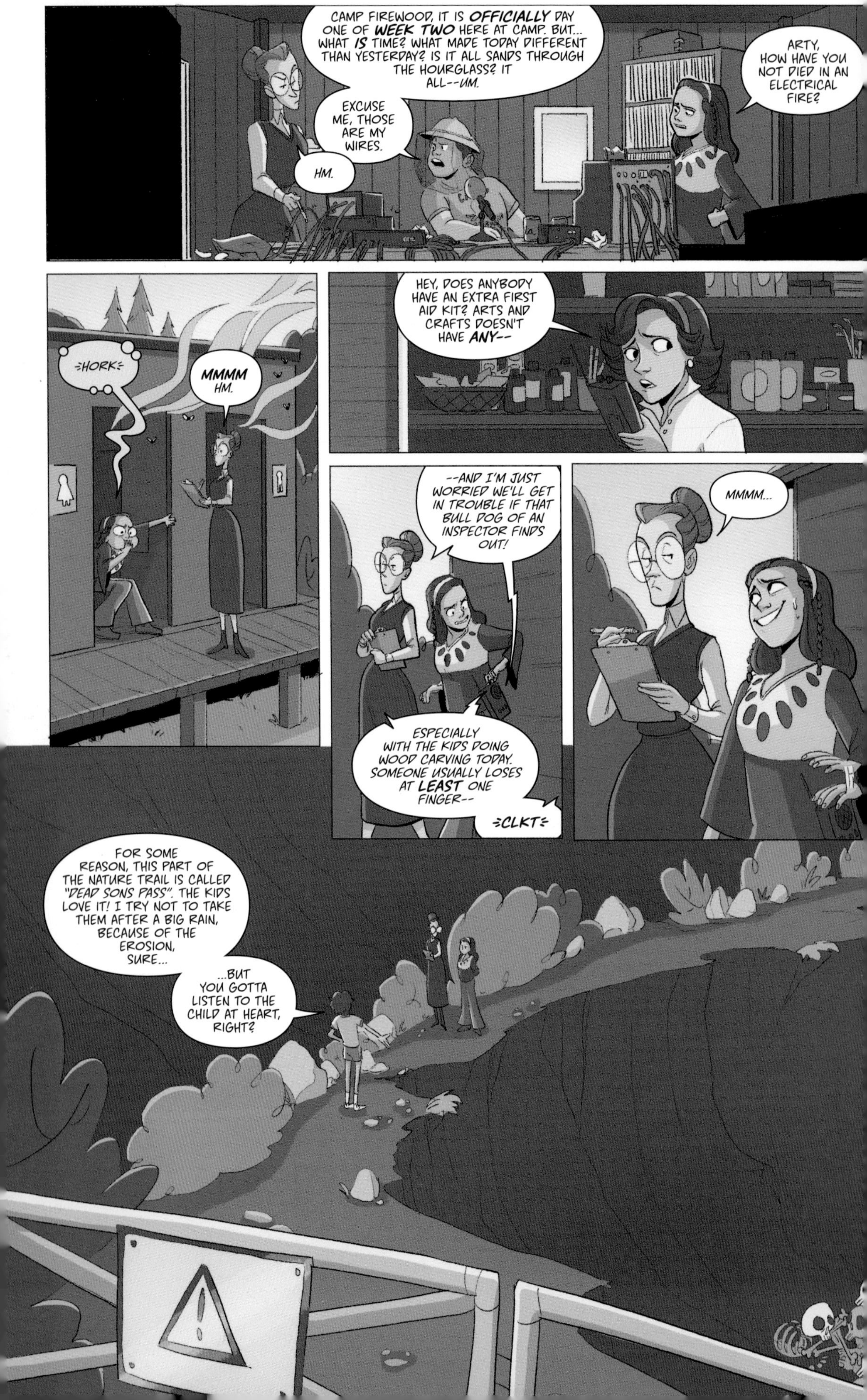

CAMP FIREWOOD, IT IS OFFICIALLY DAY ONE OF WEEK TWO HERE AT CAMP. BUT... WHAT IS TIME? WHAT MADE TODAY DIFFERENT THAN YESTERDAY? IS IT ALL SANDS THROUGH THE HOURGLASS? IT ALL--UM.
EXCUSE ME, THOSE ARE MY WIRES.
HM.
ARTY, HOW HAVE YOU NOT DIED IN AN ELECTRICAL FIRE?
HORK
MMMM HM.
HEY, DOES ANYBODY HAVE AN EXTRA FIRST AID KIT? ARTS AND CRAFTS DOESN'T HAVE ANY--
--AND I'M JUST WORRIED WE'LL GET IN TROUBLE IF THAT BULL DOG OF AN INSPECTOR FINDS OUT!
ESPECIALLY WITH THE KIDS DOING WOOD CARVING TODAY. SOMEONE USUALLY LOSES AT LEAST ONE FINGER--
CLKT
MMMM...
FOR SOME REASON, THIS PART OF THE NATURE TRAIL IS CALLED "DEAD SONS PASS". THE KIDS LOVE IT! I TRY NOT TO TAKE THEM AFTER A BIG RAIN, BECAUSE OF THE EROSION, SURE...
...BUT YOU GOTTA LISTEN TO THE CHILD AT HEART, RIGHT?

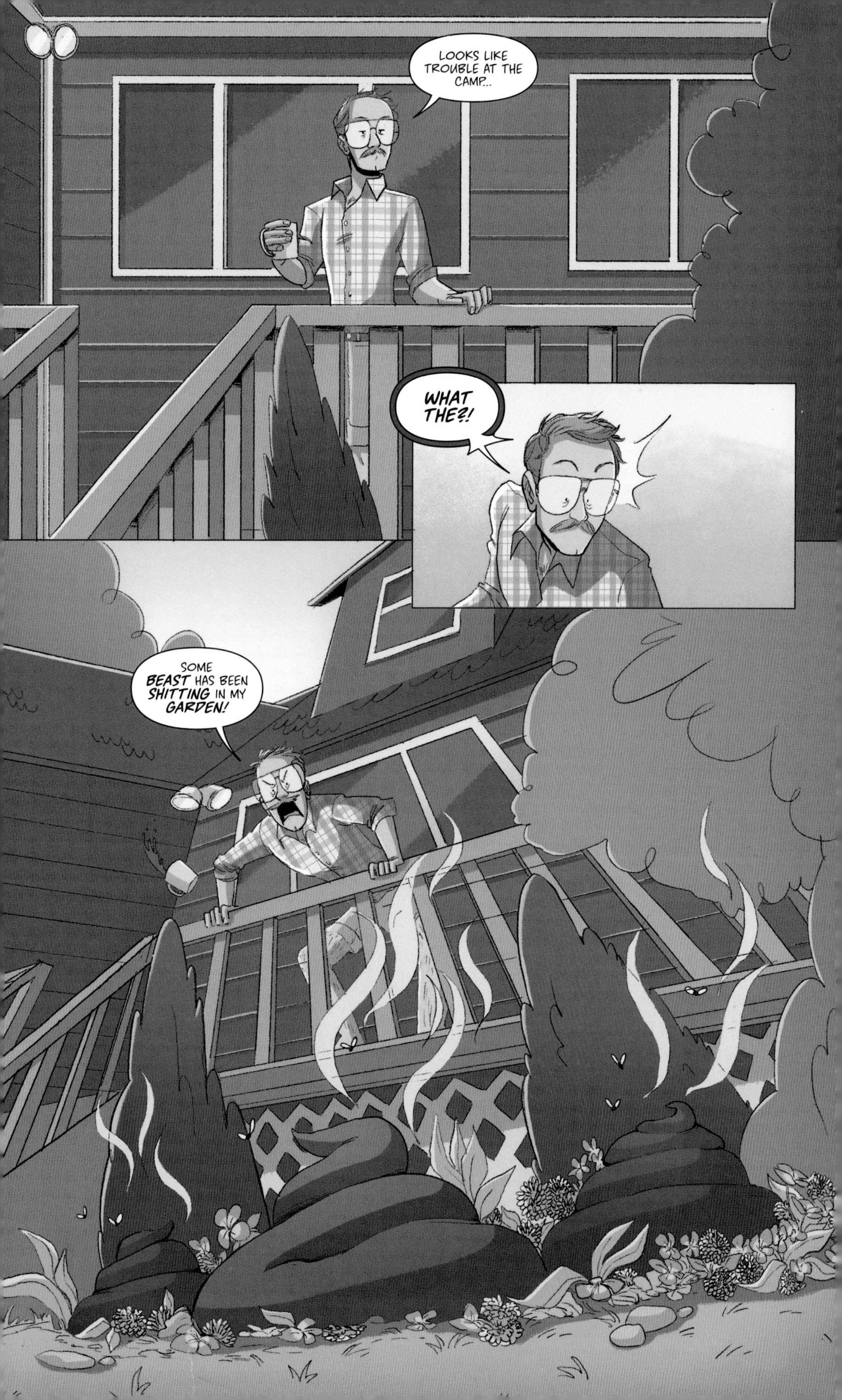
LOOKS LIKE TROUBLE AT THE CAMP...
WHAT THE?!
SOME BEAST HAS BEEN SHITTING IN MY GARDEN!

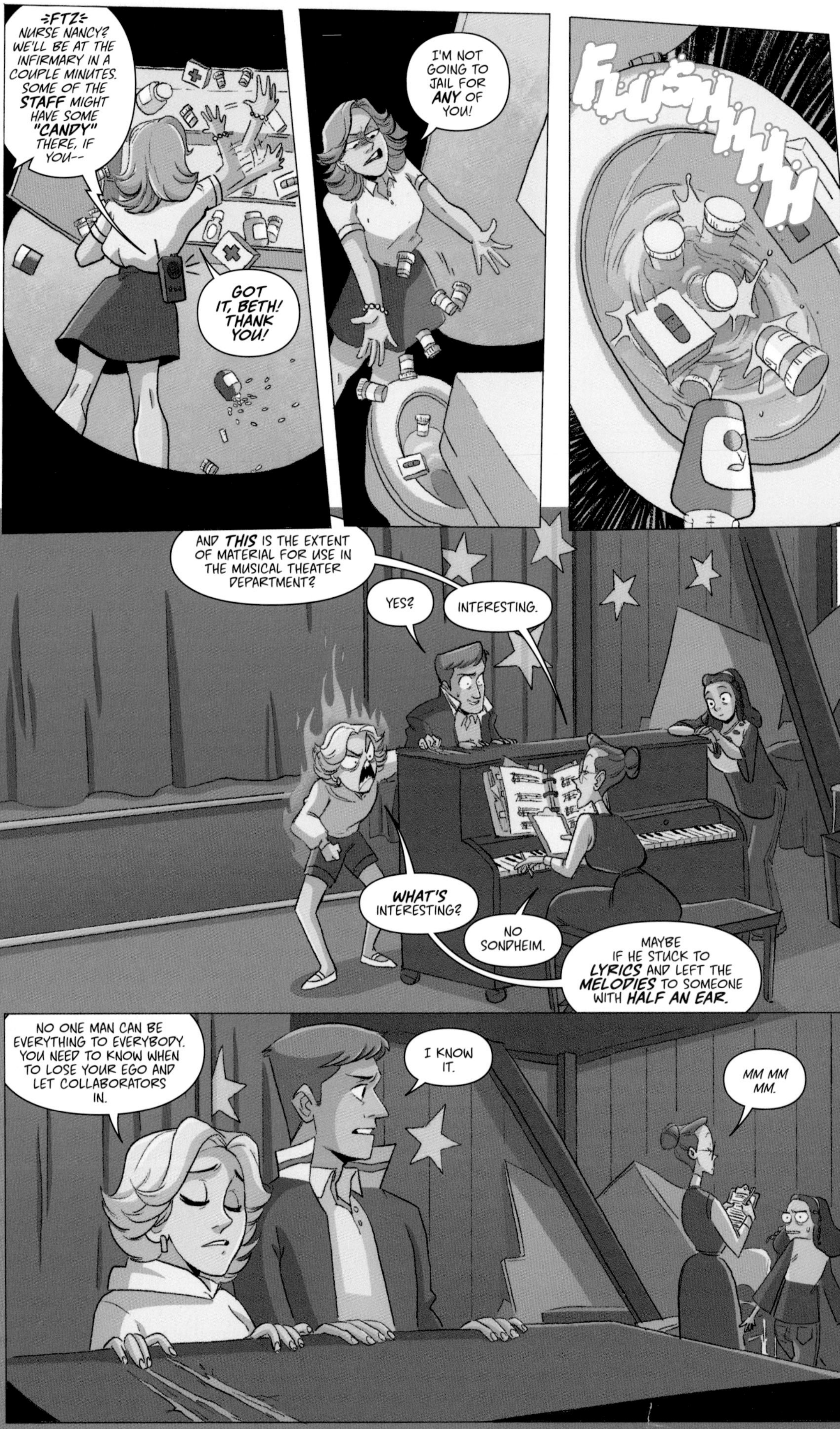
FTZ
NURSE NANCY? WE'LL BE AT THE INFIRMARY IN A COUPLE MINUTES. SOME OF THE STAFF MIGHT HAVE SOME "CANDY" THERE, IF YOU--
GOT IT, BETH! THANK YOU!
I'M NOT GOING TO JAIL FOR ANY OF YOU!
FLUSHHHHH
AND THIS IS THE EXTENT OF MATERIAL FOR USE IN THE MUSICAL THEATER DEPARTMENT?
YES?
INTERESTING.
WHAT'S INTERESTING?
NO SONDHEIM.
MAYBE IF HE STUCK TO LYRICS AND LEFT THE MELODIES TO SOMEONE WITH HALF AN EAR.
NO ONE MAN CAN BE EVERYTHING TO EVERYBODY. YOU NEED TO KNOW WHEN TO LOSE YOUR EGO AND LET COLLABORATORS IN.
I KNOW IT.
MM MM MM.

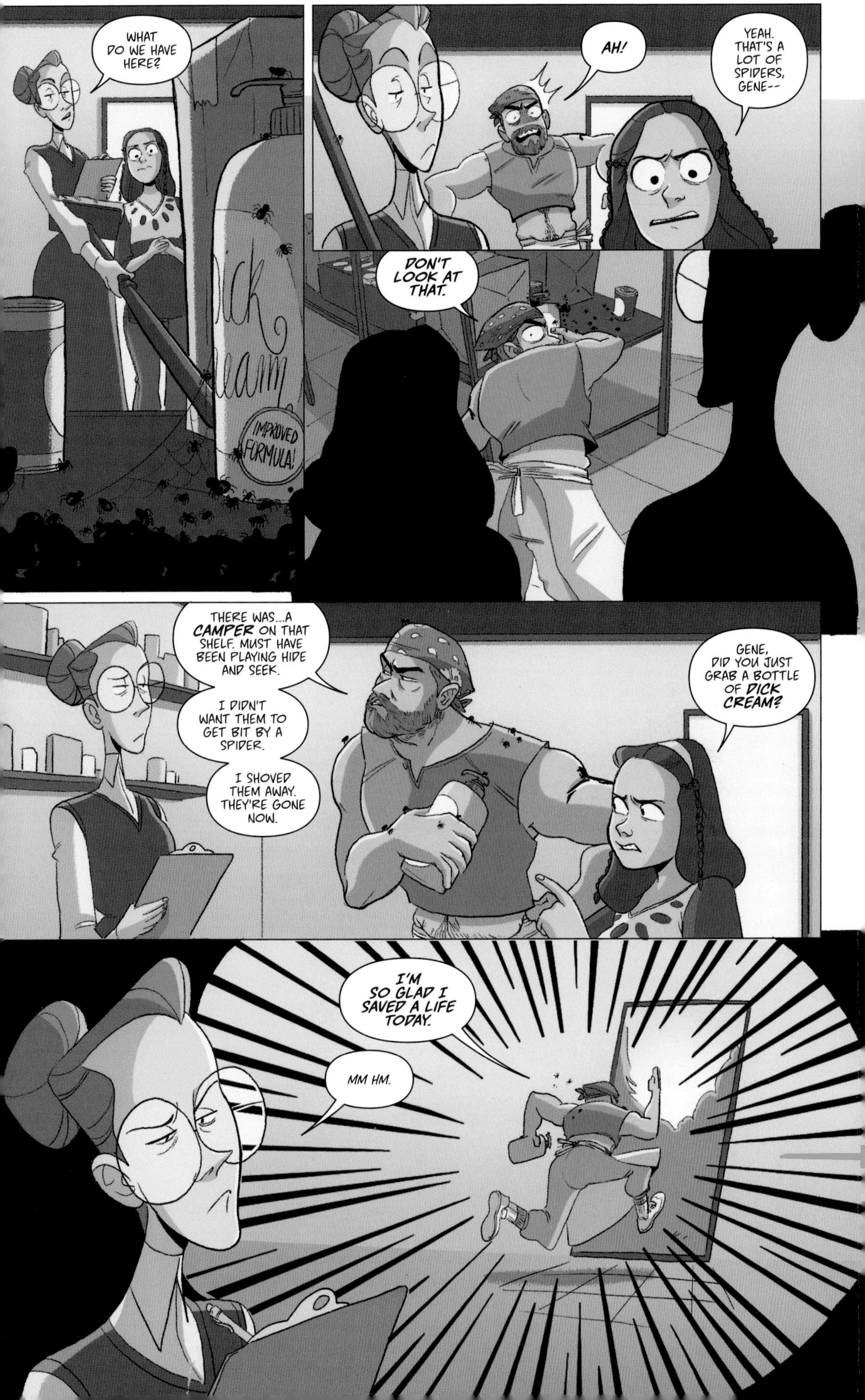

WHAT DO WE HAVE HERE?
Dick Creamy
IMPROVED FORMULA!
AH!
YEAH. THAT'S A LOT OF SPIDERS, GENE--
DON'T LOOK AT THAT.
THERE WAS...A CAMPER ON THAT SHELF. MUST HAVE BEEN PLAYING HIDE AND SEEK.
I DIDN'T WANT THEM TO GET BIT BY A SPIDER.
I SHOVED THEM AWAY. THEY'RE GONE NOW.
GENE, DID YOU JUST GRAB A BOTTLE OF DICK CREAM?
I'M SO GLAD I SAVED A LIFE TODAY.
MM HM.

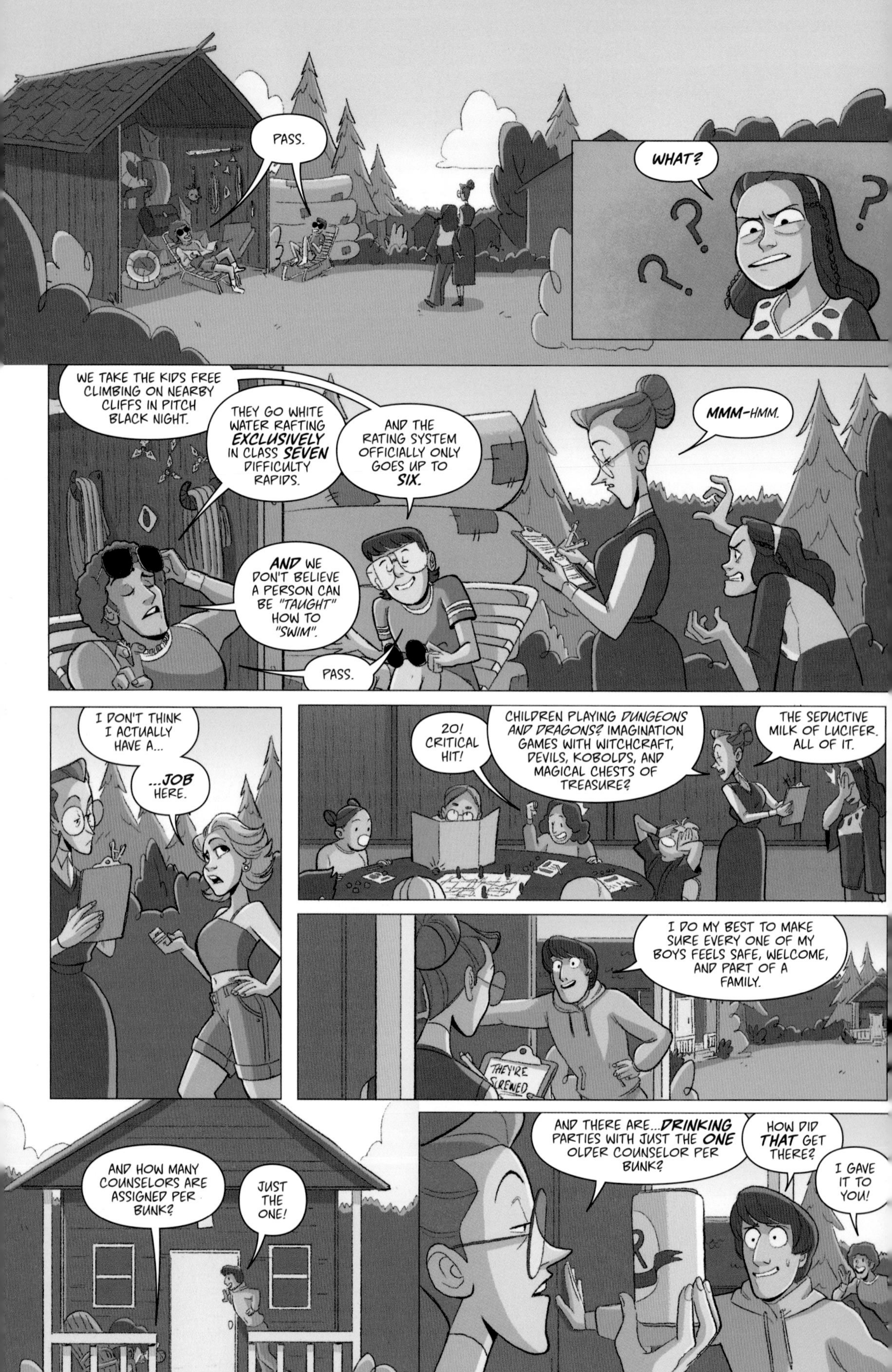

PASS.
WHAT?
WE TAKE THE KIDS FREE CLIMBING ON NEARBY CLIFFS IN PITCH BLACK NIGHT.
THEY GO WHITE WATER RAFTING EXCLUSIVELY IN CLASS SEVEN DIFFICULTY RAPIDS.
AND THE RATING SYSTEM OFFICIALLY ONLY GOES UP TO SIX.
MMM-HMM.
AND WE DON'T BELIEVE A PERSON CAN BE "TAUGHT" HOW TO "SWIM".
PASS.
I DON'T THINK I ACTUALLY HAVE A...
...JOB HERE.
20! CRITICAL HIT!
CHILDREN PLAYING DUNGEONS AND DRAGONS? IMAGINATION GAMES WITH WITCHCRAFT, DEVILS, KOBOLDS, AND MAGICAL CHESTS OF TREASURE?
THE SEDUCTIVE MILK OF LUCIFER. ALL OF IT.
I DO MY BEST TO MAKE SURE EVERY ONE OF MY BOYS FEELS SAFE, WELCOME, AND PART OF A FAMILY.
THEY'RE SCREWED
AND HOW MANY COUNSELORS ARE ASSIGNED PER BUNK?
JUST THE ONE!
AND THERE ARE...DRINKING PARTIES WITH JUST THE ONE OLDER COUNSELOR PER BUNK?
HOW DID THAT GET THERE?
I GAVE IT TO YOU!

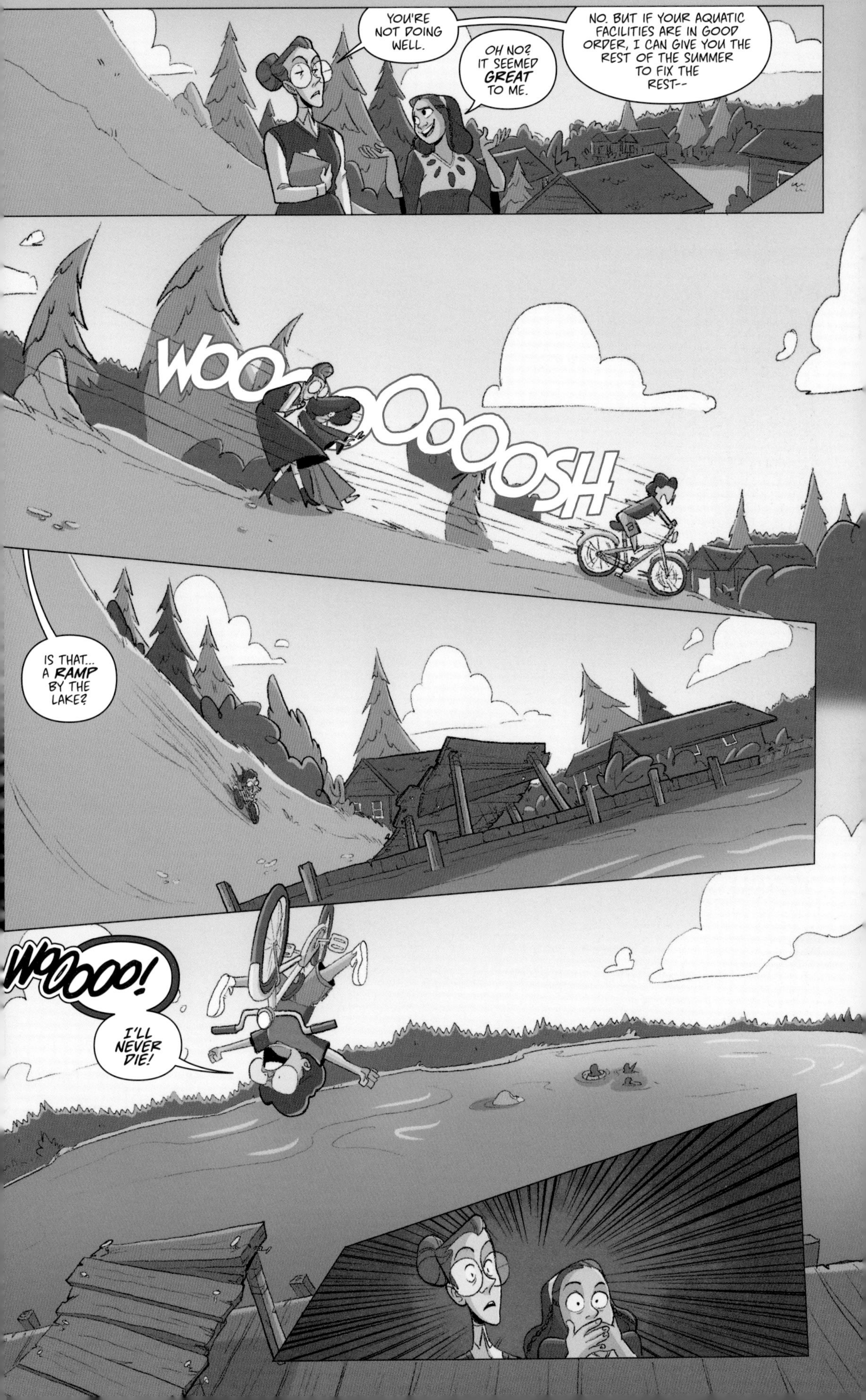
YOU'RE NOT DOING WELL.
OH NO? IT SEEMED GREAT TO ME.
NO. BUT IF YOUR AQUATIC FACILITIES ARE IN GOOD ORDER, I CAN GIVE YOU THE REST OF THE SUMMER TO FIX THE REST--
WOOOOOOOOOSH
IS THAT... A RAMP BY THE LAKE?
WOOOOO!
I'LL NEVER DIE!

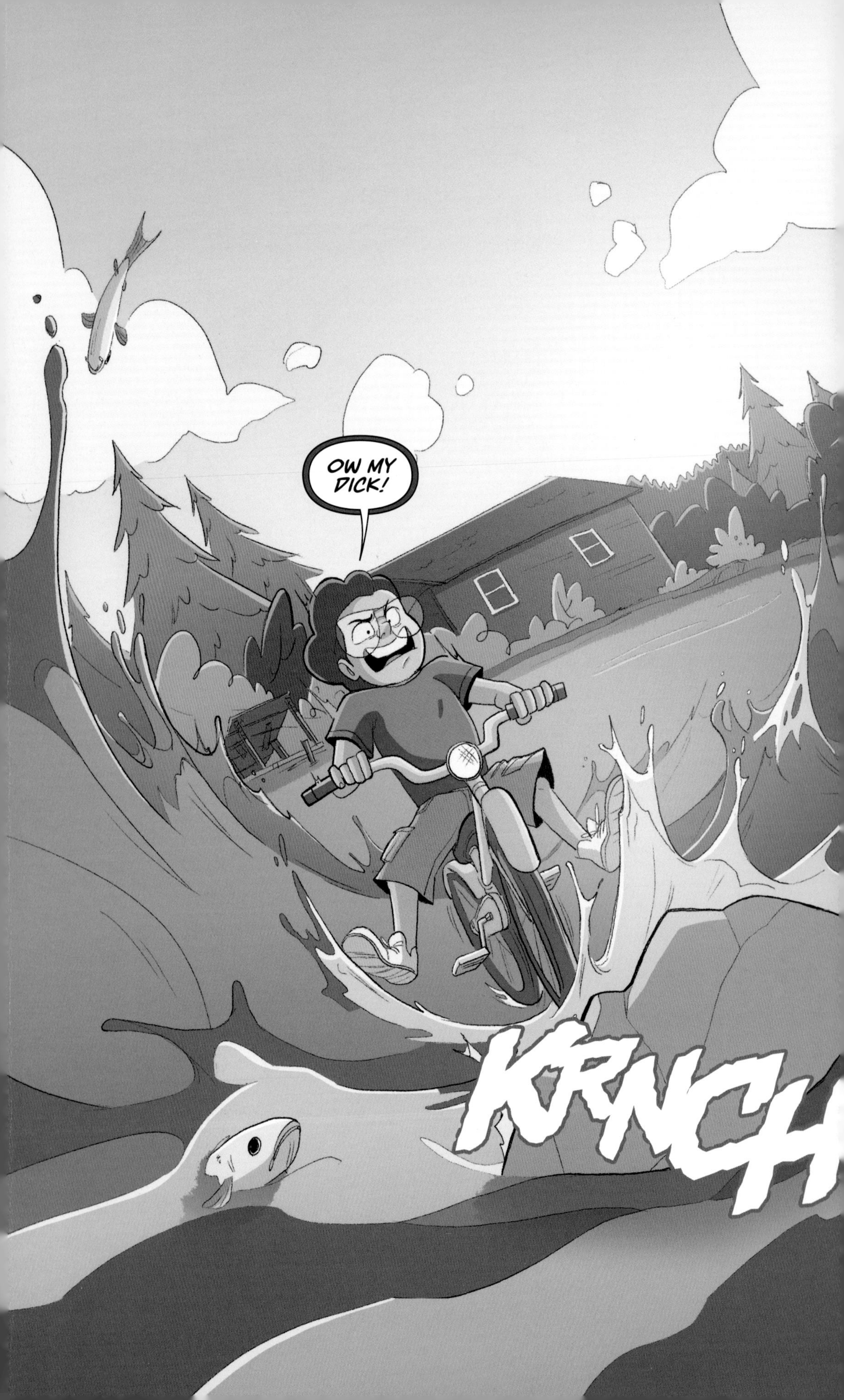
OW MY DICK!
KRNCH

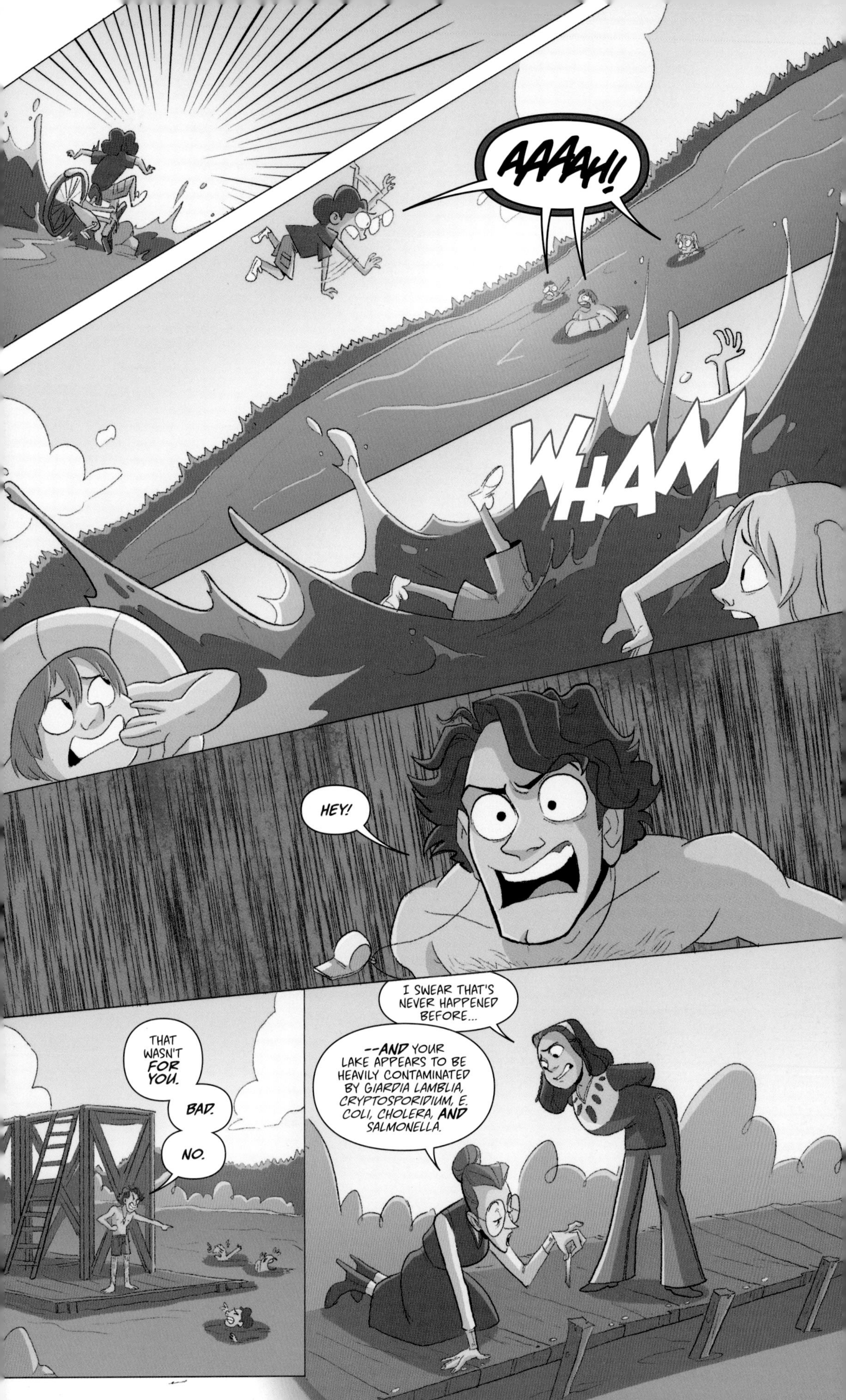
AAAAH!
WHAM
HEY!
THAT WASN'T FOR YOU.
BAD.
NO.
I SWEAR THAT'S NEVER HAPPENED BEFORE...
--AND YOUR LAKE APPEARS TO BE HEAVILY CONTAMINATED BY GIARDIA LAMBLIA, CRYPTOSPORIDIUM, E. COLI, CHOLERA, AND SALMONELLA.

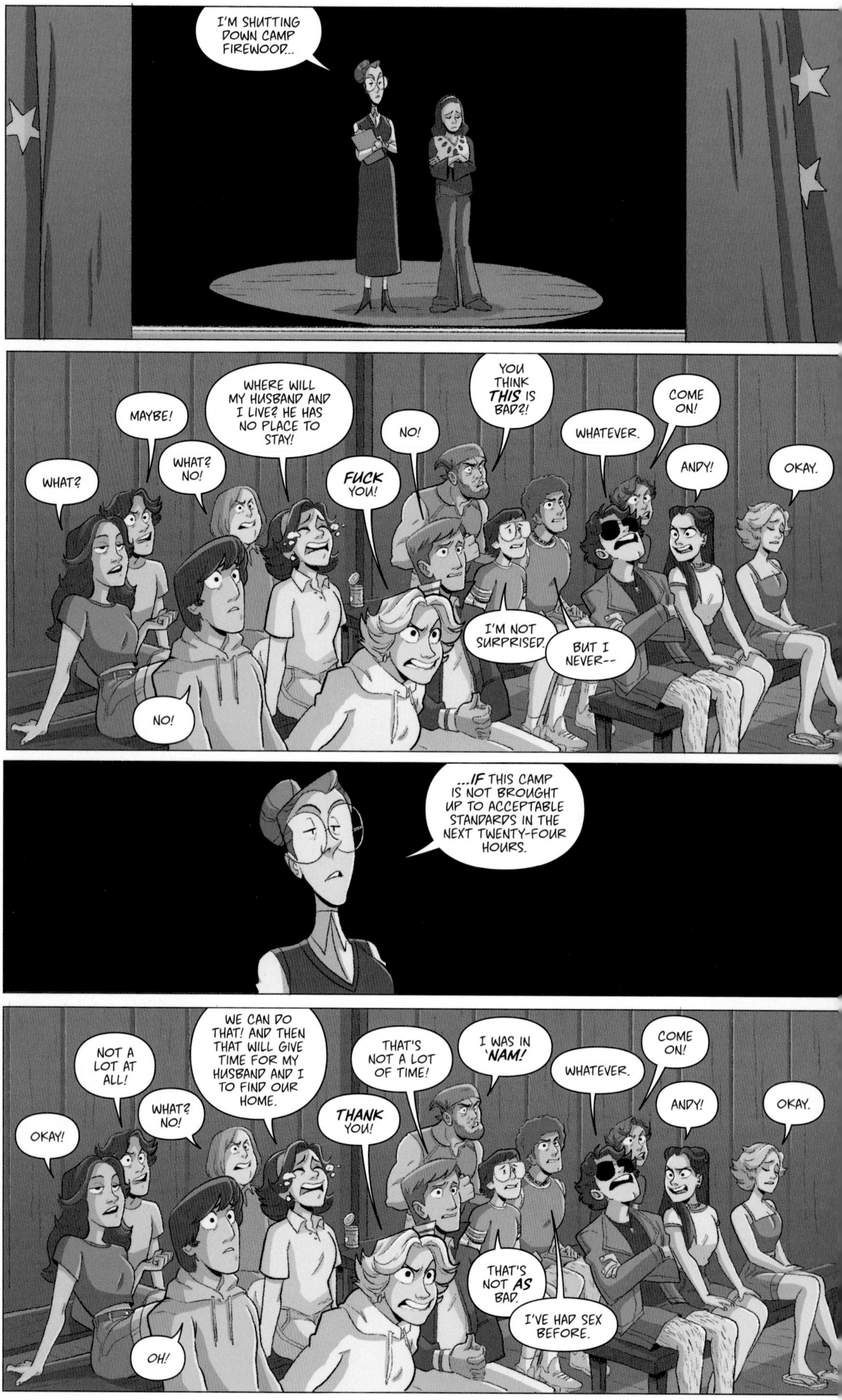
I'M SHUTTING DOWN CAMP FIREWOOD...
WHAT?
MAYBE!
WHAT? NO!
WHERE WILL MY HUSBAND AND I LIVE? HE HAS NO PLACE TO STAY!
FUCK YOU!
NO!
NO!
YOU THINK THIS IS BAD?!
I'M NOT SURPRISED.
BUT I NEVER--
WHATEVER.
COME ON!
ANDY!
OKAY.
...IF THIS CAMP IS NOT BROUGHT UP TO ACCEPTABLE STANDARDS IN THE NEXT TWENTY-FOUR HOURS.
OKAY!
NOT A LOT AT ALL!
WHAT? NO!
WE CAN DO THAT! AND THEN THAT WILL GIVE TIME FOR MY HUSBAND AND I TO FIND OUR HOME.
THANK YOU!
THAT'S NOT A LOT OF TIME!
OH!
I WAS IN 'NAM!
THAT'S NOT AS BAD.
I'VE HAD SEX BEFORE.
WHATEVER.
COME ON!
ANDY!
OKAY.

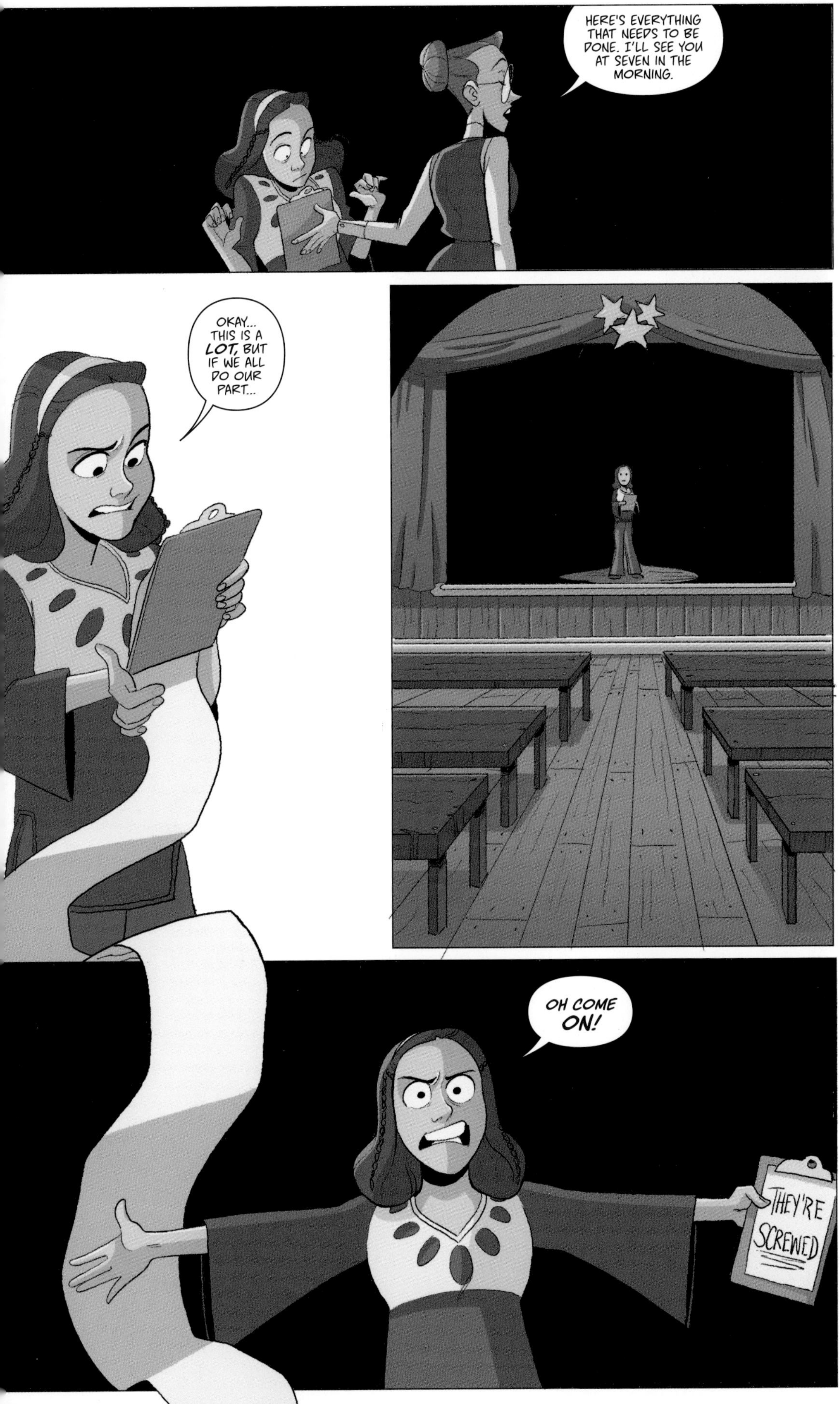
HERE'S EVERYTHING THAT NEEDS TO BE DONE. I'LL SEE YOU AT SEVEN IN THE MORNING.
OKAY... THIS IS A **LOT,** BUT IF WE ALL DO OUR PART...
OH COME **ON!**
THEY'RE SCREWED

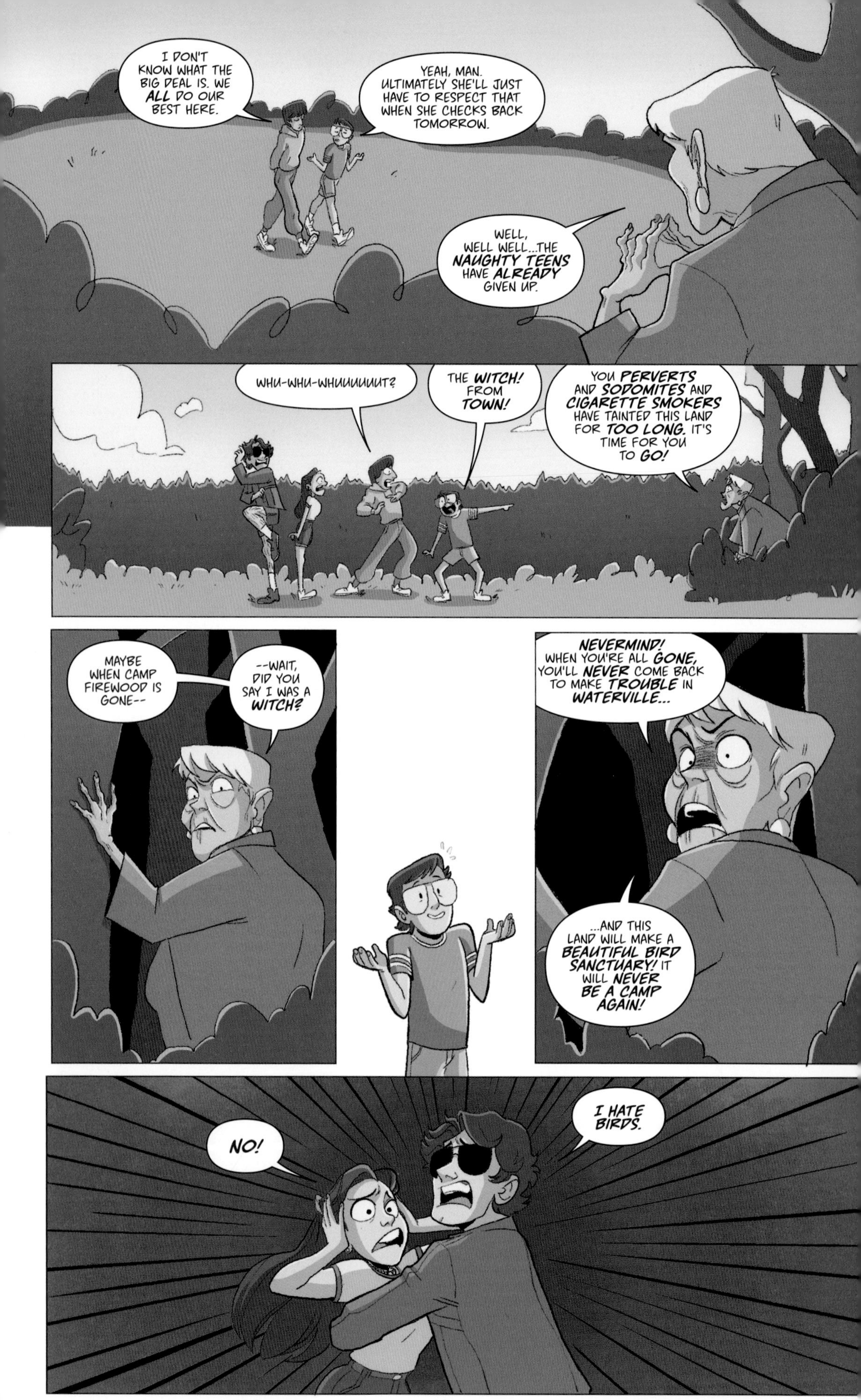
I DON'T KNOW WHAT THE BIG DEAL IS. WE ALL DO OUR BEST HERE.
YEAH, MAN. ULTIMATELY SHE'LL JUST HAVE TO RESPECT THAT WHEN SHE CHECKS BACK TOMORROW.
WELL, WELL WELL...THE NAUGHTY TEENS HAVE ALREADY GIVEN UP.
WHU-WHU-WHUUUUUUT?
THE WITCH! FROM TOWN!
YOU PERVERTS AND SODOMITES AND CIGARETTE SMOKERS HAVE TAINTED THIS LAND FOR TOO LONG. IT'S TIME FOR YOU TO GO!
MAYBE WHEN CAMP FIREWOOD IS GONE--
--WAIT, DID YOU SAY I WAS A WITCH?
NEVERMIND! WHEN YOU'RE ALL GONE, YOU'LL NEVER COME BACK TO MAKE TROUBLE IN WATERVILLE...
...AND THIS LAND WILL MAKE A BEAUTIFUL BIRD SANCTUARY! IT WILL NEVER BE A CAMP AGAIN!
NO!
I HATE BIRDS.

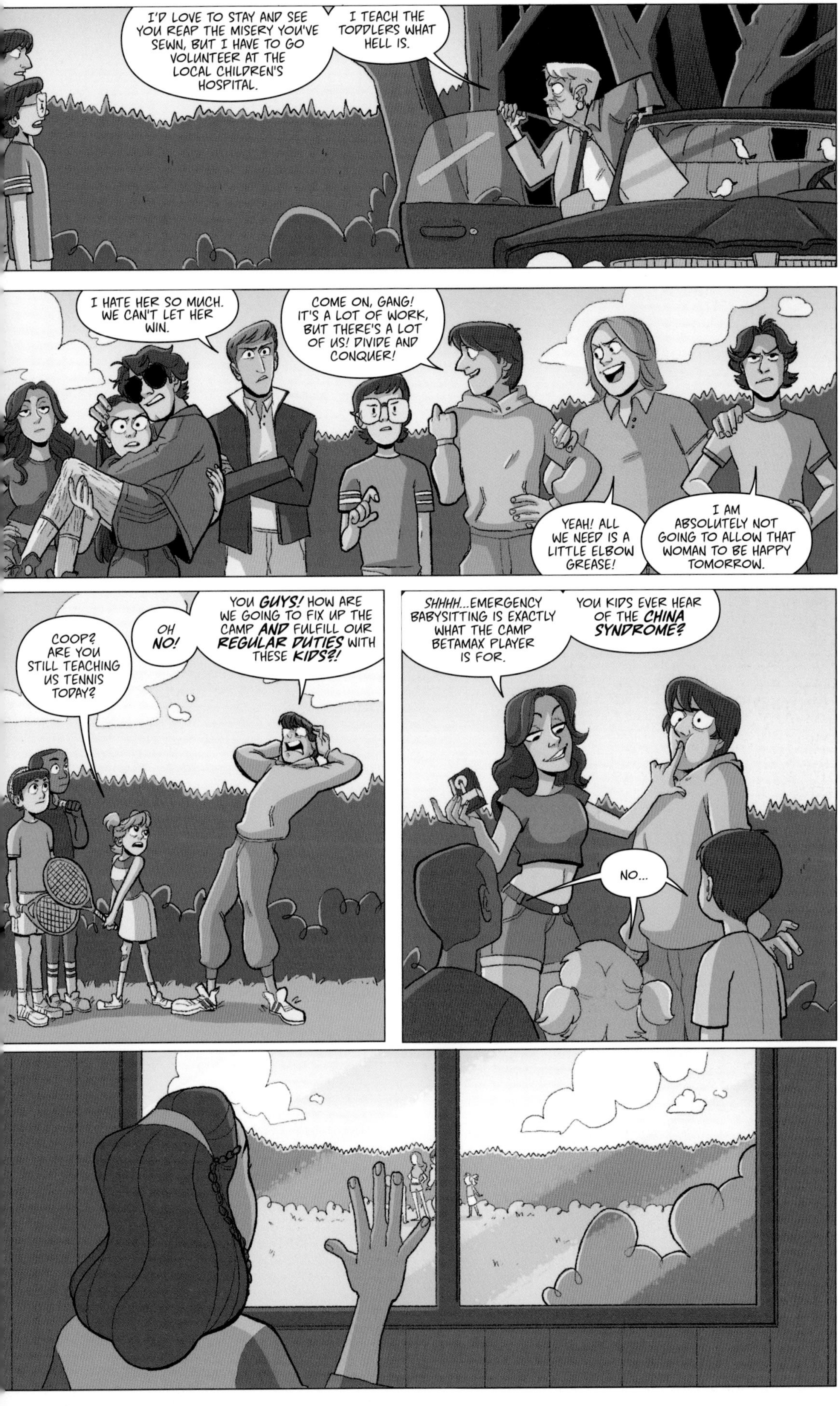
I'D LOVE TO STAY AND SEE YOU REAP THE MISERY YOU'VE SEWN, BUT I HAVE TO GO VOLUNTEER AT THE LOCAL CHILDREN'S HOSPITAL.
I TEACH THE TODDLERS WHAT HELL IS.
I HATE HER SO MUCH. WE CAN'T LET HER WIN.
COME ON, GANG! IT'S A LOT OF WORK, BUT THERE'S A LOT OF US! DIVIDE AND CONQUER!
YEAH! ALL WE NEED IS A LITTLE ELBOW GREASE!
I AM ABSOLUTELY NOT GOING TO ALLOW THAT WOMAN TO BE HAPPY TOMORROW.
COOP? ARE YOU STILL TEACHING US TENNIS TODAY?
OH NO!
YOU GUYS! HOW ARE WE GOING TO FIX UP THE CAMP AND FULFILL OUR REGULAR DUTIES WITH THESE KIDS?!
SHHHH...EMERGENCY BABYSITTING IS EXACTLY WHAT THE CAMP BETAMAX PLAYER IS FOR.
YOU KIDS EVER HEAR OF THE CHINA SYNDROME?
NO...

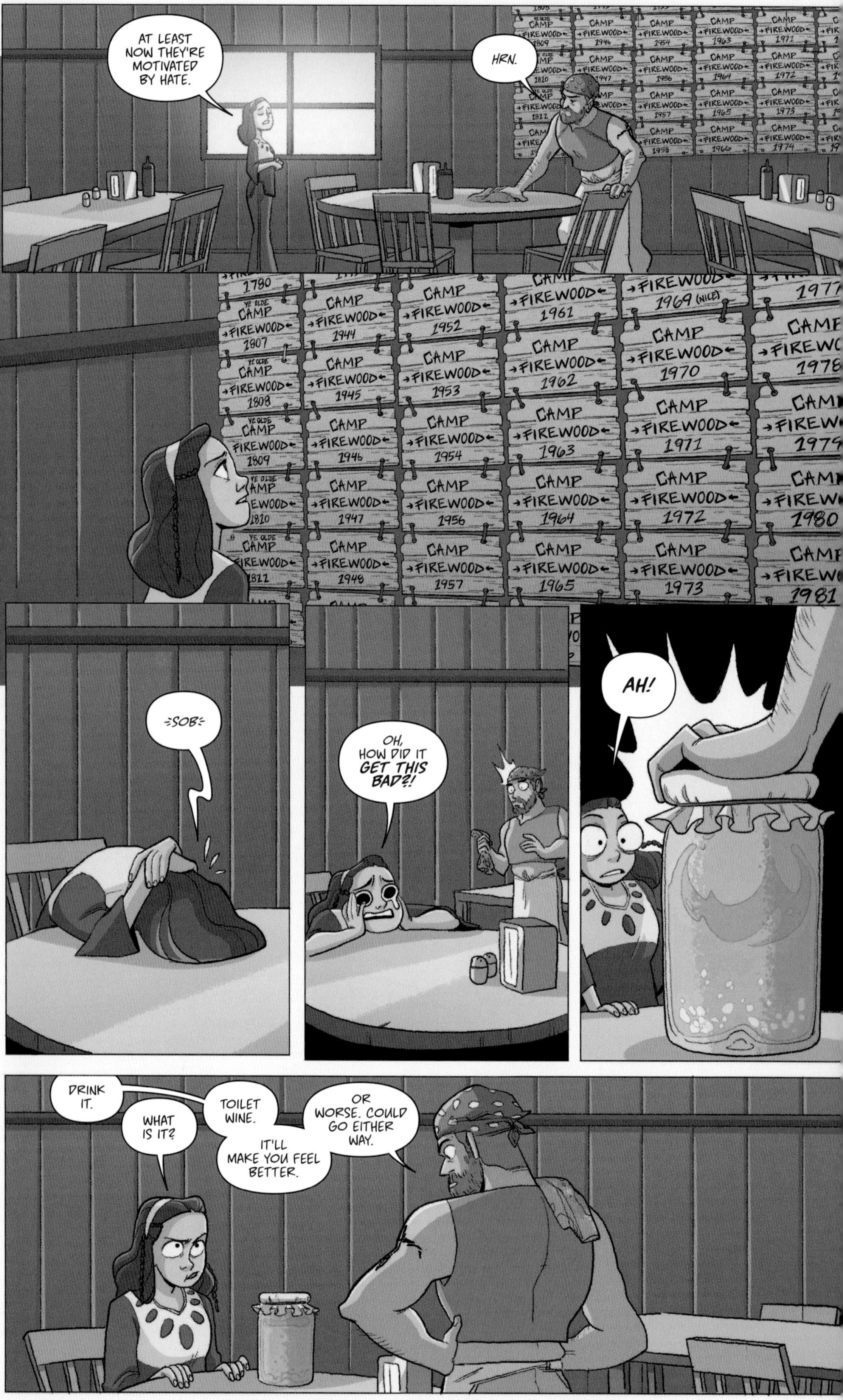
AT LEAST NOW THEY'RE MOTIVATED BY HATE.
HRN.
1969 (NICE)
SOB
OH, HOW DID IT GET THIS BAD?!
AH!
DRINK IT.
WHAT IS IT?
TOILET WINE.
IT'LL MAKE YOU FEEL BETTER.
OR WORSE. COULD GO EITHER WAY.

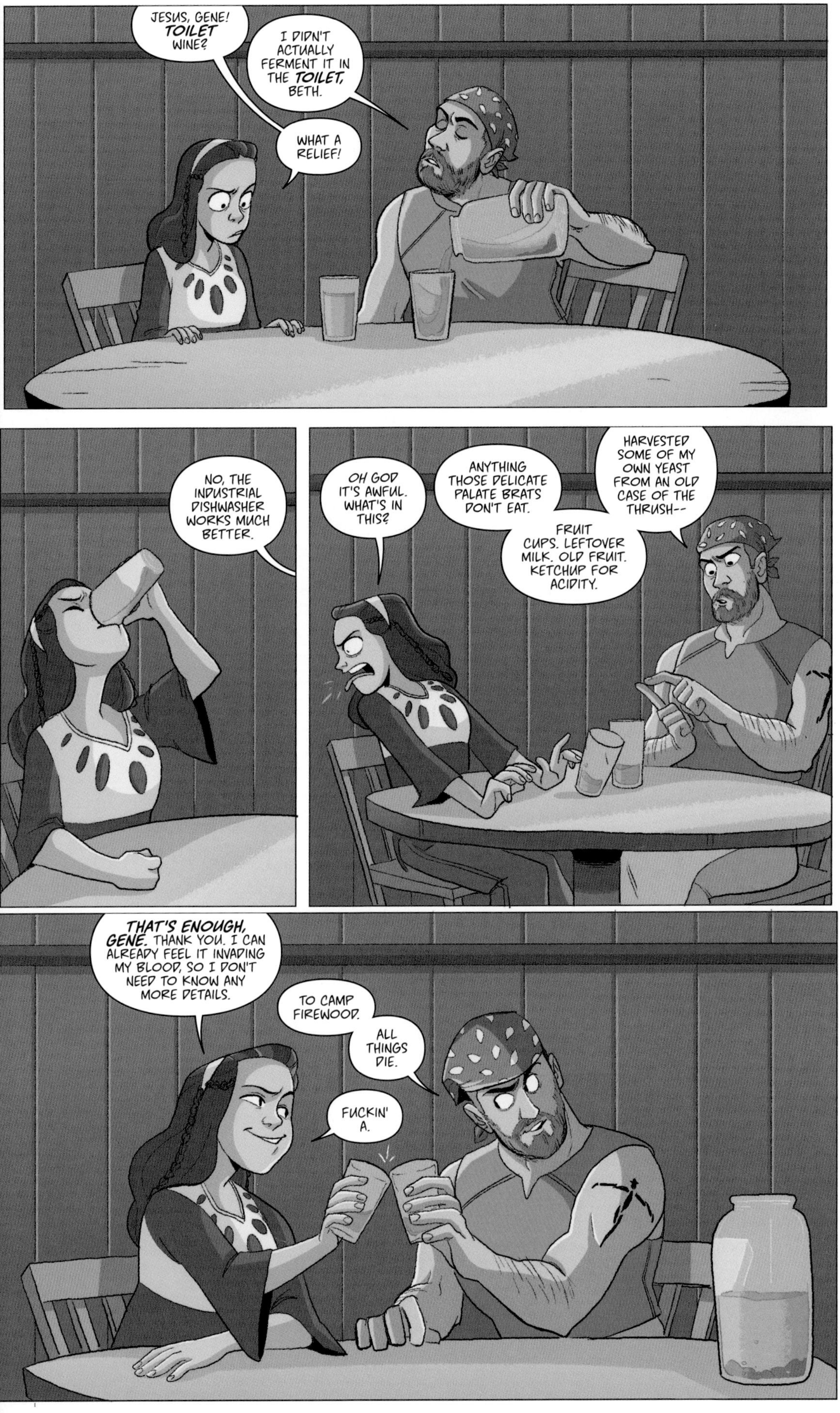

JESUS, GENE! **TOILET** WINE?
I DIDN'T ACTUALLY FERMENT IT IN THE **TOILET,** BETH.
WHAT A RELIEF!
NO, THE INDUSTRIAL DISHWASHER WORKS MUCH BETTER.
OH GOD IT'S AWFUL. WHAT'S IN THIS?
ANYTHING THOSE DELICATE PALATE BRATS DON'T EAT.
HARVESTED SOME OF MY OWN YEAST FROM AN OLD CASE OF THE THRUSH--
FRUIT CUPS. LEFTOVER MILK. OLD FRUIT. KETCHUP FOR ACIDITY.
THAT'S ENOUGH, GENE. THANK YOU. I CAN ALREADY FEEL IT INVADING MY BLOOD, SO I DON'T NEED TO KNOW ANY MORE DETAILS.
TO CAMP FIREWOOD.
ALL THINGS DIE.
FUCKIN' A.

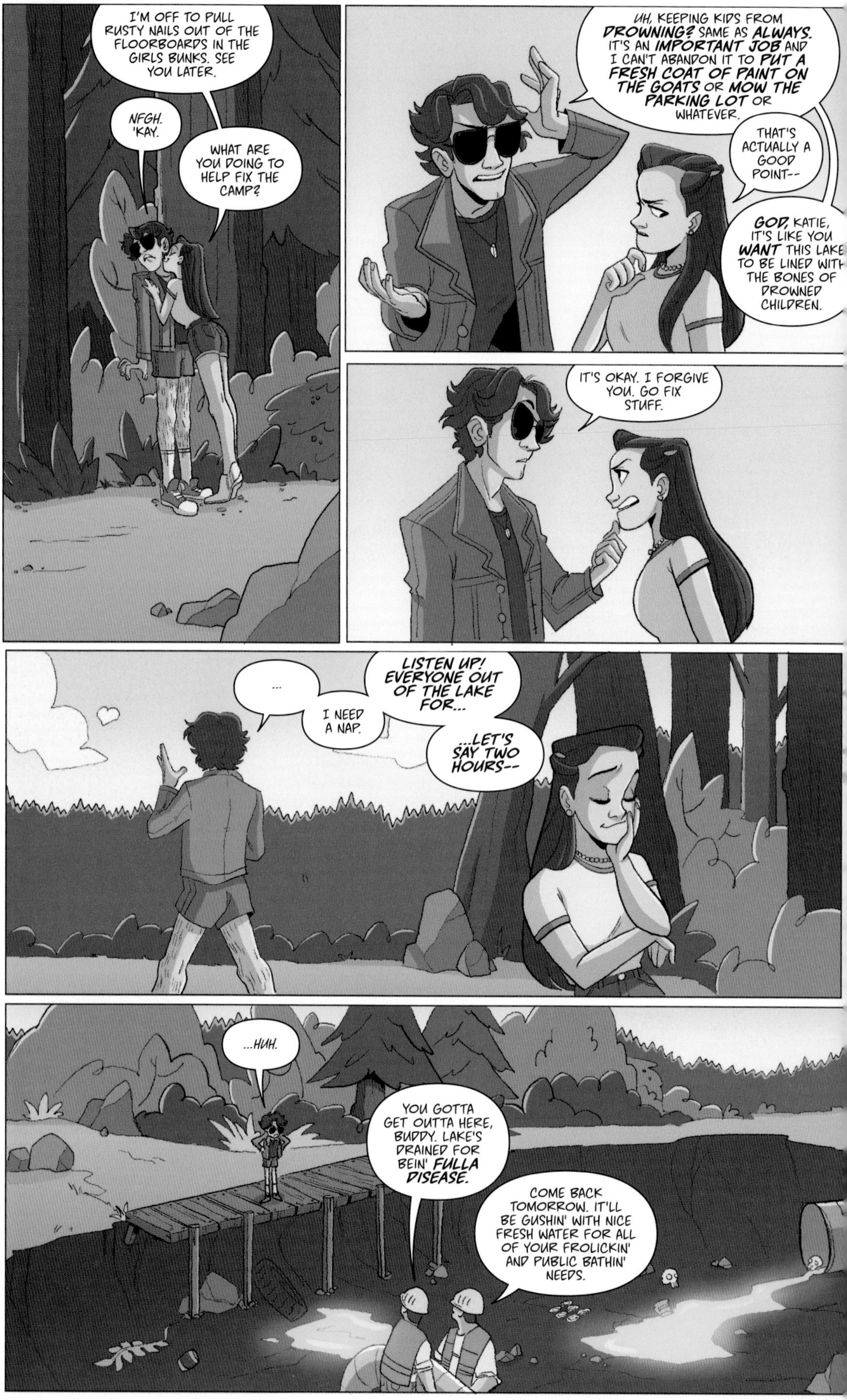
I'M OFF TO PULL RUSTY NAILS OUT OF THE FLOORBOARDS IN THE GIRLS BUNKS. SEE YOU LATER.
NFGH. 'KAY.
WHAT ARE YOU DOING TO HELP FIX THE CAMP?
UH, KEEPING KIDS FROM DROWNING? SAME AS ALWAYS. IT'S AN IMPORTANT JOB AND I CAN'T ABANDON IT TO PUT A FRESH COAT OF PAINT ON THE GOATS OR MOW THE PARKING LOT OR WHATEVER.
THAT'S ACTUALLY A GOOD POINT--
GOD, KATIE, IT'S LIKE YOU WANT THIS LAKE TO BE LINED WITH THE BONES OF DROWNED CHILDREN.
IT'S OKAY. I FORGIVE YOU. GO FIX STUFF.
...
I NEED A NAP.
LISTEN UP! EVERYONE OUT OF THE LAKE FOR...
...LET'S SAY TWO HOURS--
...HUH.
YOU GOTTA GET OUTTA HERE, BUDDY. LAKE'S DRAINED FOR BEIN' FULLA DISEASE.
COME BACK TOMORROW. IT'LL BE GUSHIN' WITH NICE FRESH WATER FOR ALL OF YOUR FROLICKIN' AND PUBLIC BATHIN' NEEDS.

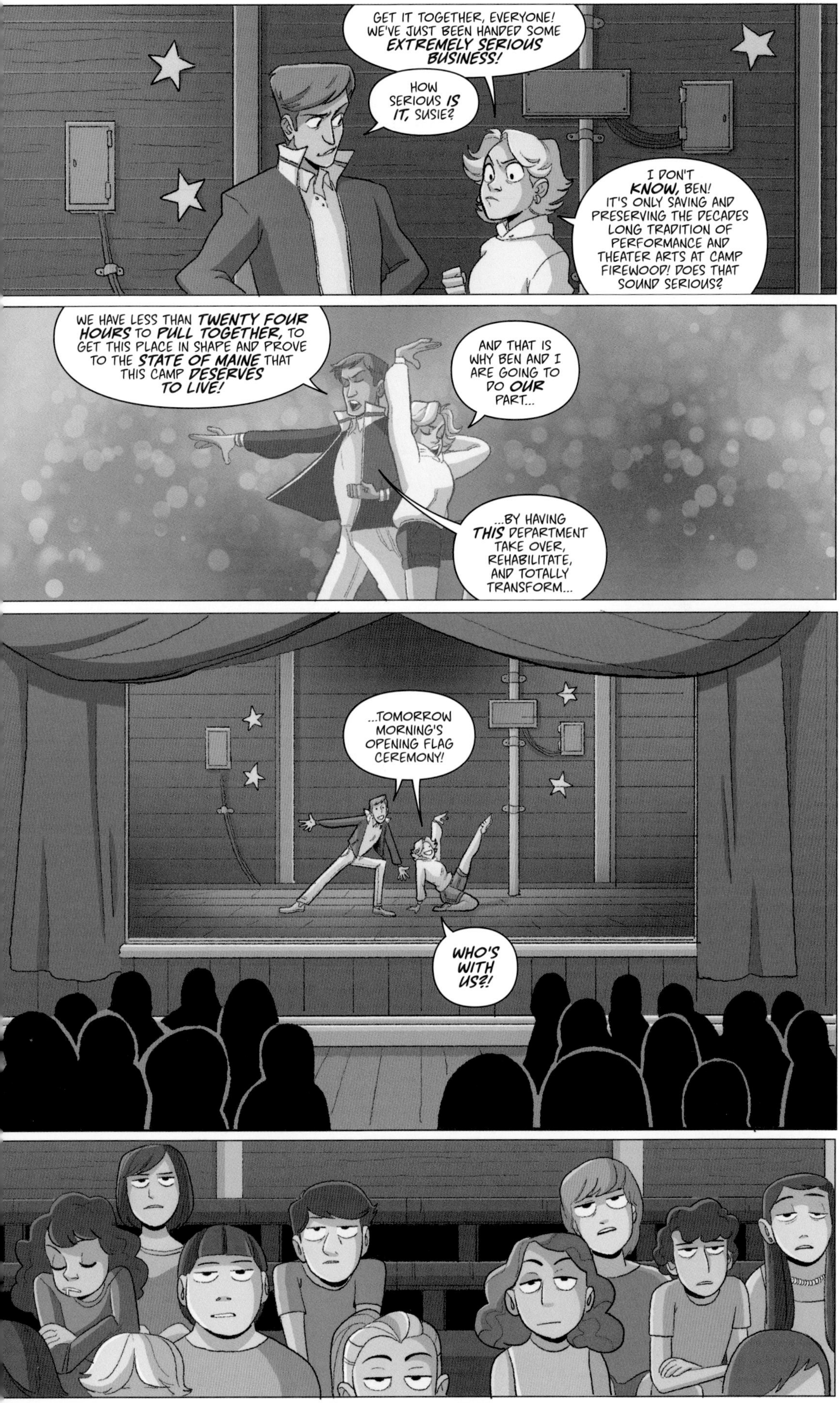
GET IT TOGETHER, EVERYONE! WE'VE JUST BEEN HANDED SOME EXTREMELY SERIOUS BUSINESS!
HOW SERIOUS IS IT, SUSIE?
I DON'T KNOW, BEN! IT'S ONLY SAVING AND PRESERVING THE DECADES LONG TRADITION OF PERFORMANCE AND THEATER ARTS AT CAMP FIREWOOD! DOES THAT SOUND SERIOUS?
WE HAVE LESS THAN TWENTY FOUR HOURS TO PULL TOGETHER, TO GET THIS PLACE IN SHAPE AND PROVE TO THE STATE OF MAINE THAT THIS CAMP DESERVES TO LIVE!
AND THAT IS WHY BEN AND I ARE GOING TO DO OUR PART...
...BY HAVING THIS DEPARTMENT TAKE OVER, REHABILITATE, AND TOTALLY TRANSFORM...
...TOMORROW MORNING'S OPENING FLAG CEREMONY!
WHO'S WITH US?!

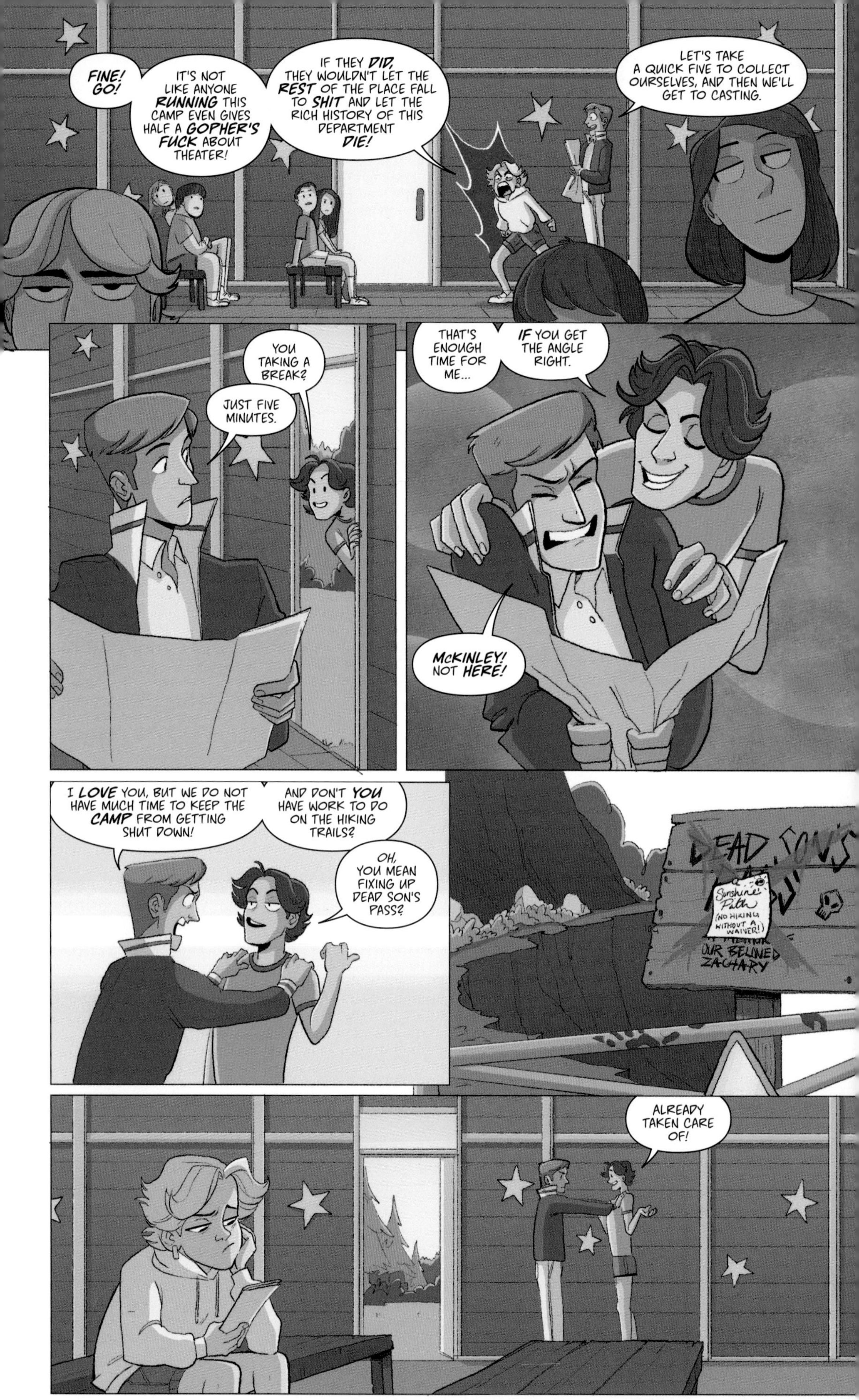

FINE! GO!
IT'S NOT LIKE ANYONE RUNNING THIS CAMP EVEN GIVES HALF A GOPHER'S FUCK ABOUT THEATER!
IF THEY DID, THEY WOULDN'T LET THE REST OF THE PLACE FALL TO SHIT AND LET THE RICH HISTORY OF THIS DEPARTMENT DIE!
LET'S TAKE A QUICK FIVE TO COLLECT OURSELVES, AND THEN WE'LL GET TO CASTING.
YOU TAKING A BREAK?
JUST FIVE MINUTES.
THAT'S ENOUGH TIME FOR ME...
IF YOU GET THE ANGLE RIGHT.
McKINLEY! NOT HERE!
I LOVE YOU, BUT WE DO NOT HAVE MUCH TIME TO KEEP THE CAMP FROM GETTING SHUT DOWN!
AND DON'T YOU HAVE WORK TO DO ON THE HIKING TRAILS?
OH, YOU MEAN FIXING UP DEAD SON'S PASS?
DEAD SON'S
Sunshine Path
(NO HIKING WITHOUT A WAIVER!)
OUR BELOVED ZACHARY
ALREADY TAKEN CARE OF!

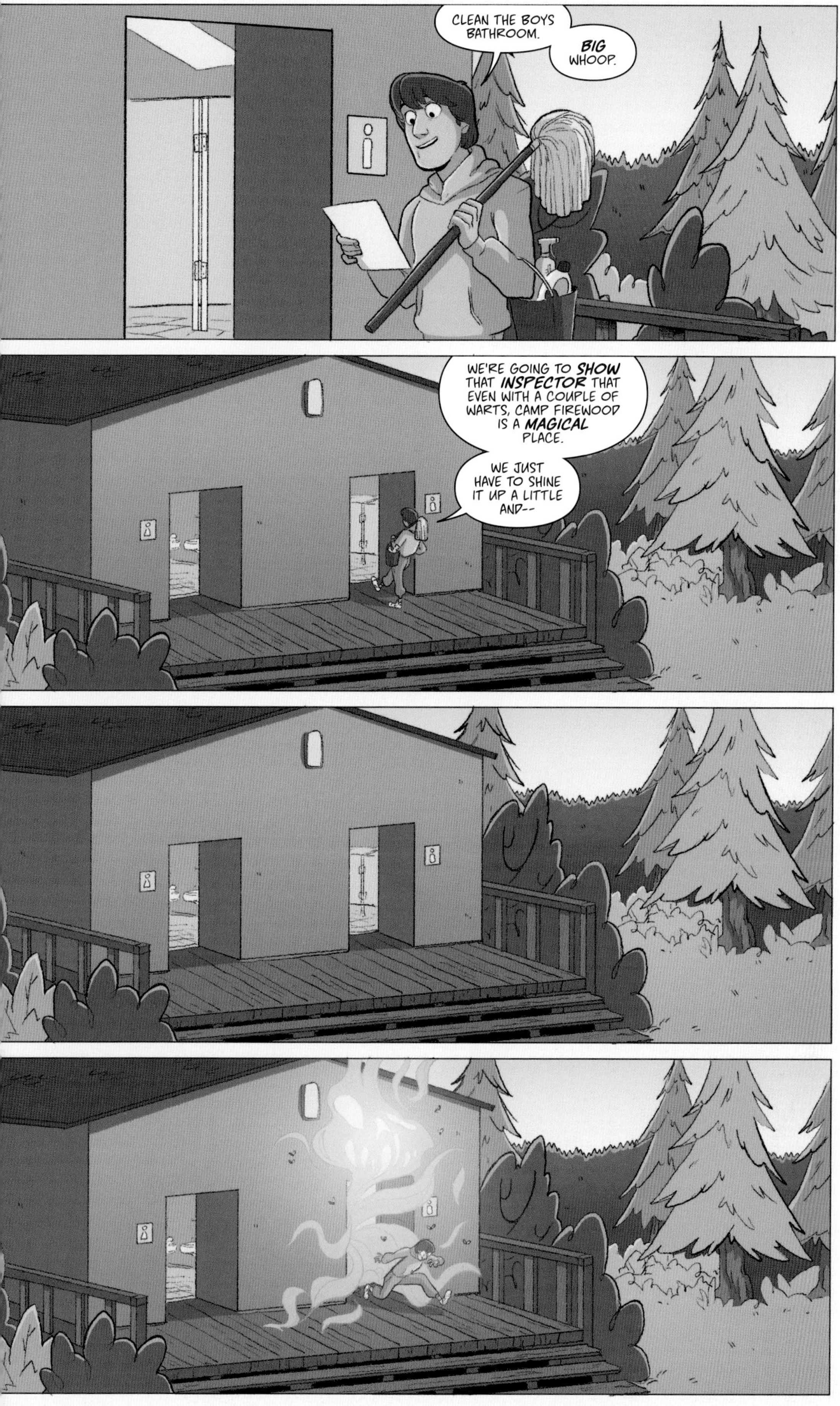
CLEAN THE BOYS BATHROOM.
BIG WHOOP.
WE'RE GOING TO SHOW THAT INSPECTOR THAT EVEN WITH A COUPLE OF WARTS, CAMP FIREWOOD IS A MAGICAL PLACE.
WE JUST HAVE TO SHINE IT UP A LITTLE AND--

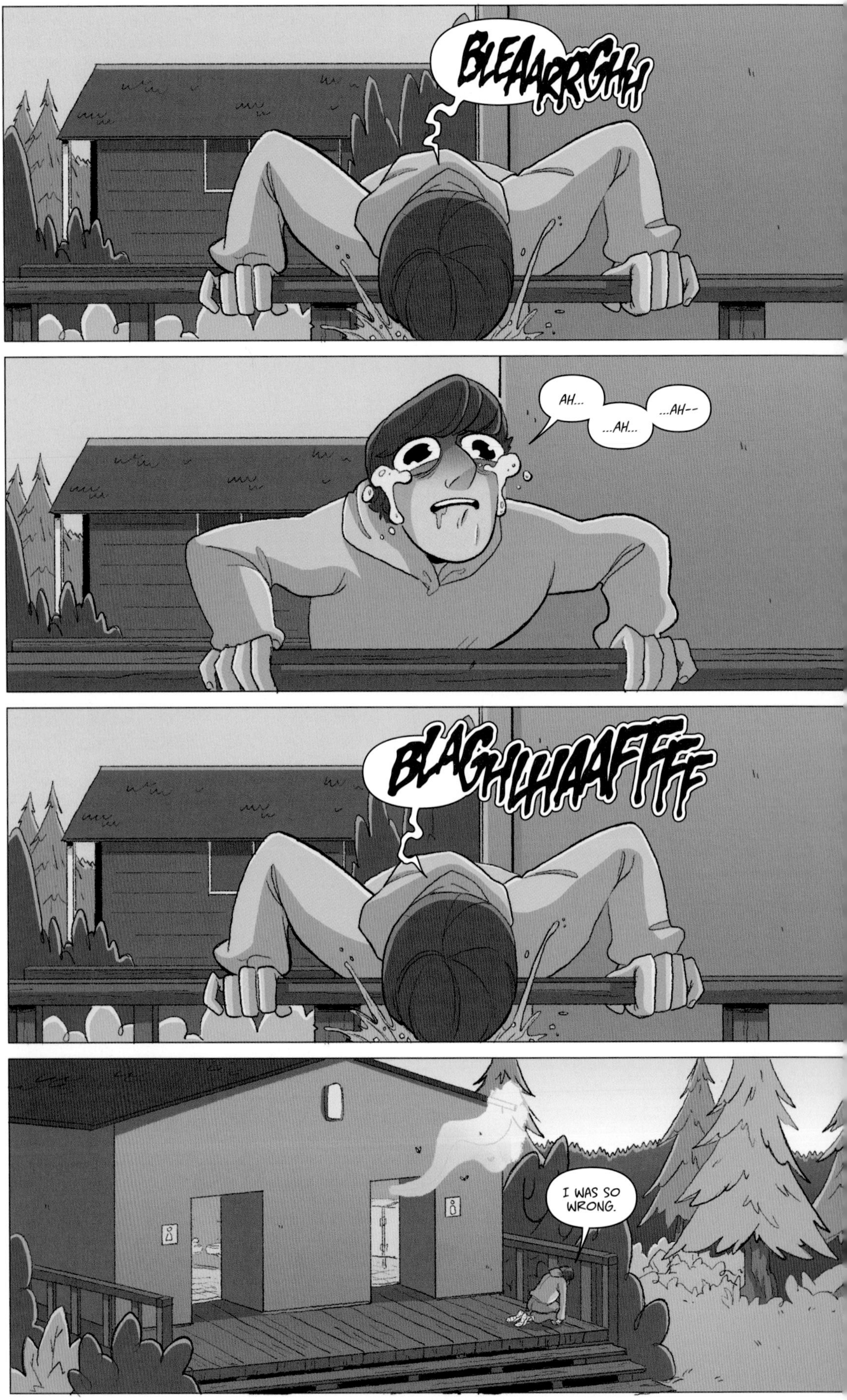

BLEAAARRGHH
AH...
...AH...
...AH--
BLAGHLHAAFFFFF
I WAS SO WRONG.

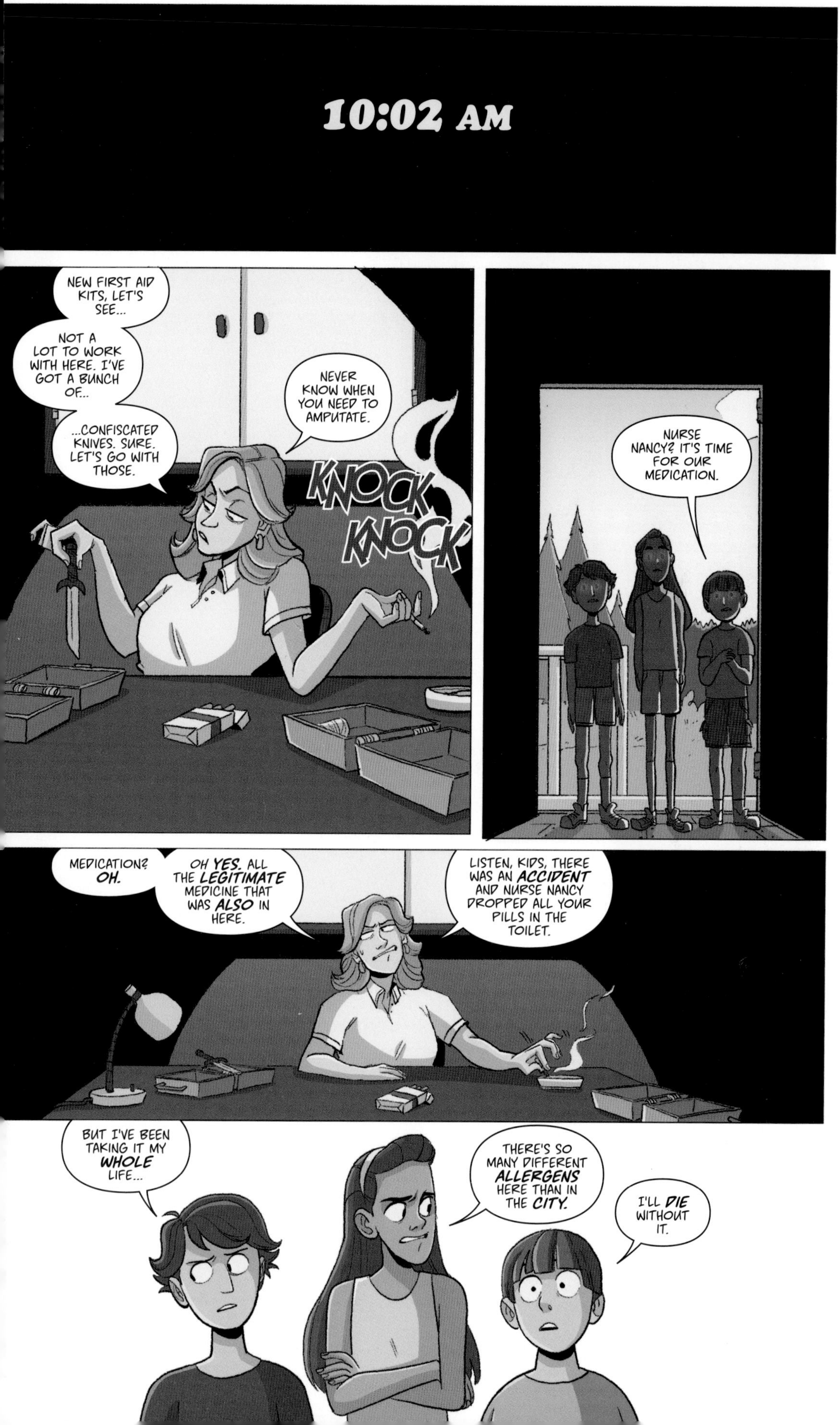
10:02 AM
NEW FIRST AID KITS, LET'S SEE...
NOT A LOT TO WORK WITH HERE. I'VE GOT A BUNCH OF...
...CONFISCATED KNIVES. SURE. LET'S GO WITH THOSE.
NEVER KNOW WHEN YOU NEED TO AMPUTATE.
KNOCK KNOCK
NURSE NANCY? IT'S TIME FOR OUR MEDICATION.
MEDICATION? OH.
OH YES. ALL THE LEGITIMATE MEDICINE THAT WAS ALSO IN HERE.
LISTEN, KIDS, THERE WAS AN ACCIDENT AND NURSE NANCY DROPPED ALL YOUR PILLS IN THE TOILET.
BUT I'VE BEEN TAKING IT MY WHOLE LIFE...
THERE'S SO MANY DIFFERENT ALLERGENS HERE THAN IN THE CITY.
I'LL DIE WITHOUT IT.

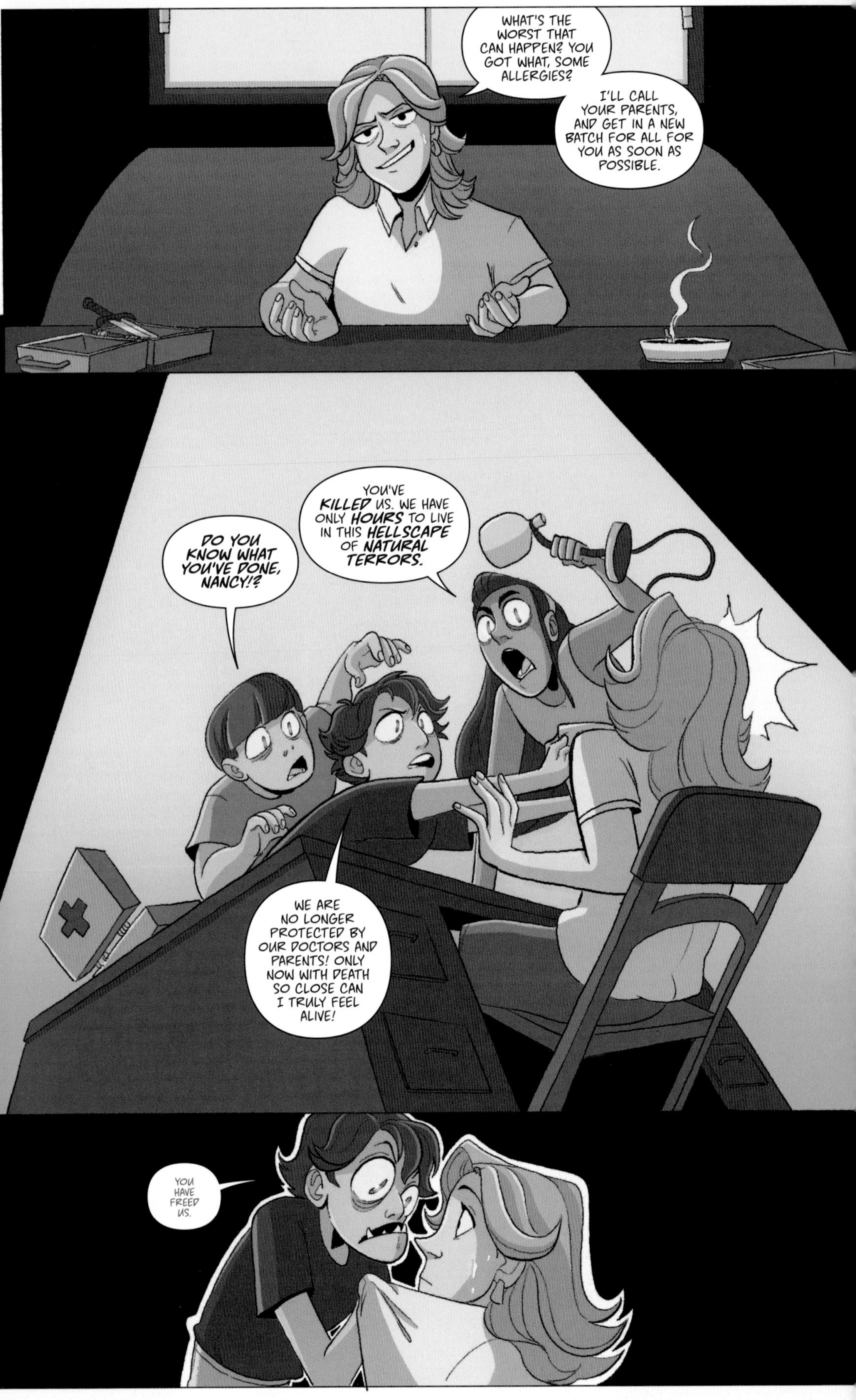
WHAT'S THE WORST THAT CAN HAPPEN? YOU GOT WHAT, SOME ALLERGIES?
I'LL CALL YOUR PARENTS, AND GET IN A NEW BATCH FOR ALL FOR YOU AS SOON AS POSSIBLE.
DO YOU KNOW WHAT YOU'VE DONE, NANCY!?
YOU'VE KILLED US. WE HAVE ONLY HOURS TO LIVE IN THIS HELLSCAPE OF NATURAL TERRORS.
WE ARE NO LONGER PROTECTED BY OUR DOCTORS AND PARENTS! ONLY NOW WITH DEATH SO CLOSE CAN I TRULY FEEL ALIVE!
YOU HAVE FREED US.

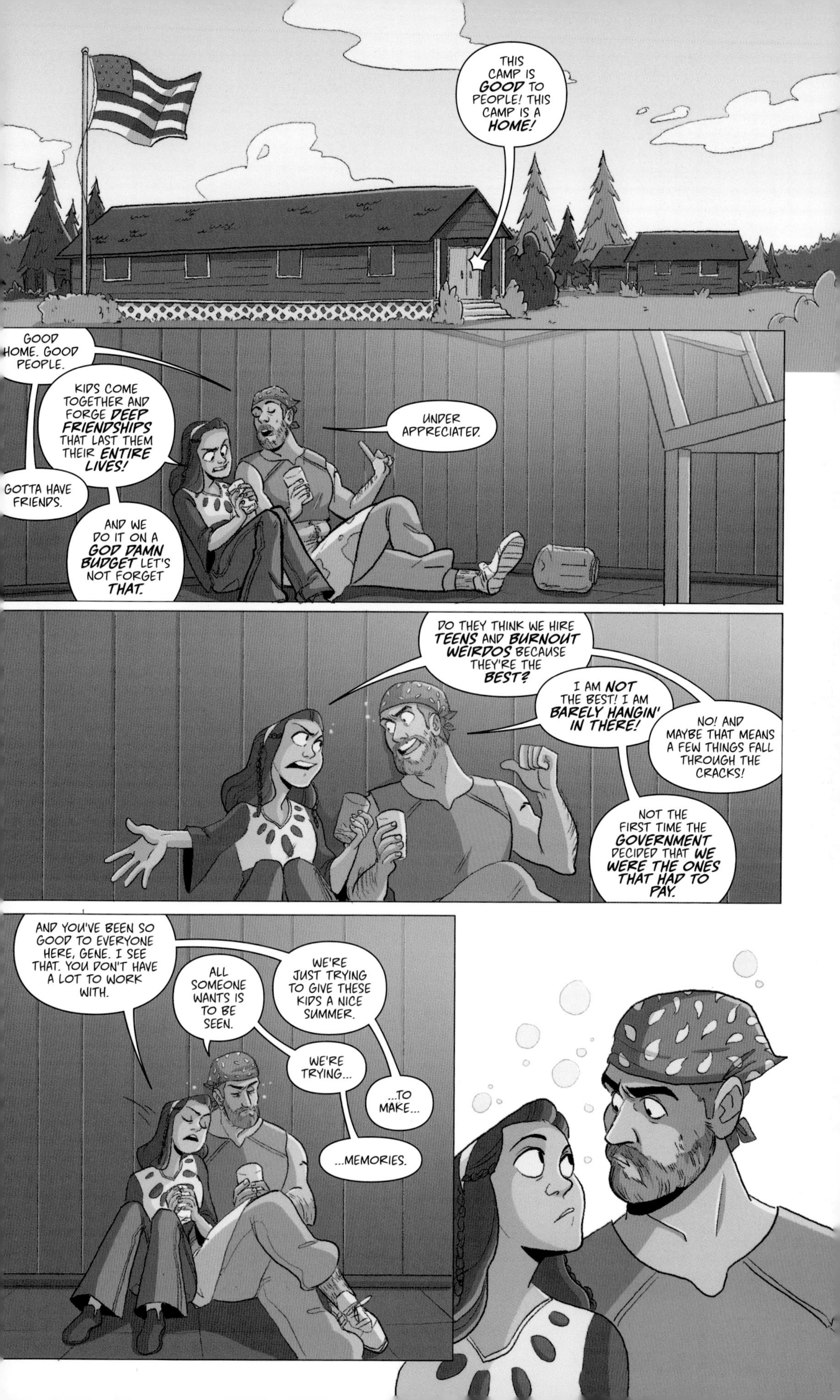

THIS CAMP IS GOOD TO PEOPLE! THIS CAMP IS A HOME!
GOOD HOME. GOOD PEOPLE.
KIDS COME TOGETHER AND FORGE DEEP FRIENDSHIPS THAT LAST THEM THEIR ENTIRE LIVES!
UNDER APPRECIATED.
GOTTA HAVE FRIENDS.
AND WE DO IT ON A GOD DAMN BUDGET LET'S NOT FORGET THAT.
DO THEY THINK WE HIRE TEENS AND BURNOUT WEIRDOS BECAUSE THEY'RE THE BEST?
I AM NOT THE BEST! I AM BARELY HANGIN' IN THERE!
NO! AND MAYBE THAT MEANS A FEW THINGS FALL THROUGH THE CRACKS!
NOT THE FIRST TIME THE GOVERNMENT DECIDED THAT WE WERE THE ONES THAT HAD TO PAY.
AND YOU'VE BEEN SO GOOD TO EVERYONE HERE, GENE. I SEE THAT. YOU DON'T HAVE A LOT TO WORK WITH.
ALL SOMEONE WANTS IS TO BE SEEN.
WE'RE JUST TRYING TO GIVE THESE KIDS A NICE SUMMER.
WE'RE TRYING...
...TO MAKE...
...MEMORIES.

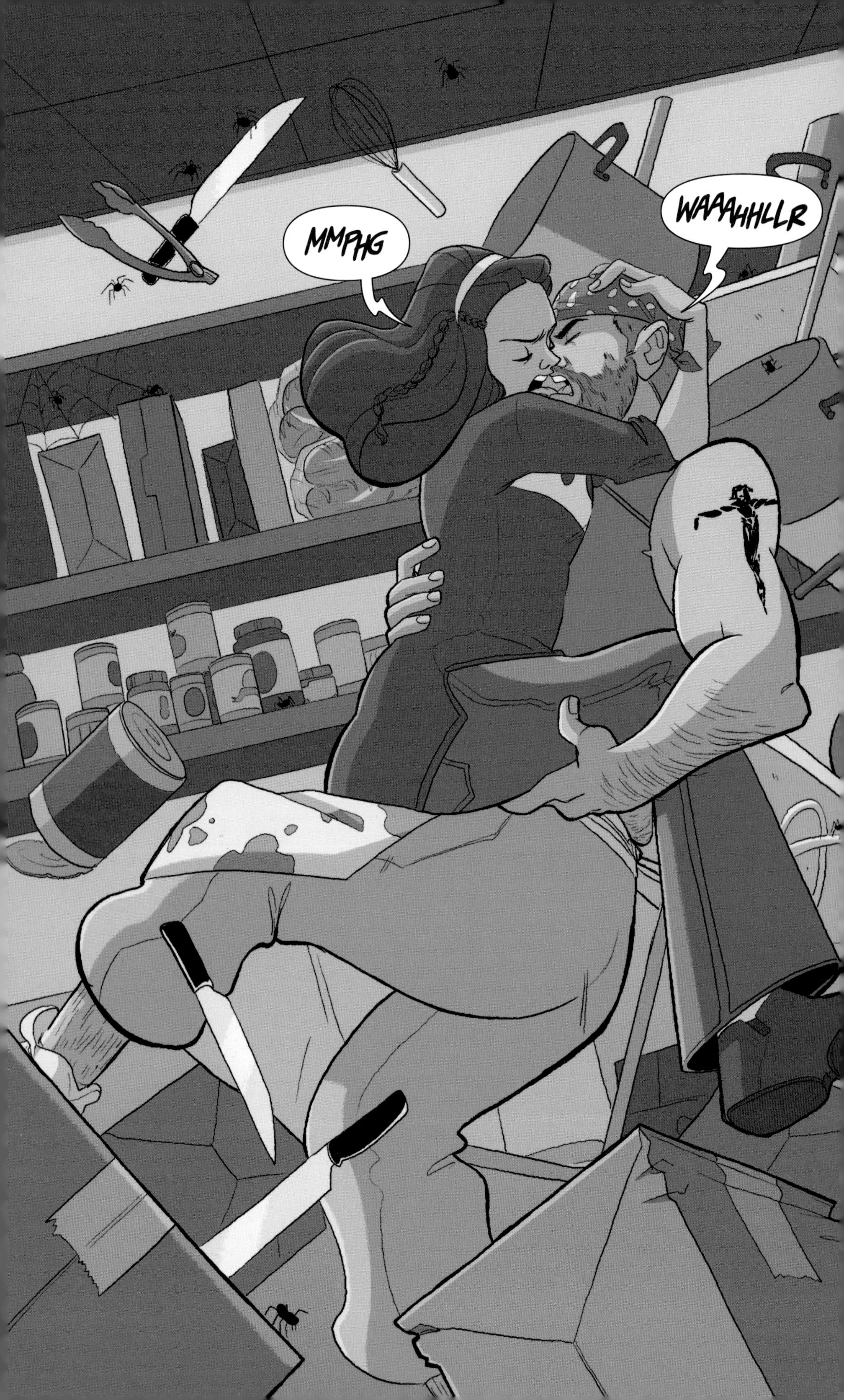
MMPHG
WAAAHHLLR

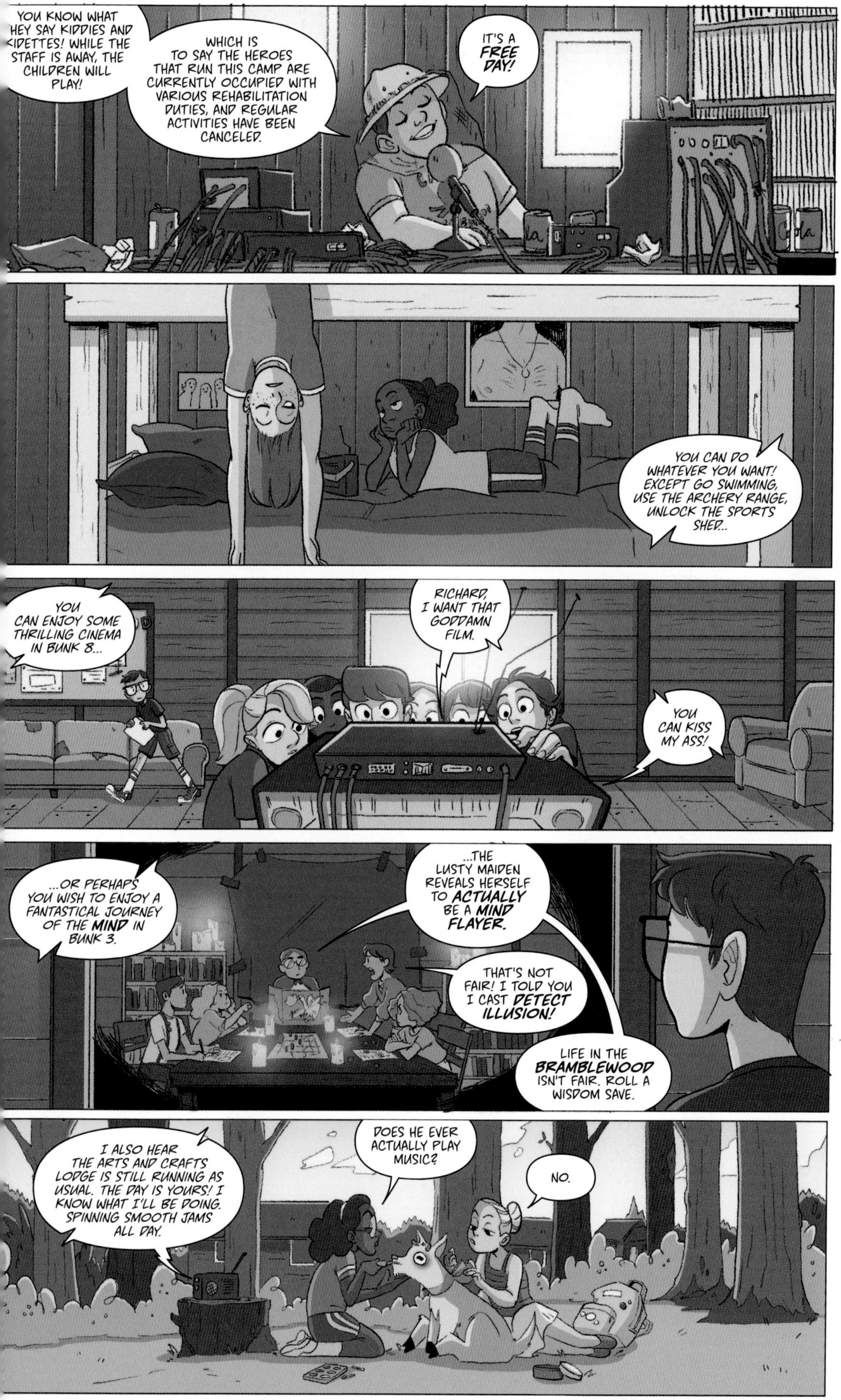
YOU KNOW WHAT HEY SAY KIDDIES AND IDETTES! WHILE THE STAFF IS AWAY, THE CHILDREN WILL PLAY!
WHICH IS TO SAY THE HEROES THAT RUN THIS CAMP ARE CURRENTLY OCCUPIED WITH VARIOUS REHABILITATION DUTIES, AND REGULAR ACTIVITIES HAVE BEEN CANCELED.
IT'S A FREE DAY!
YOU CAN DO WHATEVER YOU WANT! EXCEPT GO SWIMMING, USE THE ARCHERY RANGE, UNLOCK THE SPORTS SHED...
YOU CAN ENJOY SOME THRILLING CINEMA IN BUNK 8...
RICHARD, I WANT THAT GODDAMN FILM.
YOU CAN KISS MY ASS!
...OR PERHAPS YOU WISH TO ENJOY A FANTASTICAL JOURNEY OF THE MIND IN BUNK 3.
...THE LUSTY MAIDEN REVEALS HERSELF TO ACTUALLY BE A MIND FLAYER.
THAT'S NOT FAIR! I TOLD YOU I CAST DETECT ILLUSION!
LIFE IN THE BRAMBLEWOOD ISN'T FAIR. ROLL A WISDOM SAVE.
I ALSO HEAR THE ARTS AND CRAFTS LODGE IS STILL RUNNING AS USUAL. THE DAY IS YOURS! I KNOW WHAT I'LL BE DOING. SPINNING SMOOTH JAMS ALL DAY.
DOES HE EVER ACTUALLY PLAY MUSIC?
NO.

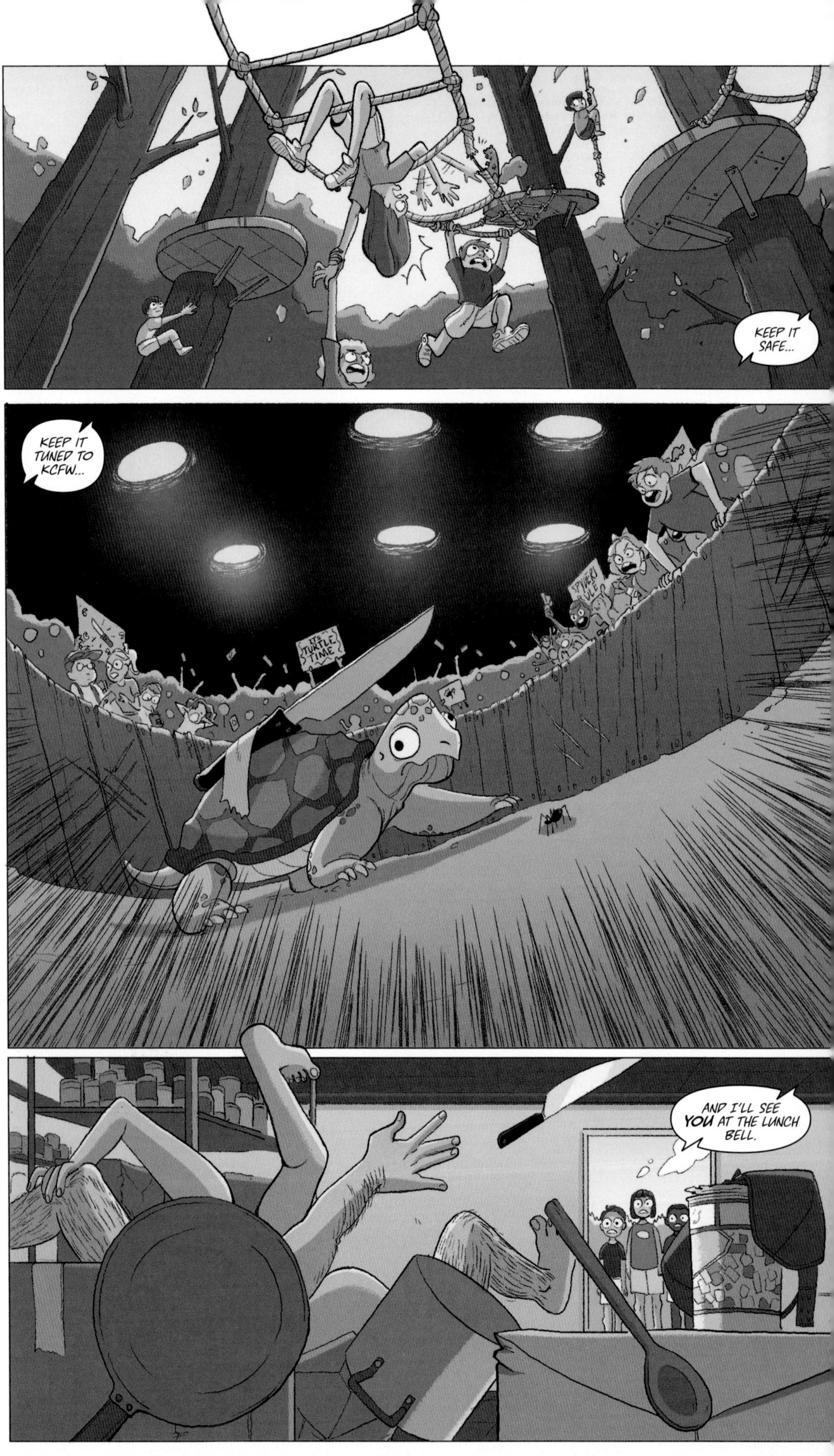
KEEP IT SAFE...
KEEP IT TUNED TO KCFW...
IT'S TURTLE TIME
AND I'LL SEE **YOU** AT THE LUNCH BELL.

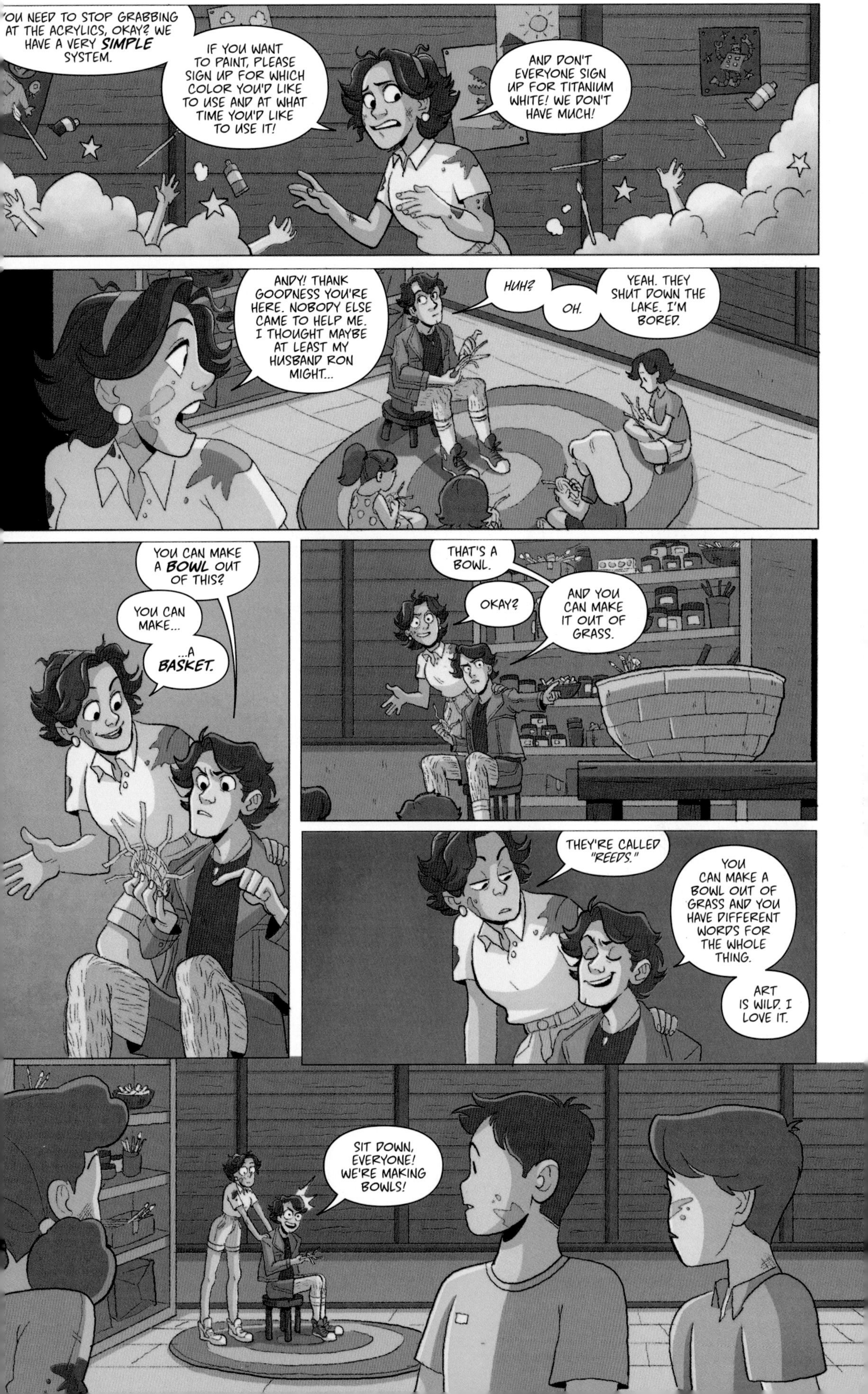
YOU NEED TO STOP GRABBING AT THE ACRYLICS, OKAY? WE HAVE A VERY SIMPLE SYSTEM.
IF YOU WANT TO PAINT, PLEASE SIGN UP FOR WHICH COLOR YOU'D LIKE TO USE AND AT WHAT TIME YOU'D LIKE TO USE IT!
AND DON'T EVERYONE SIGN UP FOR TITANIUM WHITE! WE DON'T HAVE MUCH!
ANDY! THANK GOODNESS YOU'RE HERE. NOBODY ELSE CAME TO HELP ME. I THOUGHT MAYBE AT LEAST MY HUSBAND RON MIGHT...
HUH?
OH.
YEAH. THEY SHUT DOWN THE LAKE. I'M BORED.
YOU CAN MAKE A BOWL OUT OF THIS?
YOU CAN MAKE...
...A BASKET.
THAT'S A BOWL.
OKAY?
AND YOU CAN MAKE IT OUT OF GRASS.
THEY'RE CALLED "REEDS."
YOU CAN MAKE A BOWL OUT OF GRASS AND YOU HAVE DIFFERENT WORDS FOR THE WHOLE THING.
ART IS WILD. I LOVE IT.
SIT DOWN, EVERYONE! WE'RE MAKING BOWLS!

EXCUSE ME, LADIES AND GERMS. I HAPPENED TO NOTICE YOU WERE ENGAGED IN SOME *GAMING* OF THE PEN AND PAPER VARIETY...

PERHAPS YOUR PARTY MIGHT BE INTERESTED IN A VISIT FROM "BULLENWOLF DINDIDDLE?"

HE APPEARS TO BE BUT A LOWLY DWARF SONGSMITH, ONE WHO TRAVELS FROM TOWN TO TOWN, EARNING HIS ALE WITH NIGHTLY MUSIC AND RIBALDRY.

BUT IN *FACT*, HE IS A DUAL CLASS BARD MAGE FROM AN ANCIENT LINEAGE OF--

THE PARTY'S FULL. START A NEW GAME WITH SOMEONE ELSE.

EXCELLENT INITIATIVE, NARCELIA. YOUR "CIRCLE OF PROTECTION VERSUS *LOSERS*" WORKS WITHOUT FLAW.

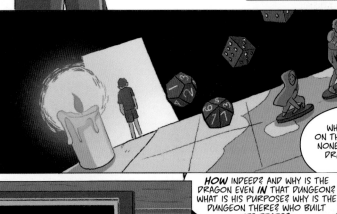

UNFORTUNATELY, WHILE YOUR PARTY RESTS ON THE DARK DUNGEON FLOOR, NONE OF YOU HEAR THE WHITE DRAGON APPROACH FROM THE CORRIDOR.

ALL OF YOU TAKE 57 POINTS OF DAMAGE FROM T[ ] CONE OF COLD THE DRAGON UNLEASHES FROM ITS JOWLS--

BUT THAT KILLS MY CLERIC!

WHAT?! NO!

HOW DID WE NOT HEAR A *DRAGON* WALKING DOWN THE HALL?

HOW INDEED? AND WHY IS THE DRAGON EVEN *IN* THAT DUNGEON? WHAT IS HIS PURPOSE? WHY IS THE DUNGEON THERE? WHO BUILT ITS TRAPS?

WHAT? I DON'T KNOW. WHO CARES?

YOUR *PLAYERS* CARE. AND AS AN OFFICIALLY RECOGNIZED CLASS 'C' DUNGEON MASTER, *I CHALLENGE YOU FOR CUSTODY OF YOUR CAMPAIGN!*

LET THE BATTLE BEGIN!

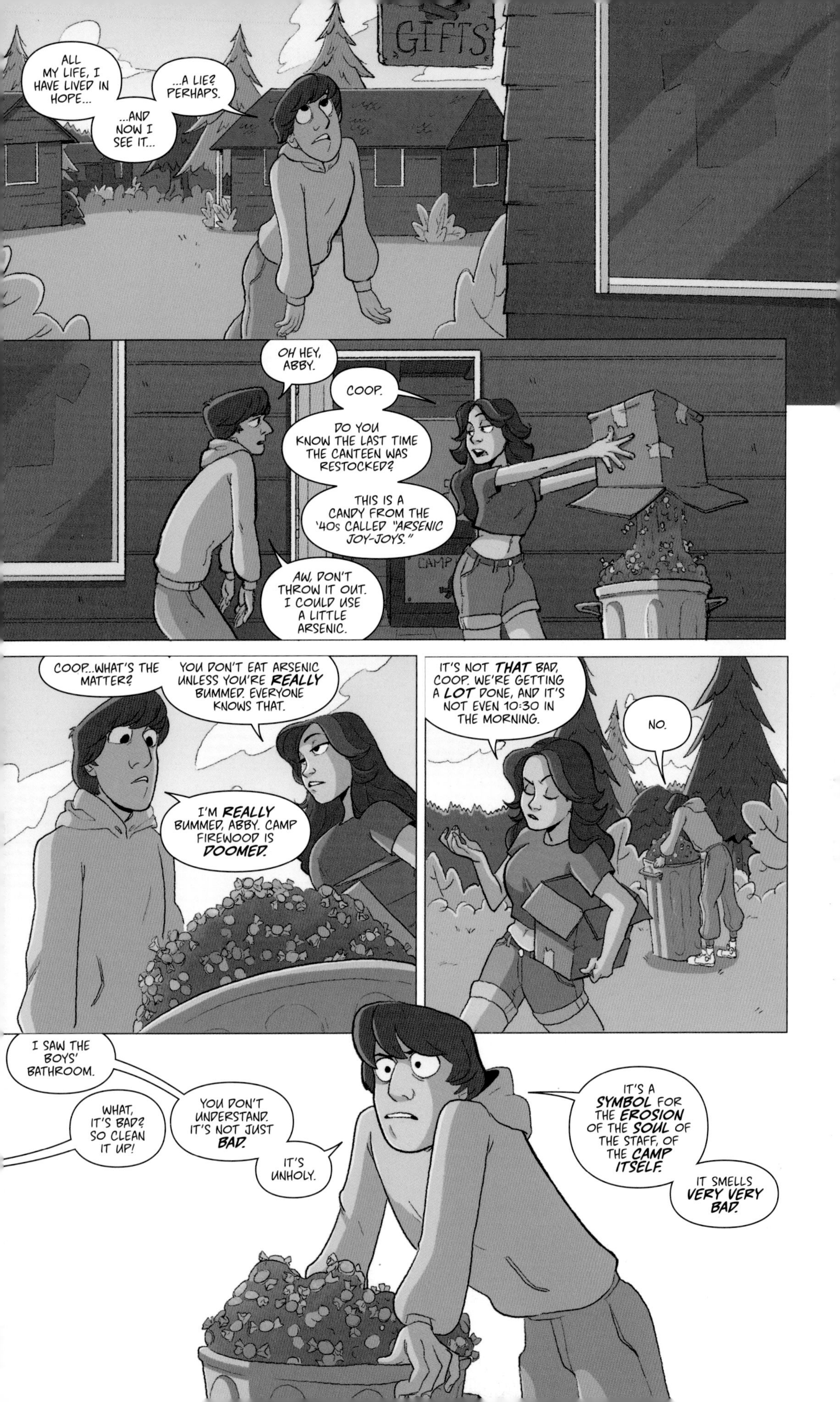
GIFTS
ALL MY LIFE, I HAVE LIVED IN HOPE...
...AND NOW I SEE IT...
...A LIE? PERHAPS.
OH HEY, ABBY.
COOP.
DO YOU KNOW THE LAST TIME THE CANTEEN WAS RESTOCKED?
THIS IS A CANDY FROM THE '40s CALLED "ARSENIC JOY-JOYS."
AW, DON'T THROW IT OUT. I COULD USE A LITTLE ARSENIC.
CAMP
COOP...WHAT'S THE MATTER?
YOU DON'T EAT ARSENIC UNLESS YOU'RE REALLY BUMMED. EVERYONE KNOWS THAT.
I'M REALLY BUMMED, ABBY. CAMP FIREWOOD IS DOOMED.
IT'S NOT THAT BAD, COOP. WE'RE GETTING A LOT DONE, AND IT'S NOT EVEN 10:30 IN THE MORNING.
NO.
I SAW THE BOYS' BATHROOM.
WHAT, IT'S BAD? SO CLEAN IT UP!
YOU DON'T UNDERSTAND. IT'S NOT JUST BAD.
IT'S UNHOLY.
IT'S A SYMBOL FOR THE EROSION OF THE SOUL OF THE STAFF, OF THE CAMP ITSELF.
IT SMELLS VERY VERY BAD.

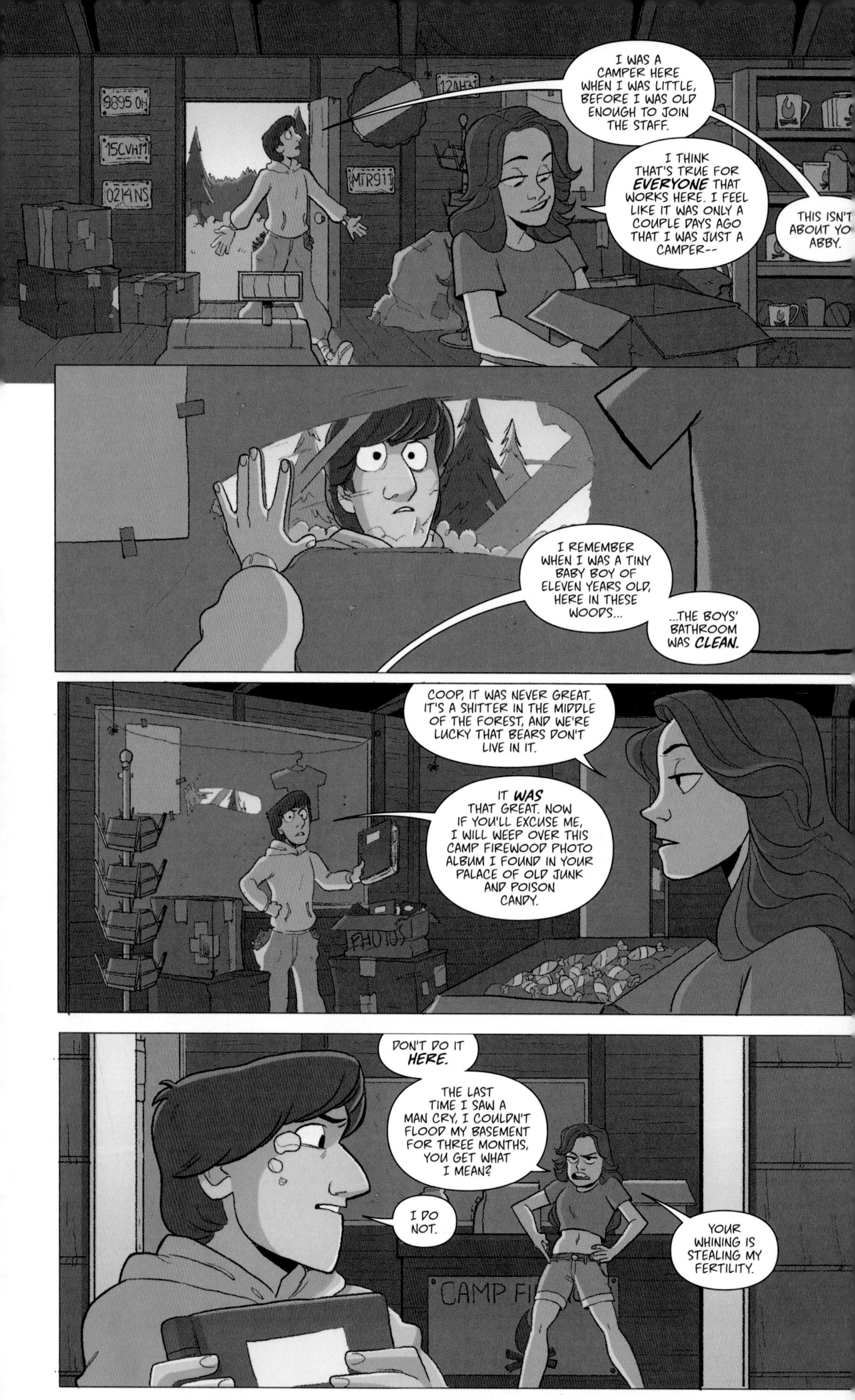

9895 OH
15CVH11
0214NS
MTR911
12AH31
I WAS A CAMPER HERE WHEN I WAS LITTLE, BEFORE I WAS OLD ENOUGH TO JOIN THE STAFF.
I THINK THAT'S TRUE FOR EVERYONE THAT WORKS HERE. I FEEL LIKE IT WAS ONLY A COUPLE DAYS AGO THAT I WAS JUST A CAMPER--
THIS ISN'T ABOUT YO ABBY.
I REMEMBER WHEN I WAS A TINY BABY BOY OF ELEVEN YEARS OLD, HERE IN THESE WOODS...
...THE BOYS' BATHROOM WAS CLEAN.
COOP, IT WAS NEVER GREAT. IT'S A SHITTER IN THE MIDDLE OF THE FOREST, AND WE'RE LUCKY THAT BEARS DON'T LIVE IN IT.
IT WAS THAT GREAT. NOW IF YOU'LL EXCUSE ME, I WILL WEEP OVER THIS CAMP FIREWOOD PHOTO ALBUM I FOUND IN YOUR PALACE OF OLD JUNK AND POISON CANDY.
PHOTOS
DON'T DO IT HERE.
THE LAST TIME I SAW A MAN CRY, I COULDN'T FLOOD MY BASEMENT FOR THREE MONTHS, YOU GET WHAT I MEAN?
I DO NOT.
YOUR WHINING IS STEALING MY FERTILITY.
CAMP FI

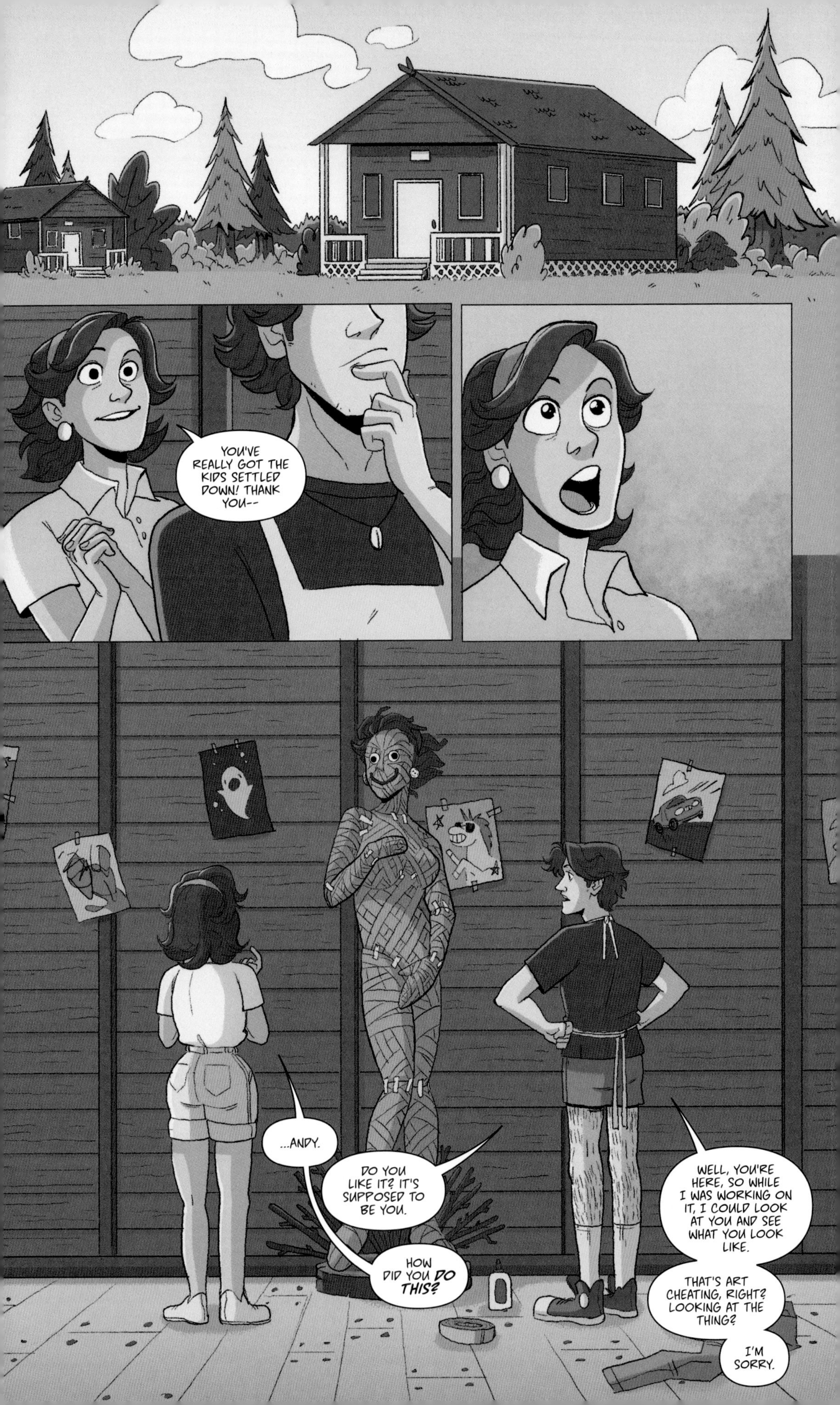
YOU'VE REALLY GOT THE KIDS SETTLED DOWN! THANK YOU--
...ANDY.
DO YOU LIKE IT? IT'S SUPPOSED TO BE YOU.
HOW DID YOU *DO THIS?*
WELL, YOU'RE HERE, SO WHILE I WAS WORKING ON IT, I COULD LOOK AT YOU AND SEE WHAT YOU LOOK LIKE.
THAT'S ART CHEATING, RIGHT? LOOKING AT THE THING?
I'M SORRY.

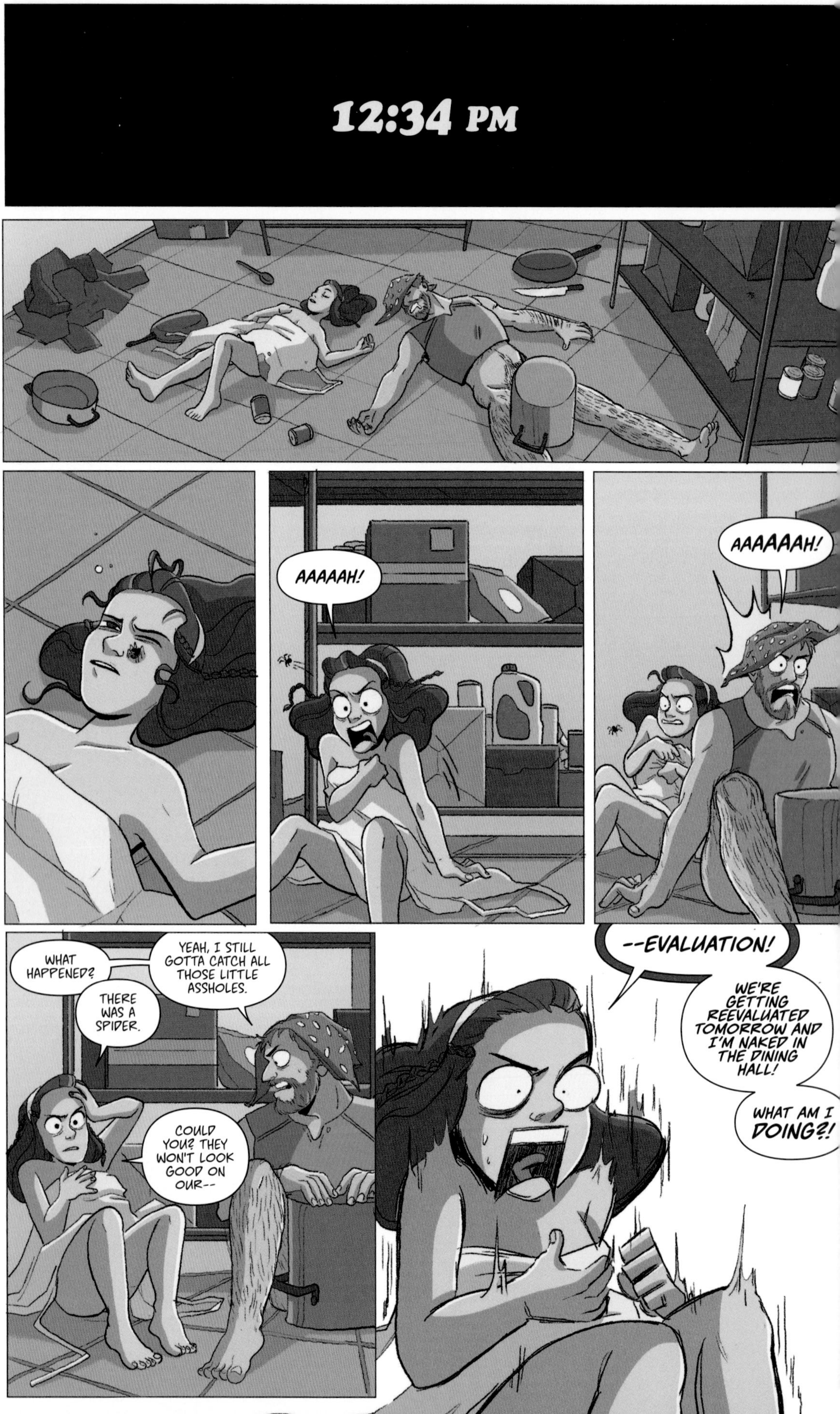
12:34 PM
AAAAAH!
AAAAAAH!
WHAT HAPPENED?
THERE WAS A SPIDER.
YEAH, I STILL GOTTA CATCH ALL THOSE LITTLE ASSHOLES.
COULD YOU? THEY WON'T LOOK GOOD ON OUR--
--EVALUATION!
WE'RE GETTING REEVALUATED TOMORROW AND I'M NAKED IN THE DINING HALL!
WHAT AM I DOING?!

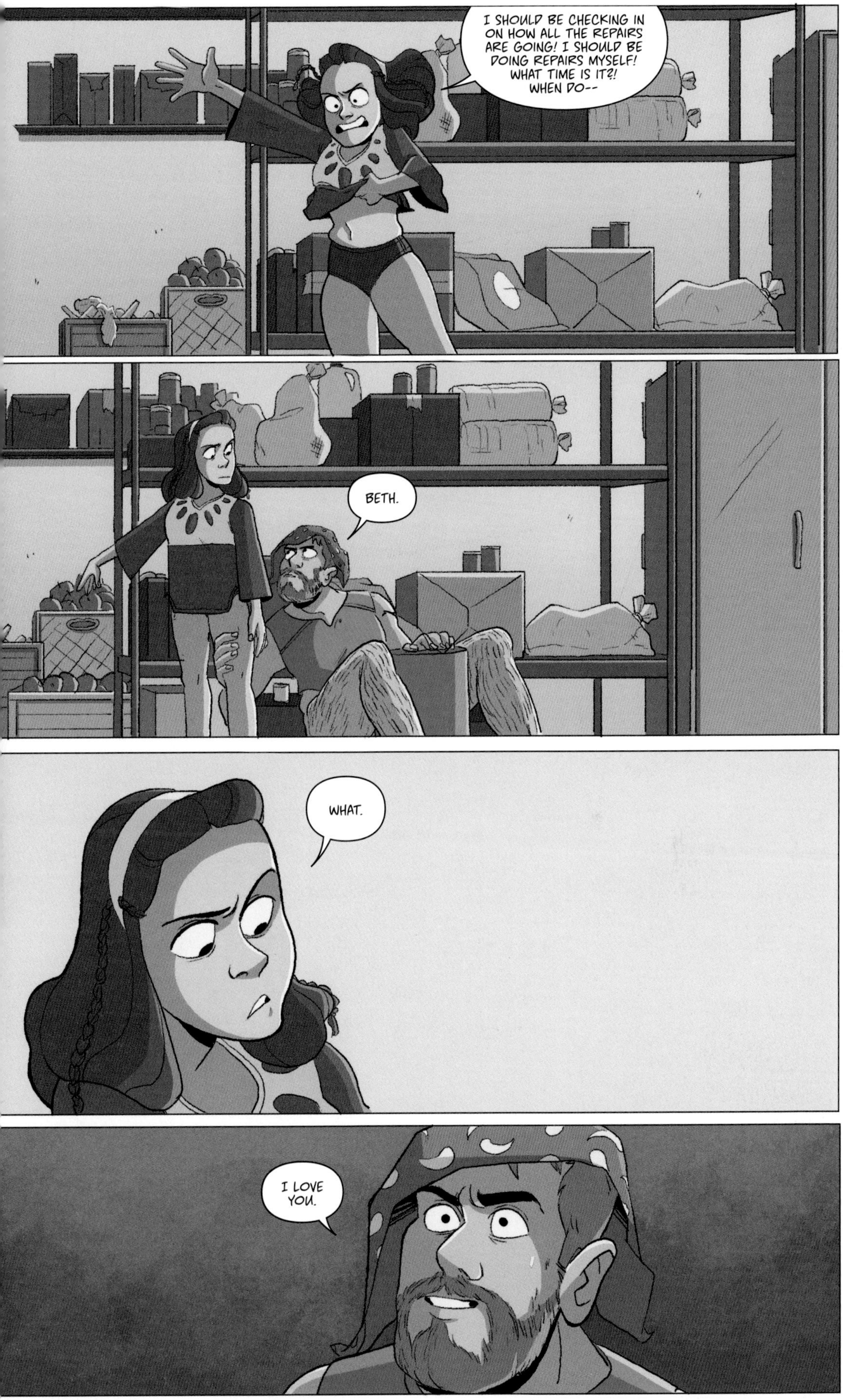
I SHOULD BE CHECKING IN ON HOW ALL THE REPAIRS ARE GOING! I SHOULD BE DOING REPAIRS MYSELF! WHAT TIME IS IT?! WHEN DO--
BETH.
WHAT.
I LOVE YOU.

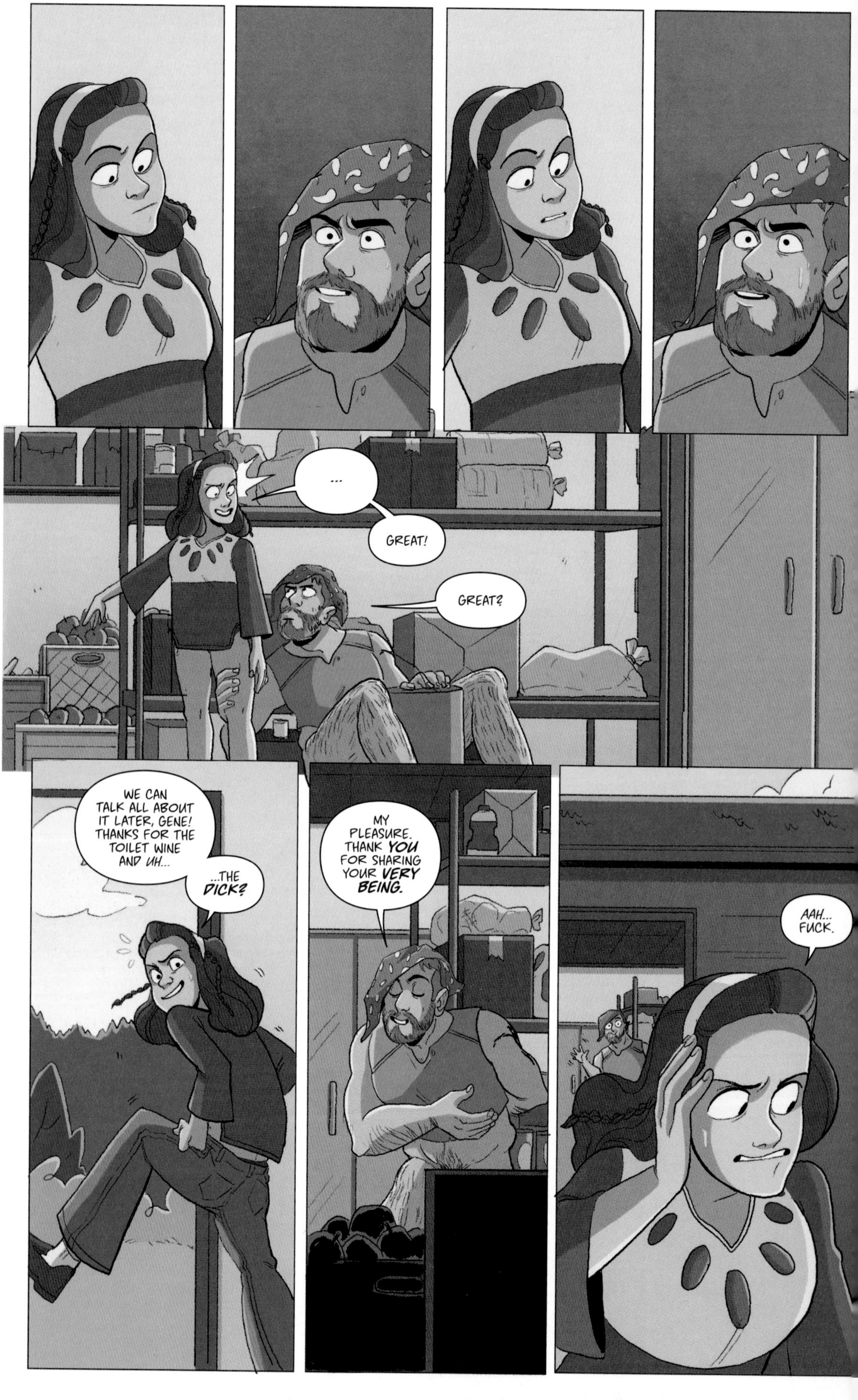
...
GREAT!
GREAT?
WE CAN TALK ALL ABOUT IT LATER, GENE! THANKS FOR THE TOILET WINE AND UH...
...THE DICK?
MY PLEASURE. THANK YOU FOR SHARING YOUR VERY BEING.
AAH... FUCK.

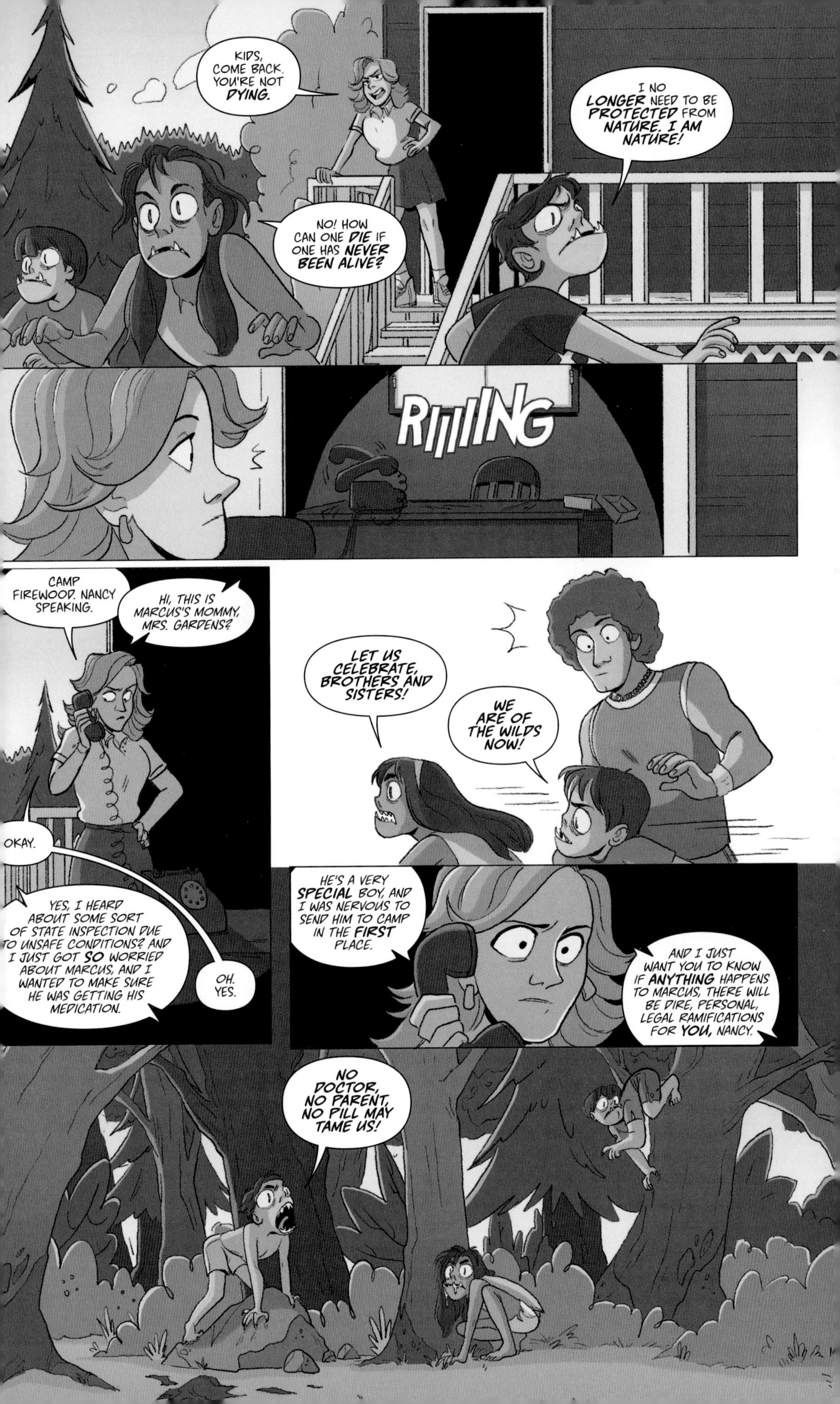
KIDS, COME BACK. YOU'RE NOT DYING.
I NO LONGER NEED TO BE PROTECTED FROM NATURE. I AM NATURE!
NO! HOW CAN ONE DIE IF ONE HAS NEVER BEEN ALIVE?
RIIIING
CAMP FIREWOOD. NANCY SPEAKING.
HI, THIS IS MARCUS'S MOMMY, MRS. GARDENS?
LET US CELEBRATE, BROTHERS AND SISTERS!
WE ARE OF THE WILDS NOW!
OKAY.
YES, I HEARD ABOUT SOME SORT OF STATE INSPECTION DUE TO UNSAFE CONDITIONS? AND I JUST GOT SO WORRIED ABOUT MARCUS, AND I WANTED TO MAKE SURE HE WAS GETTING HIS MEDICATION.
OH. YES.
HE'S A VERY SPECIAL BOY, AND I WAS NERVOUS TO SEND HIM TO CAMP IN THE FIRST PLACE.
AND I JUST WANT YOU TO KNOW IF ANYTHING HAPPENS TO MARCUS, THERE WILL BE DIRE, PERSONAL, LEGAL RAMIFICATIONS FOR YOU, NANCY.
NO DOCTOR, NO PARENT, NO PILL MAY TAME US!

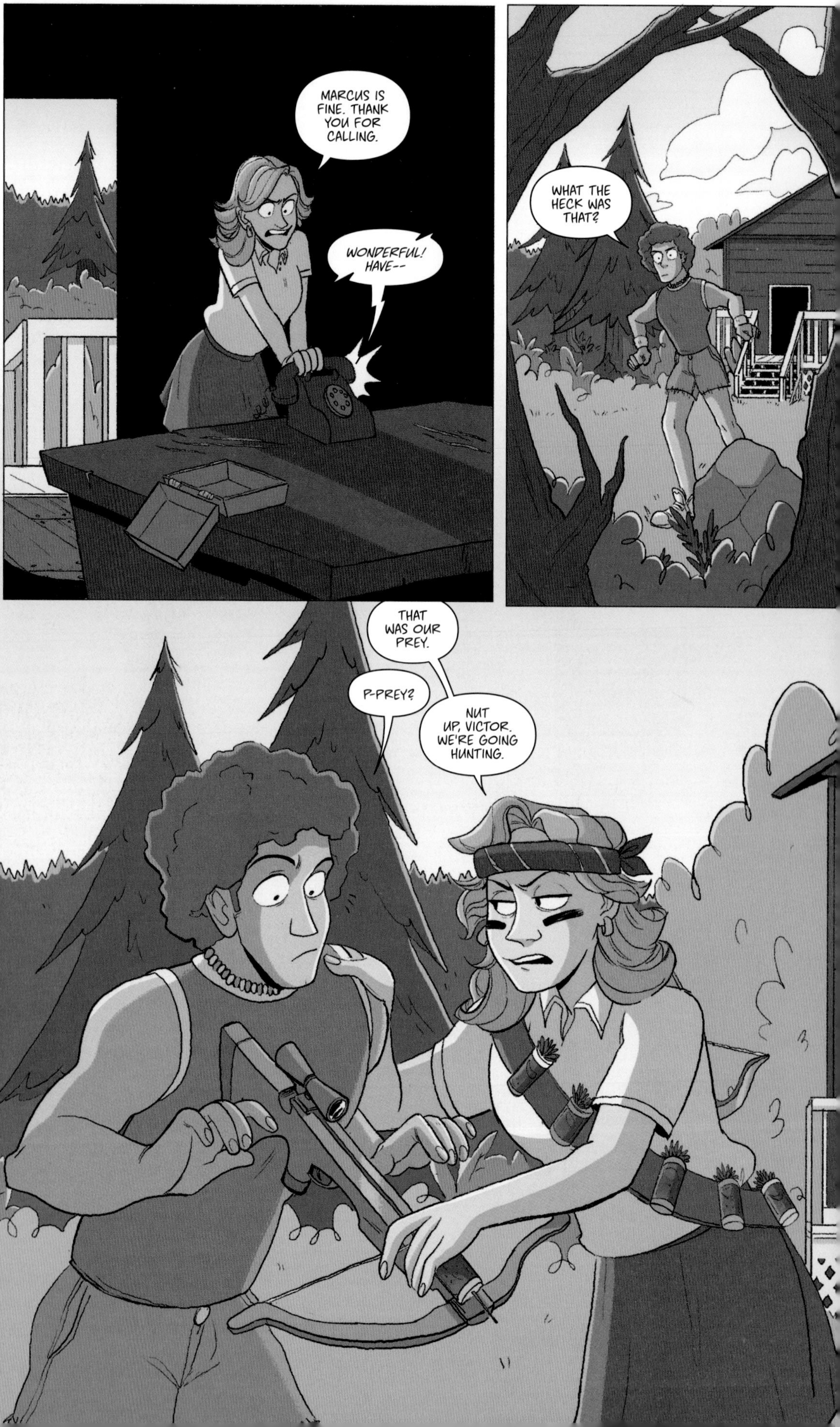
MARCUS IS FINE. THANK YOU FOR CALLING.
WONDERFUL! HAVE--
WHAT THE HECK WAS THAT?
THAT WAS OUR PREY.
P-PREY?
NUT UP, VICTOR. WE'RE GOING HUNTING.

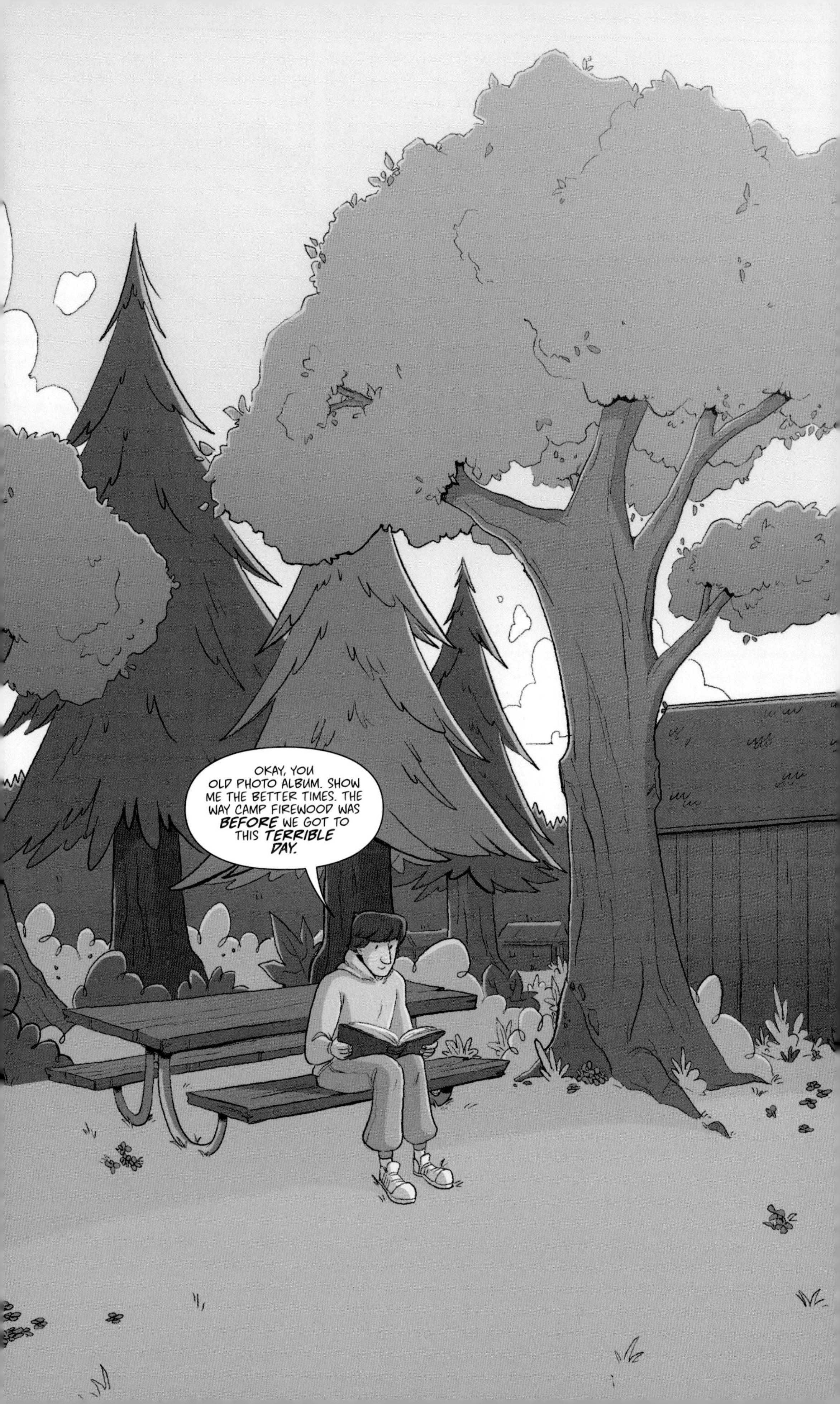
OKAY, YOU OLD PHOTO ALBUM. SHOW ME THE BETTER TIMES. THE WAY CAMP FIREWOOD WAS BEFORE WE GOT TO THIS TERRIBLE DAY.

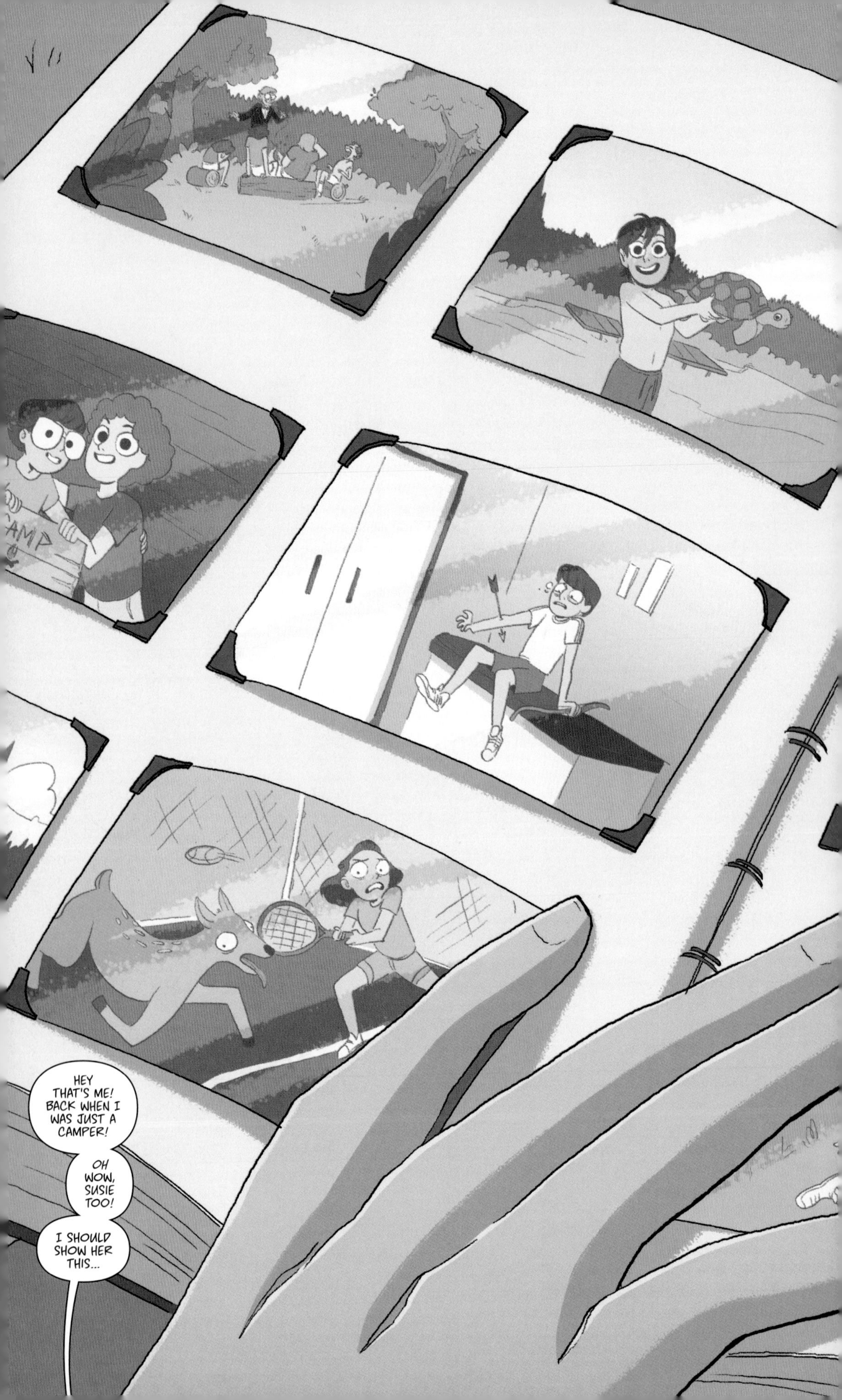
CAMP
HEY THAT'S ME! BACK WHEN I WAS JUST A CAMPER!
OH WOW, SUSIE TOO!
I SHOULD SHOW HER THIS...

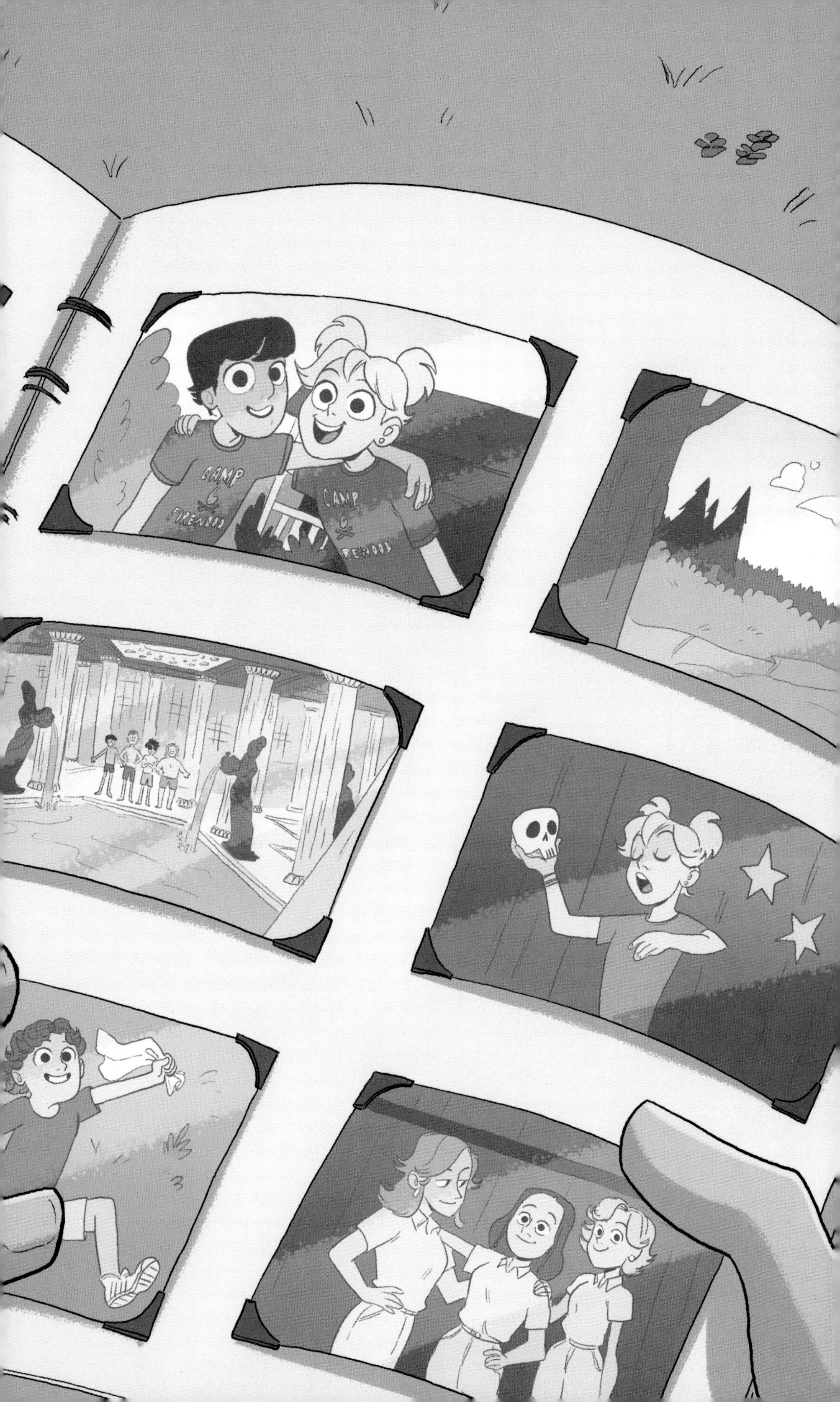
CAMP
FIREWOOD
CAMP
FIREWOOD

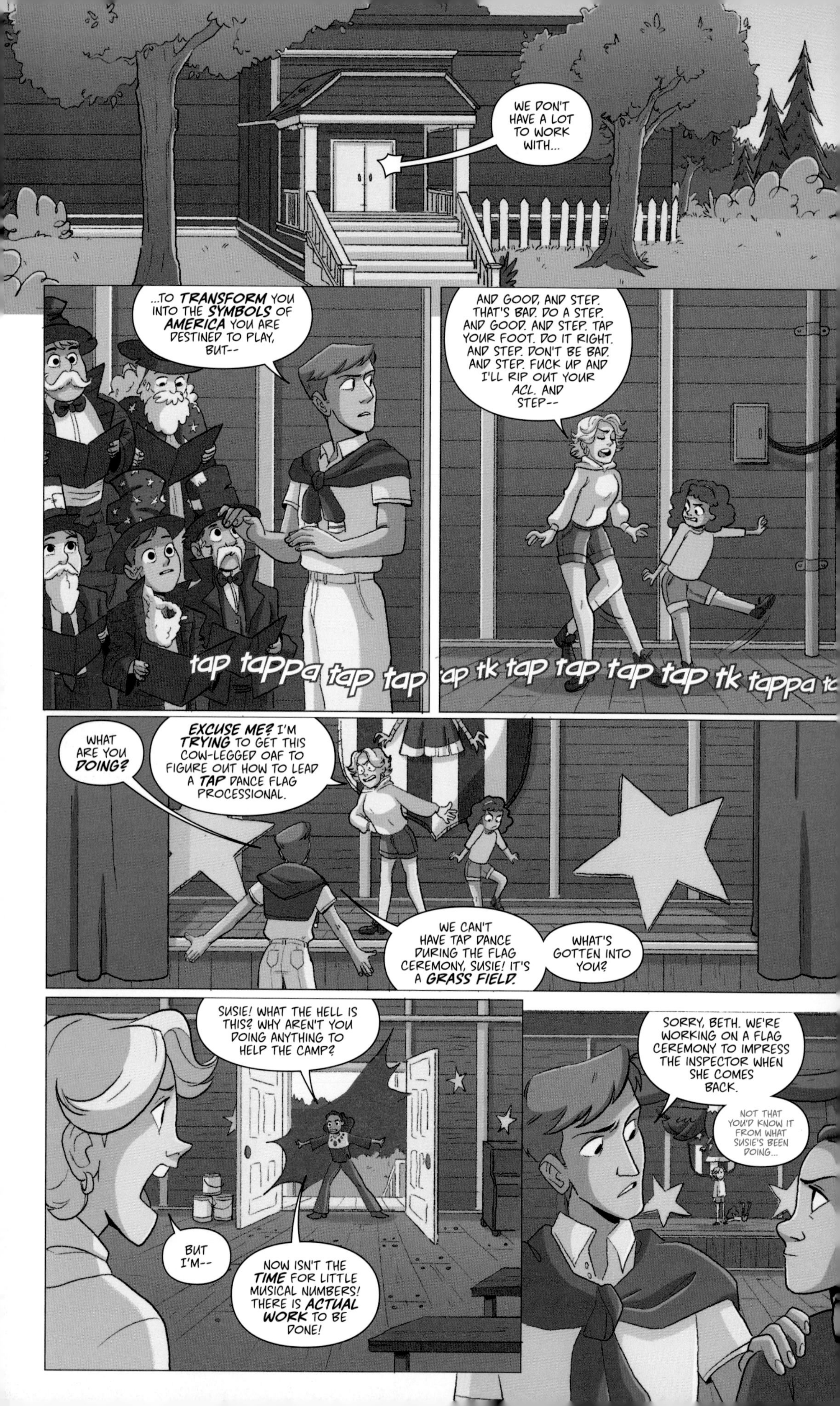
WE DON'T HAVE A LOT TO WORK WITH...
...TO TRANSFORM YOU INTO THE SYMBOLS OF AMERICA YOU ARE DESTINED TO PLAY, BUT--
tap tappa tap tap
AND GOOD, AND STEP. THAT'S BAD. DO A STEP. AND GOOD. AND STEP. TAP YOUR FOOT. DO IT RIGHT. AND STEP. DON'T BE BAD. AND STEP. FUCK UP AND I'LL RIP OUT YOUR ACL. AND STEP--
tap tk tap tap tap tap tk tappa ta
WHAT ARE YOU DOING?
EXCUSE ME? I'M TRYING TO GET THIS COW-LEGGED OAF TO FIGURE OUT HOW TO LEAD A TAP DANCE FLAG PROCESSIONAL.
WE CAN'T HAVE TAP DANCE DURING THE FLAG CEREMONY, SUSIE! IT'S A GRASS FIELD.
WHAT'S GOTTEN INTO YOU?
SUSIE! WHAT THE HELL IS THIS? WHY AREN'T YOU DOING ANYTHING TO HELP THE CAMP?
BUT I'M--
NOW ISN'T THE TIME FOR LITTLE MUSICAL NUMBERS! THERE IS ACTUAL WORK TO BE DONE!
SORRY, BETH. WE'RE WORKING ON A FLAG CEREMONY TO IMPRESS THE INSPECTOR WHEN SHE COMES BACK.
NOT THAT YOU'D KNOW IT FROM WHAT SUSIE'S BEEN DOING...

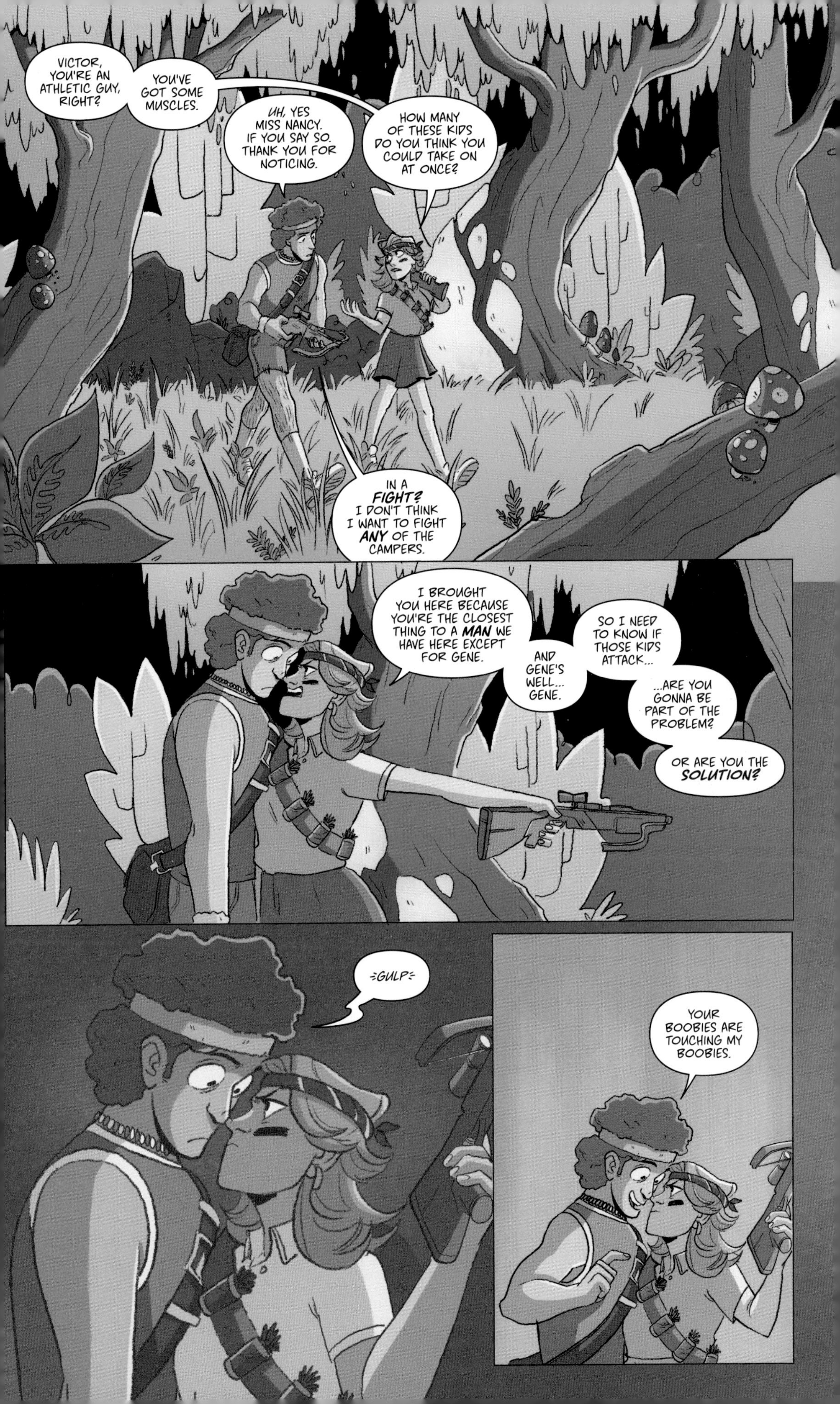
VICTOR, YOU'RE AN ATHLETIC GUY, RIGHT?
YOU'VE GOT SOME MUSCLES.
UH, YES MISS NANCY. IF YOU SAY SO. THANK YOU FOR NOTICING.
HOW MANY OF THESE KIDS DO YOU THINK YOU COULD TAKE ON AT ONCE?
IN A FIGHT? I DON'T THINK I WANT TO FIGHT ANY OF THE CAMPERS.
I BROUGHT YOU HERE BECAUSE YOU'RE THE CLOSEST THING TO A MAN WE HAVE HERE EXCEPT FOR GENE.
AND GENE'S WELL... GENE.
SO I NEED TO KNOW IF THOSE KIDS ATTACK...
...ARE YOU GONNA BE PART OF THE PROBLEM?
OR ARE YOU THE SOLUTION?
GULP
YOUR BOOBIES ARE TOUCHING MY BOOBIES.

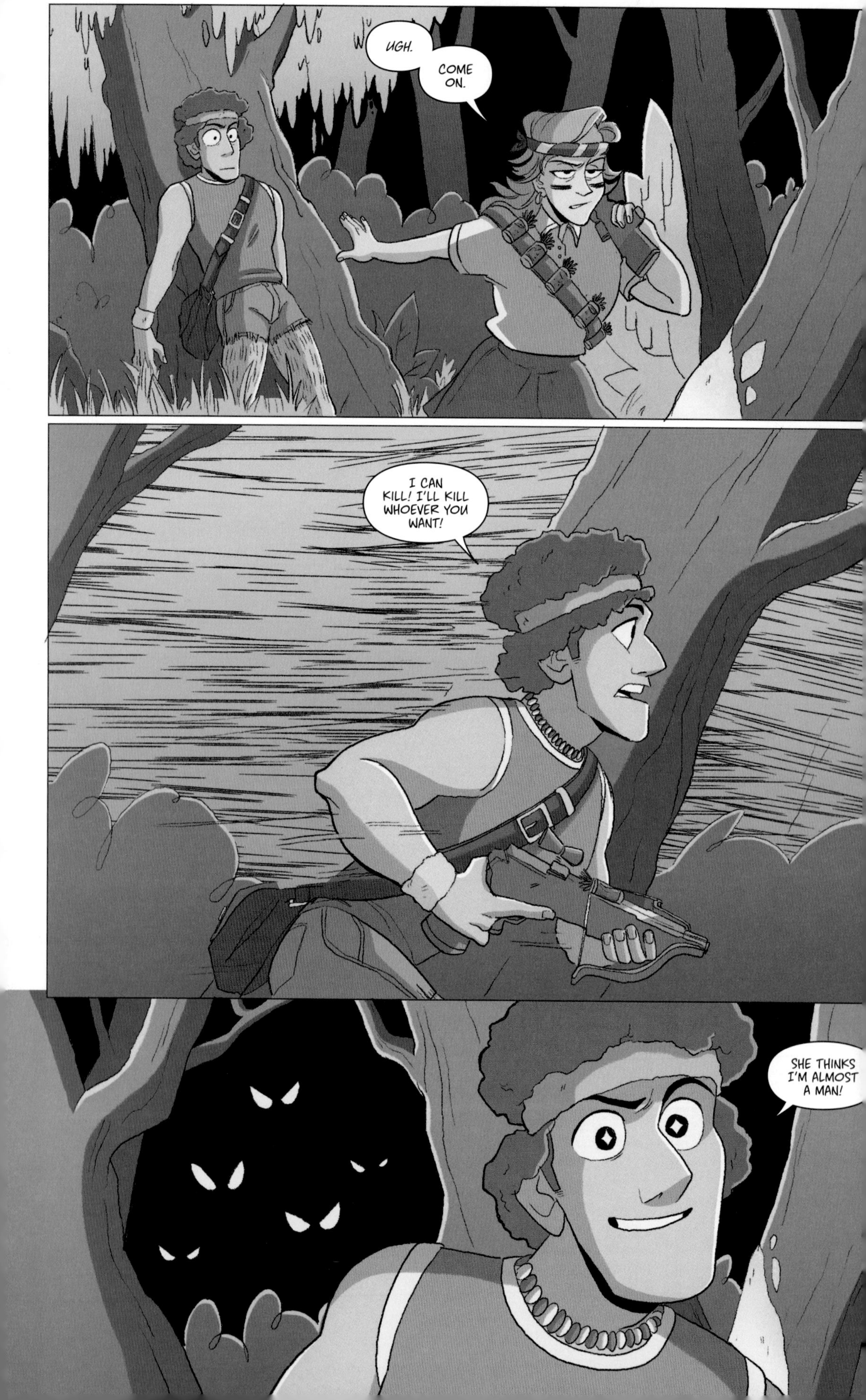
UGH.
COME ON.
I CAN KILL! I'LL KILL WHOEVER YOU WANT!
SHE THINKS I'M ALMOST A MAN!

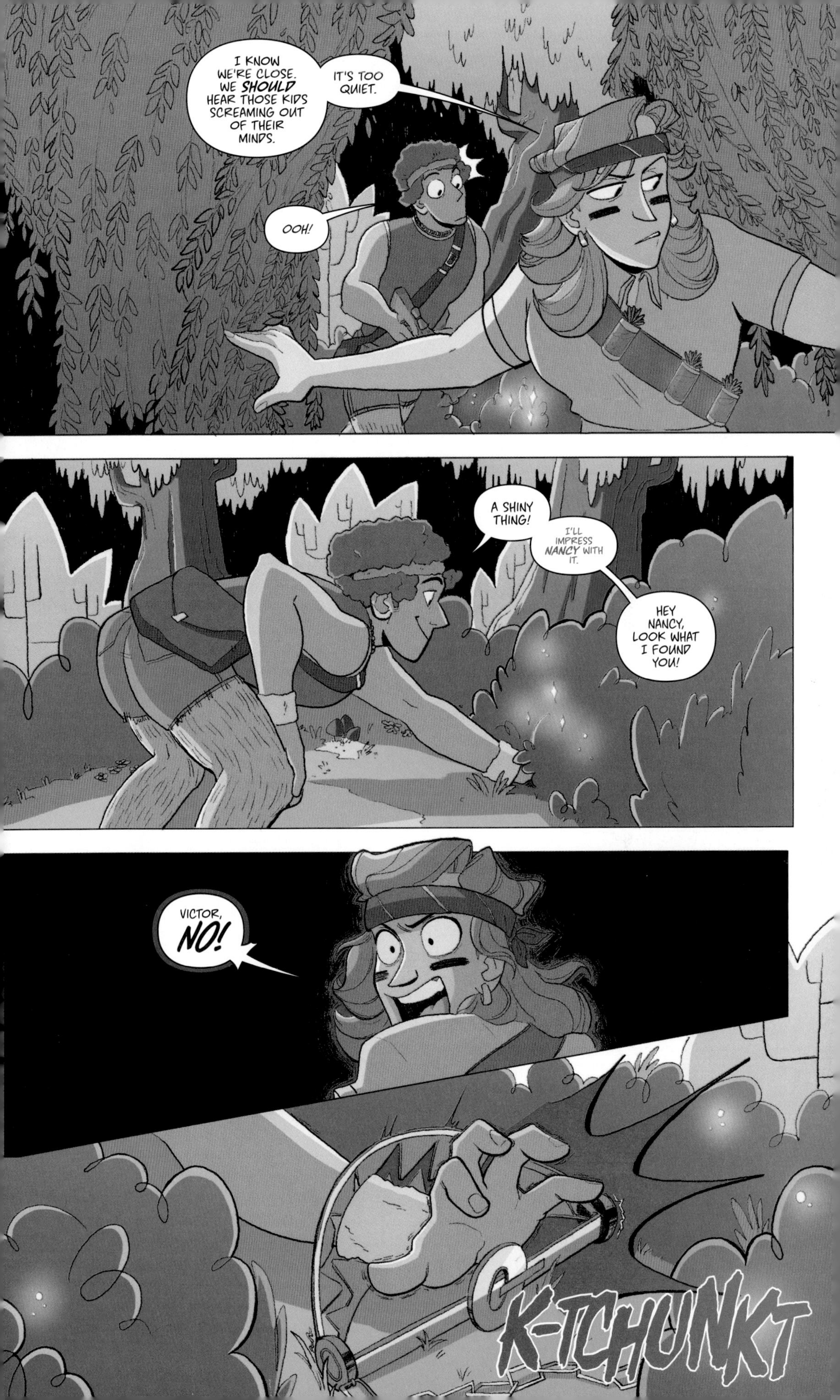
I KNOW WE'RE CLOSE. WE SHOULD HEAR THOSE KIDS SCREAMING OUT OF THEIR MINDS.
IT'S TOO QUIET.
OOH!
A SHINY THING!
I'LL IMPRESS NANCY WITH IT.
HEY NANCY, LOOK WHAT I FOUND YOU!
VICTOR, NO!
K-TCHUNK

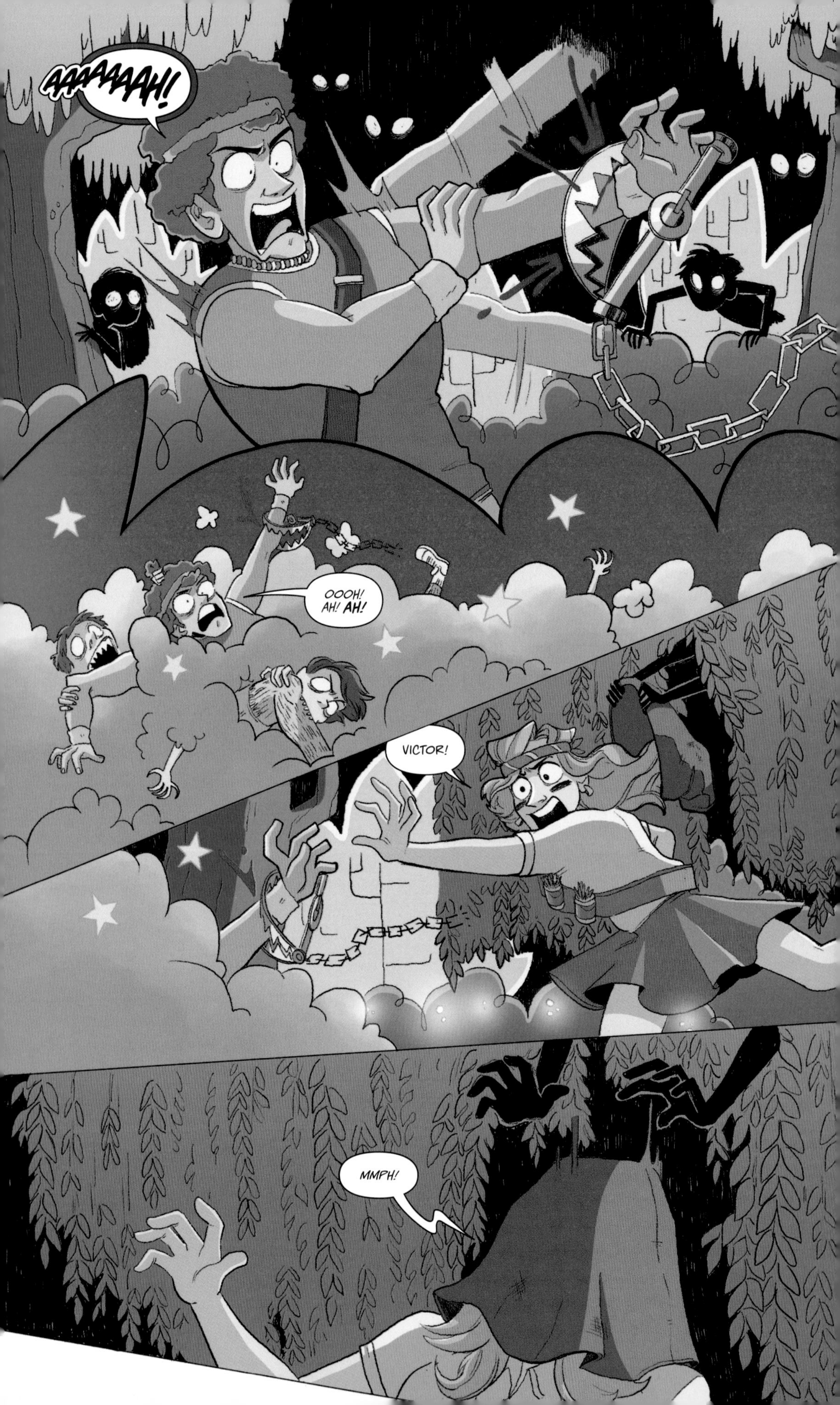
AAAAAAAH!
OOOH! AH! AH!
VICTOR!
MMPH!

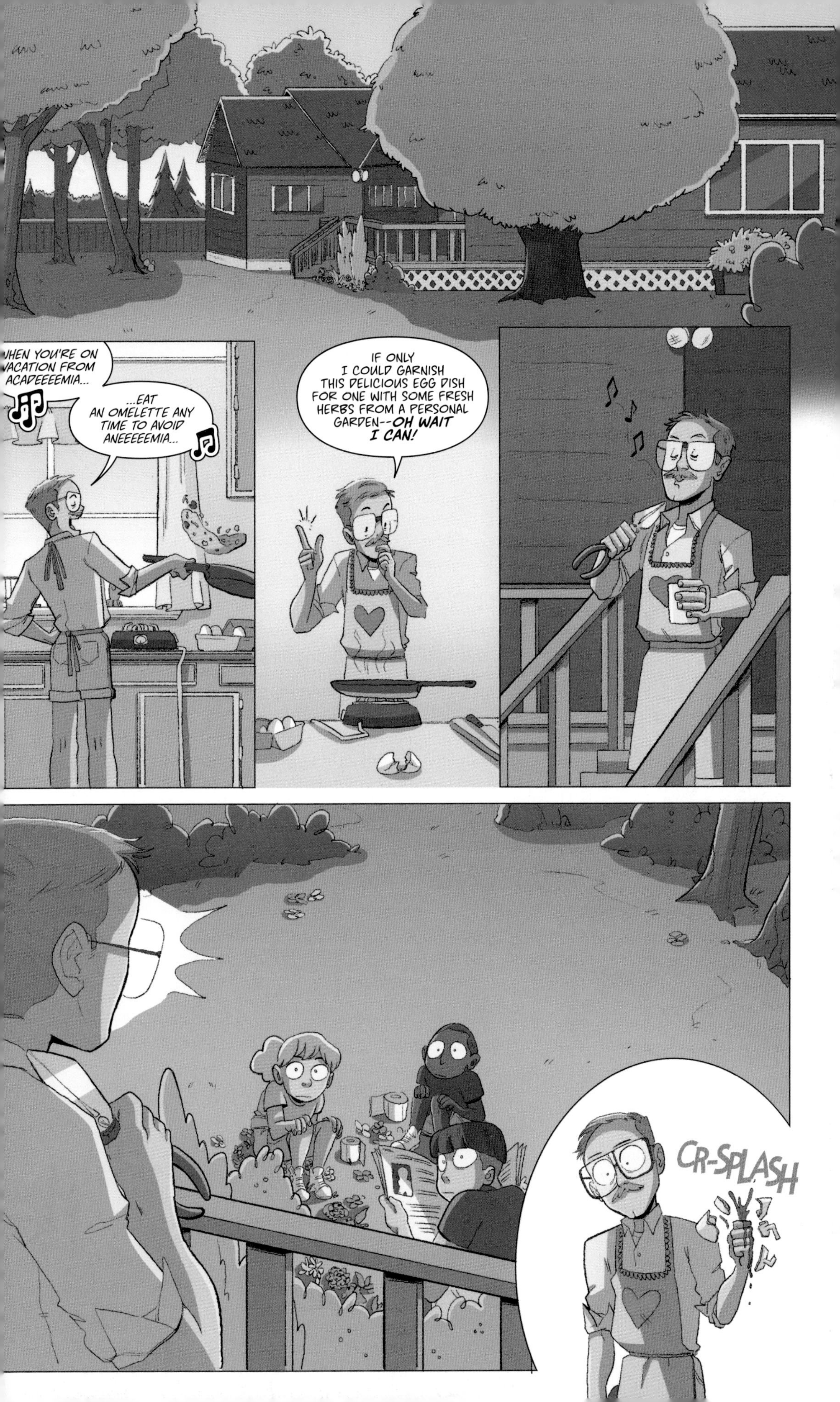

WHEN YOU'RE ON VACATION FROM ACADEEEEMIA...
...EAT AN OMELETTE ANY TIME TO AVOID ANEEEEEMIA...
IF ONLY I COULD GARNISH THIS DELICIOUS EGG DISH FOR ONE WITH SOME FRESH HERBS FROM A PERSONAL GARDEN--OH WAIT I CAN!
CR-SPLASH

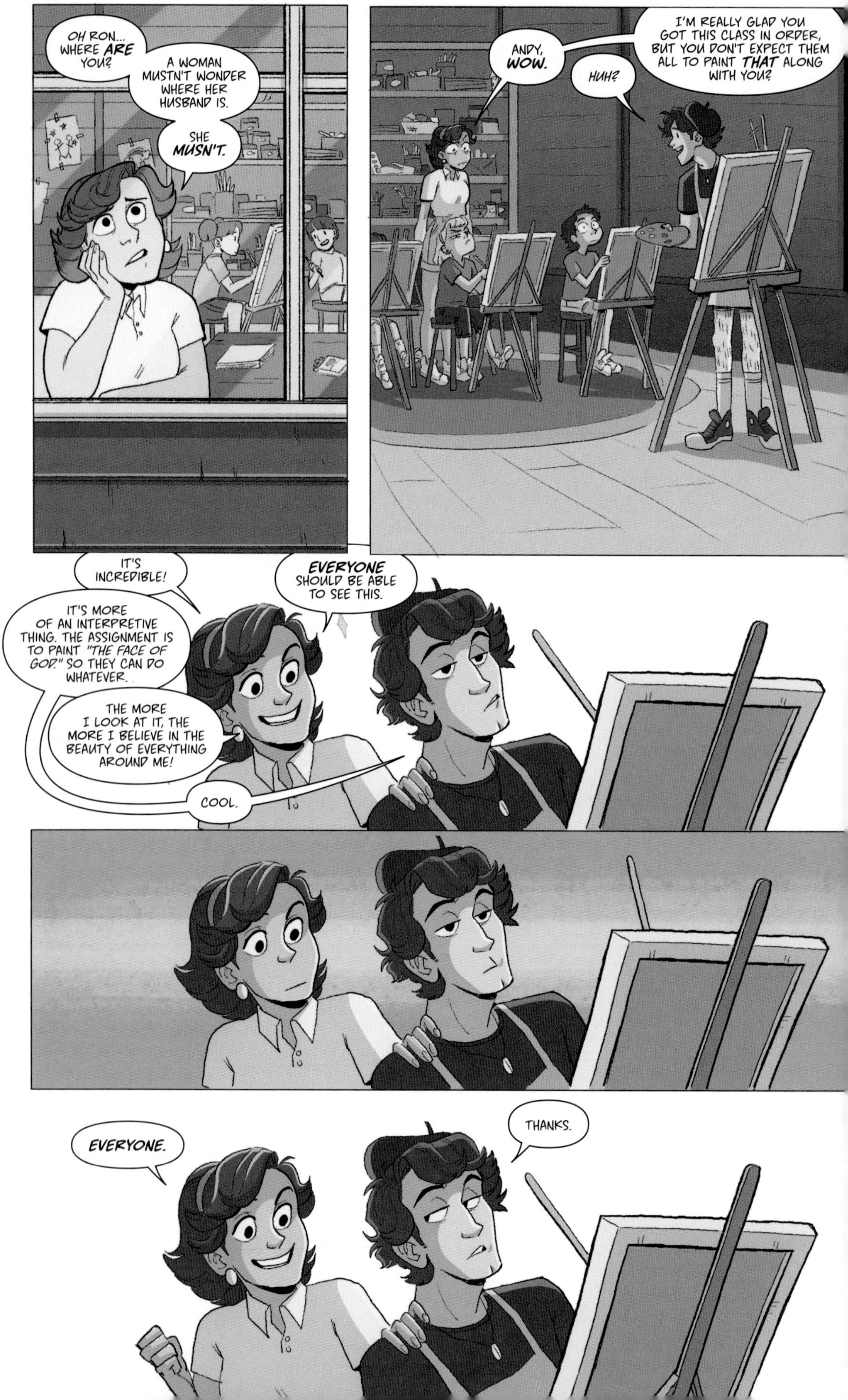
OH RON... WHERE ARE YOU?
A WOMAN MUSTN'T WONDER WHERE HER HUSBAND IS.
SHE MUSN'T.
ANDY, WOW.
HUH?
I'M REALLY GLAD YOU GOT THIS CLASS IN ORDER, BUT YOU DON'T EXPECT THEM ALL TO PAINT THAT ALONG WITH YOU?
IT'S MORE OF AN INTERPRETIVE THING. THE ASSIGNMENT IS TO PAINT "THE FACE OF GOD," SO THEY CAN DO WHATEVER.
IT'S INCREDIBLE!
EVERYONE SHOULD BE ABLE TO SEE THIS.
THE MORE I LOOK AT IT, THE MORE I BELIEVE IN THE BEAUTY OF EVERYTHING AROUND ME!
COOL.
EVERYONE.
THANKS.

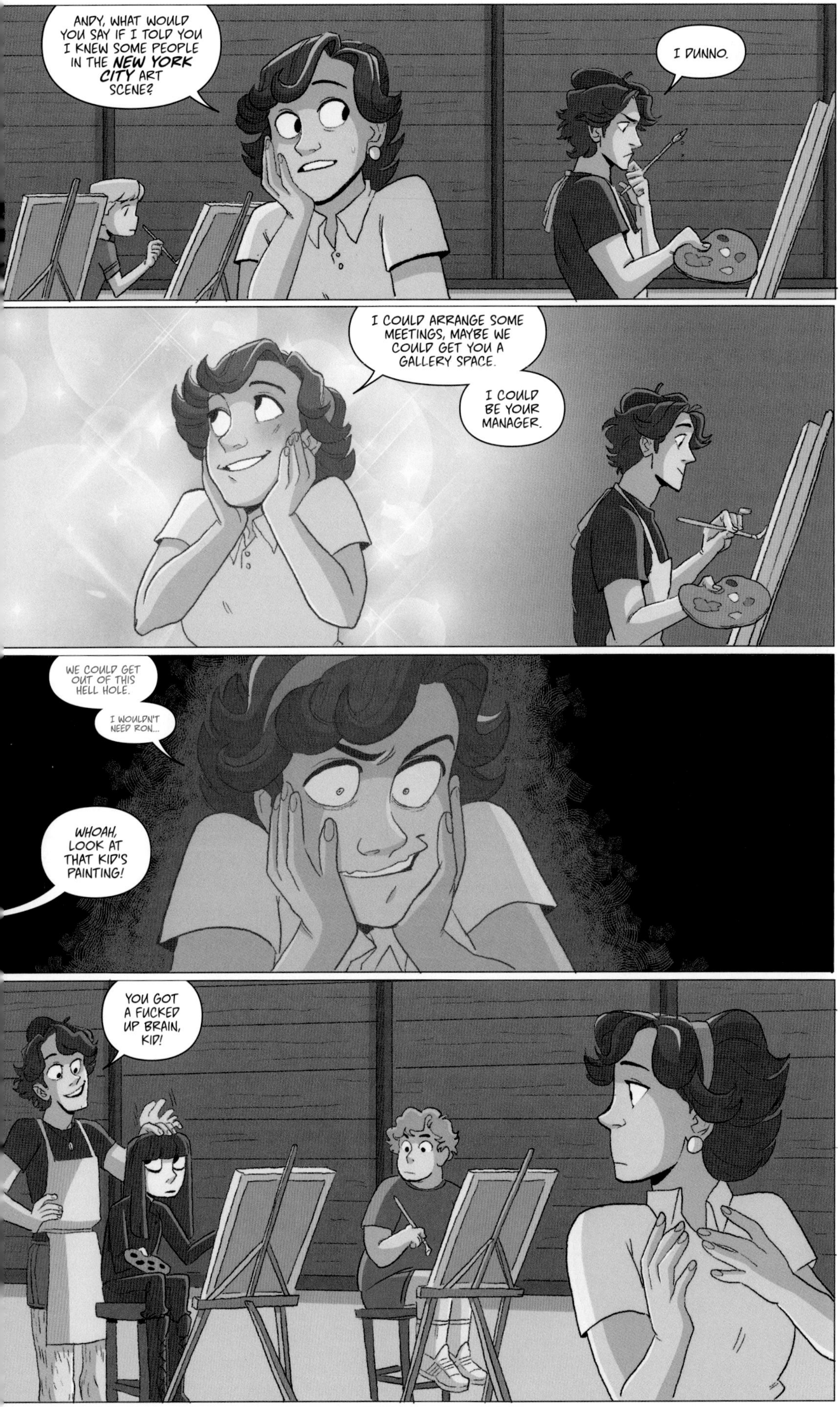
ANDY, WHAT WOULD YOU SAY IF I TOLD YOU I KNEW SOME PEOPLE IN THE NEW YORK CITY ART SCENE?
I DUNNO.
I COULD ARRANGE SOME MEETINGS, MAYBE WE COULD GET YOU A GALLERY SPACE.
I COULD BE YOUR MANAGER.
WE COULD GET OUT OF THIS HELL HOLE.
I WOULDN'T NEED RON...
WHOAH, LOOK AT THAT KID'S PAINTING!
YOU GOT A FUCKED UP BRAIN, KID!

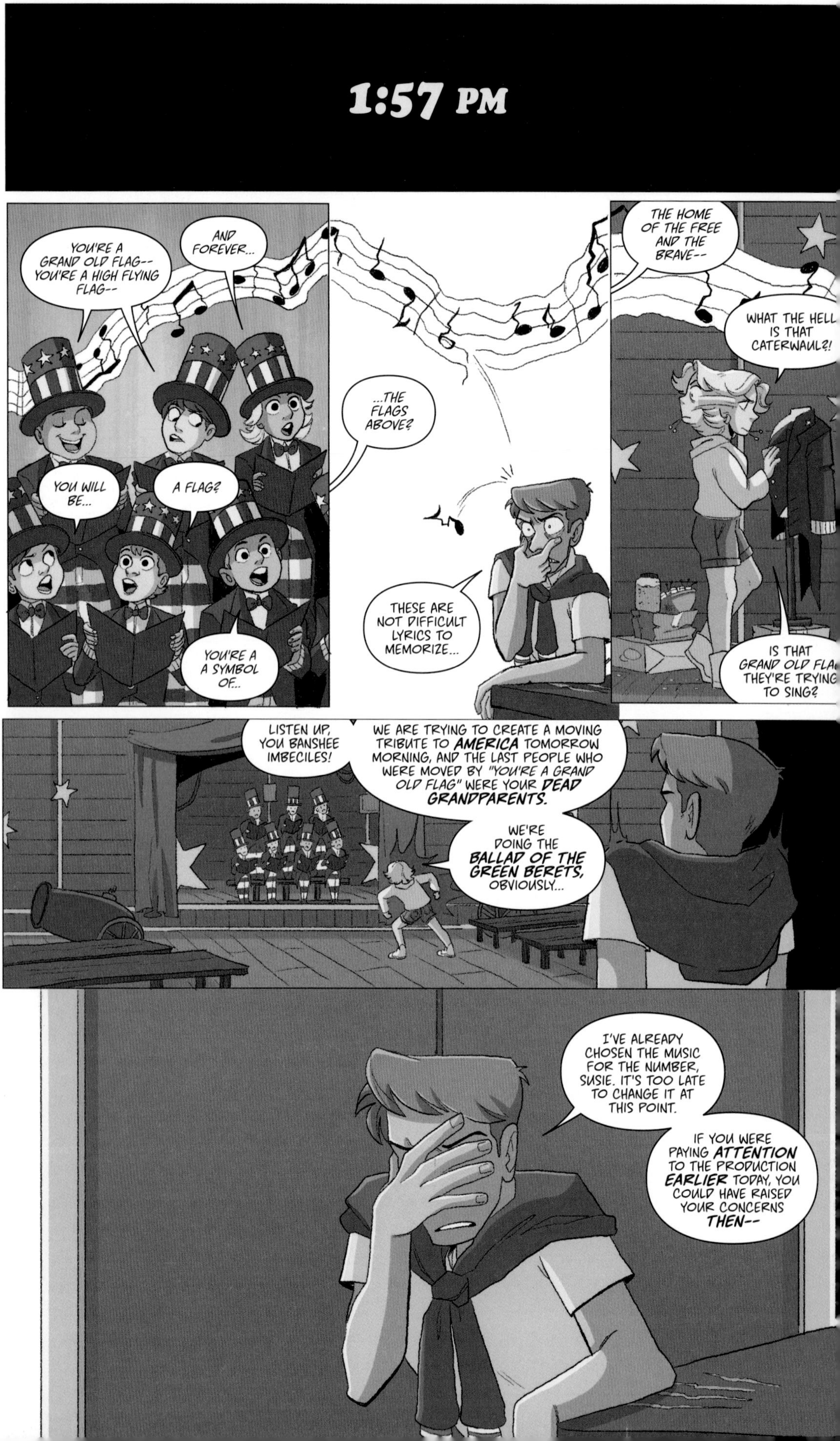
1:57 PM
YOU'RE A GRAND OLD FLAG-- YOU'RE A HIGH FLYING FLAG--
AND FOREVER...
YOU WILL BE...
A FLAG?
YOU'RE A A SYMBOL OF...
...THE FLAGS ABOVE?
THESE ARE NOT DIFFICULT LYRICS TO MEMORIZE...
THE HOME OF THE FREE AND THE BRAVE--
WHAT THE HELL IS THAT CATERWAUL?!
IS THAT GRAND OLD FLA THEY'RE TRYING TO SING?
LISTEN UP, YOU BANSHEE IMBECILES!
WE ARE TRYING TO CREATE A MOVING TRIBUTE TO AMERICA TOMORROW MORNING, AND THE LAST PEOPLE WHO WERE MOVED BY "YOU'RE A GRAND OLD FLAG" WERE YOUR DEAD GRANDPARENTS.
WE'RE DOING THE BALLAD OF THE GREEN BERETS, OBVIOUSLY...
I'VE ALREADY CHOSEN THE MUSIC FOR THE NUMBER, SUSIE. IT'S TOO LATE TO CHANGE IT AT THIS POINT.
IF YOU WERE PAYING ATTENTION TO THE PRODUCTION EARLIER TODAY, YOU COULD HAVE RAISED YOUR CONCERNS THEN--

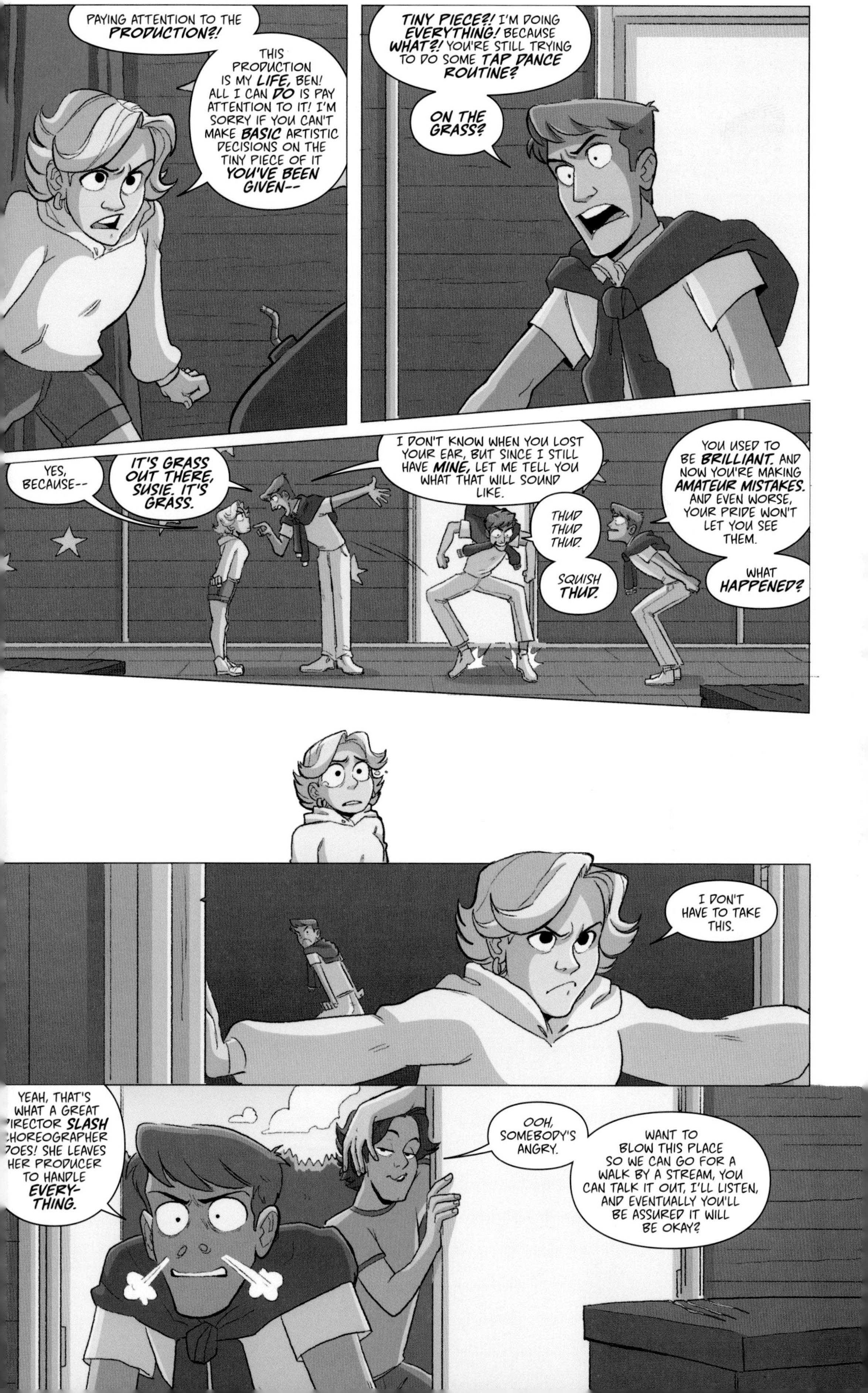
PAYING ATTENTION TO THE PRODUCTION?!
THIS PRODUCTION IS MY LIFE, BEN! ALL I CAN DO IS PAY ATTENTION TO IT! I'M SORRY IF YOU CAN'T MAKE BASIC ARTISTIC DECISIONS ON THE TINY PIECE OF IT YOU'VE BEEN GIVEN--
TINY PIECE?! I'M DOING EVERYTHING! BECAUSE WHAT?! YOU'RE STILL TRYING TO DO SOME TAP DANCE ROUTINE?
ON THE GRASS?
YES, BECAUSE--
IT'S GRASS OUT THERE, SUSIE. IT'S GRASS.
I DON'T KNOW WHEN YOU LOST YOUR EAR, BUT SINCE I STILL HAVE MINE, LET ME TELL YOU WHAT THAT WILL SOUND LIKE.
THUD THUD THUD.
SQUISH THUD.
YOU USED TO BE BRILLIANT. AND NOW YOU'RE MAKING AMATEUR MISTAKES. AND EVEN WORSE, YOUR PRIDE WON'T LET YOU SEE THEM.
WHAT HAPPENED?
I DON'T HAVE TO TAKE THIS.
YEAH, THAT'S WHAT A GREAT DIRECTOR SLASH CHOREOGRAPHER DOES! SHE LEAVES HER PRODUCER TO HANDLE EVERY-THING.
OOH, SOMEBODY'S ANGRY.
WANT TO BLOW THIS PLACE SO WE CAN GO FOR A WALK BY A STREAM, YOU CAN TALK IT OUT, I'LL LISTEN, AND EVENTUALLY YOU'LL BE ASSURED IT WILL BE OKAY?

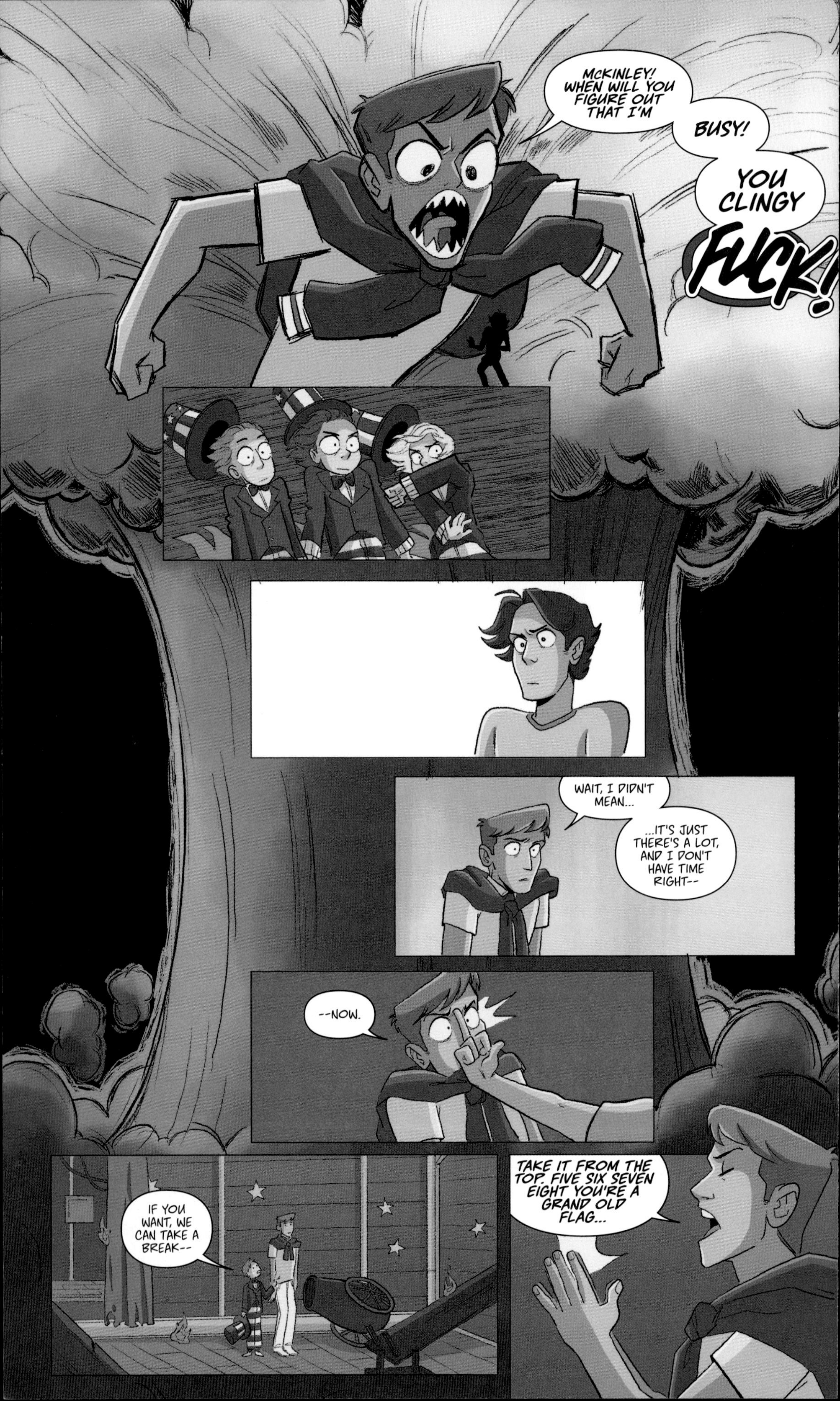
McKINLEY! WHEN WILL YOU FIGURE OUT THAT I'M
BUSY!
YOU CLINGY
FUCK!
WAIT, I DIDN'T MEAN...
...IT'S JUST THERE'S A LOT, AND I DON'T HAVE TIME RIGHT--
--NOW.
IF YOU WANT, WE CAN TAKE A BREAK--
TAKE IT FROM THE TOP. FIVE SIX SEVEN EIGHT YOU'RE A GRAND OLD FLAG...

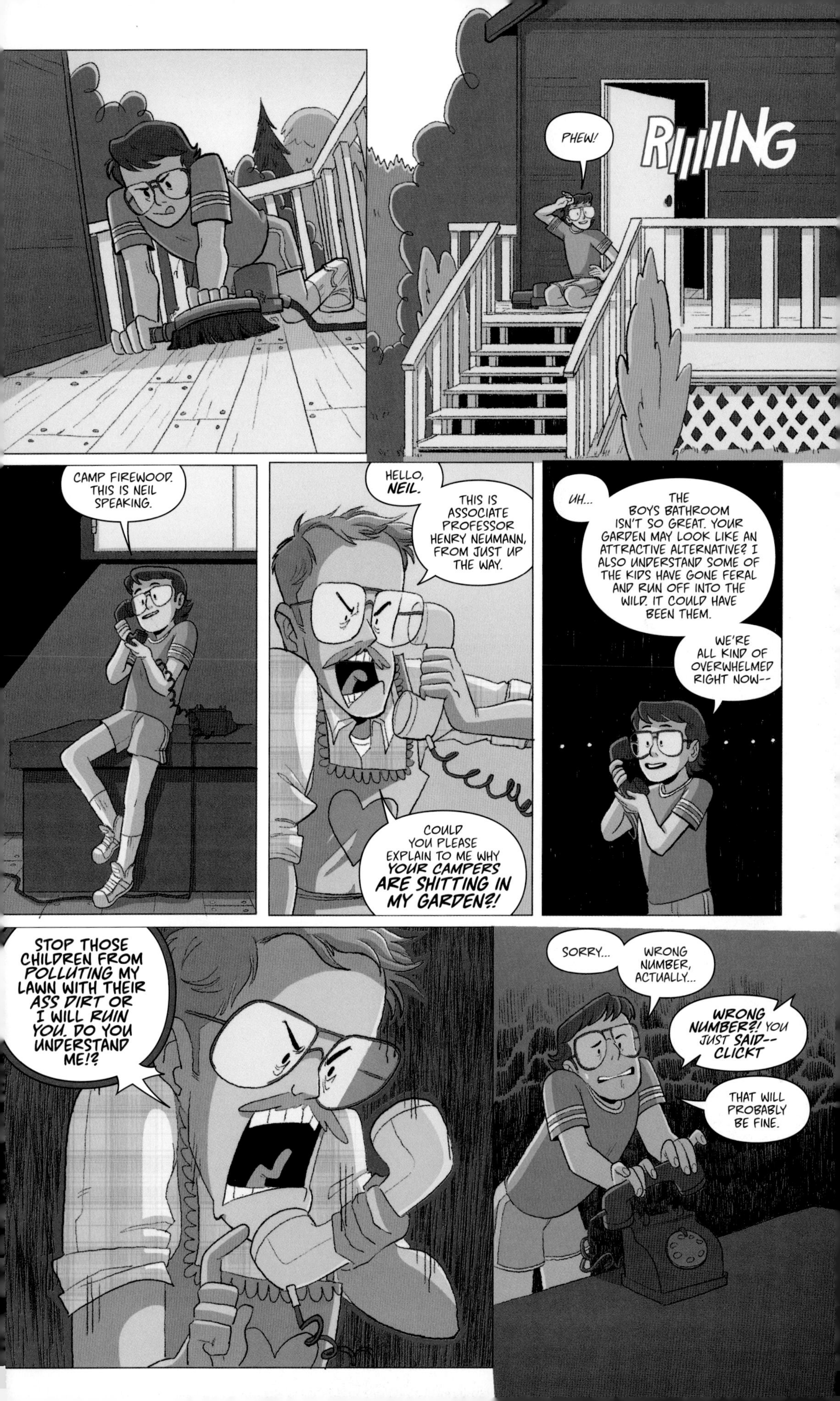
PHEW!
RIIIIING
CAMP FIREWOOD. THIS IS NEIL SPEAKING.
HELLO, NEIL.
THIS IS ASSOCIATE PROFESSOR HENRY NEUMANN, FROM JUST UP THE WAY.
COULD YOU PLEASE EXPLAIN TO ME WHY YOUR CAMPERS ARE SHITTING IN MY GARDEN?!
UH...
THE BOYS BATHROOM ISN'T SO GREAT. YOUR GARDEN MAY LOOK LIKE AN ATTRACTIVE ALTERNATIVE? I ALSO UNDERSTAND SOME OF THE KIDS HAVE GONE FERAL AND RUN OFF INTO THE WILD. IT COULD HAVE BEEN THEM.
WE'RE ALL KIND OF OVERWHELMED RIGHT NOW--
STOP THOSE CHILDREN FROM POLLUTING MY LAWN WITH THEIR ASS DIRT OR I WILL RUIN YOU. DO YOU UNDERSTAND ME!?
SORRY...
WRONG NUMBER, ACTUALLY...
WRONG NUMBER?! YOU JUST SAID-- CLICKT
THAT WILL PROBABLY BE FINE.

J'TARRAN HAS ANGERED THE KING BELOW. THE FATES MUST BE CALLED.

THANK YOU, DUNGEON JUDGE.

I DIDN'T *MEAN* TO ANGER THE KING BELOW.

QUIET, J'TARREN. A RUMBLING VOICE SPEAKS FROM THE UNDERKING'S MOLTEN LIPS.

"I AM THE KING BELOW, AND I HAVE BEEN DISTURBED BY--WHAT'S THAT?

"IS THAT J'TARREN, THE ELVEN RANGER MADE TO DANCE IN NOTHING BUT KNICKERS IN THE QUIVERING ELK'S PUB NOT TWELVE MOONS AGO? HA *HA!* TALES OF THIS LAD HAVE SPREAD FAR AND WIDE!

"YOU MAY PASS! AND TAKE SOME OF THESE ENCHANTED WEAPONS ON YOUR WAY! THE CAVE KING OF MOLTEN ROCK HAS NO NEED FOR THEM!"

CLAP

YES!

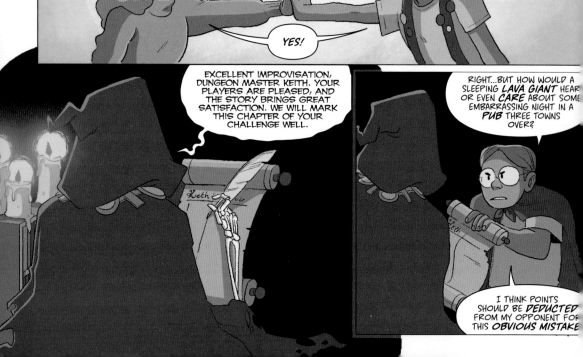

EXCELLENT IMPROVISATION, DUNGEON MASTER KEITH. YOUR PLAYERS ARE PLEASED, AND THE STORY BRINGS GREAT SATISFACTION. WE WILL MARK THIS CHAPTER OF YOUR CHALLENGE WELL.

RIGHT...BUT HOW WOULD A SLEEPING *LAVA GIANT* HEAR OR EVEN *CARE* ABOUT SOME EMBARRASSING NIGHT IN A *PUB* THREE TOWNS OVER?

I THINK POINTS SHOULD BE *DEDUCTED* FROM MY OPPONENT FOR THIS *OBVIOUS MISTAKE*

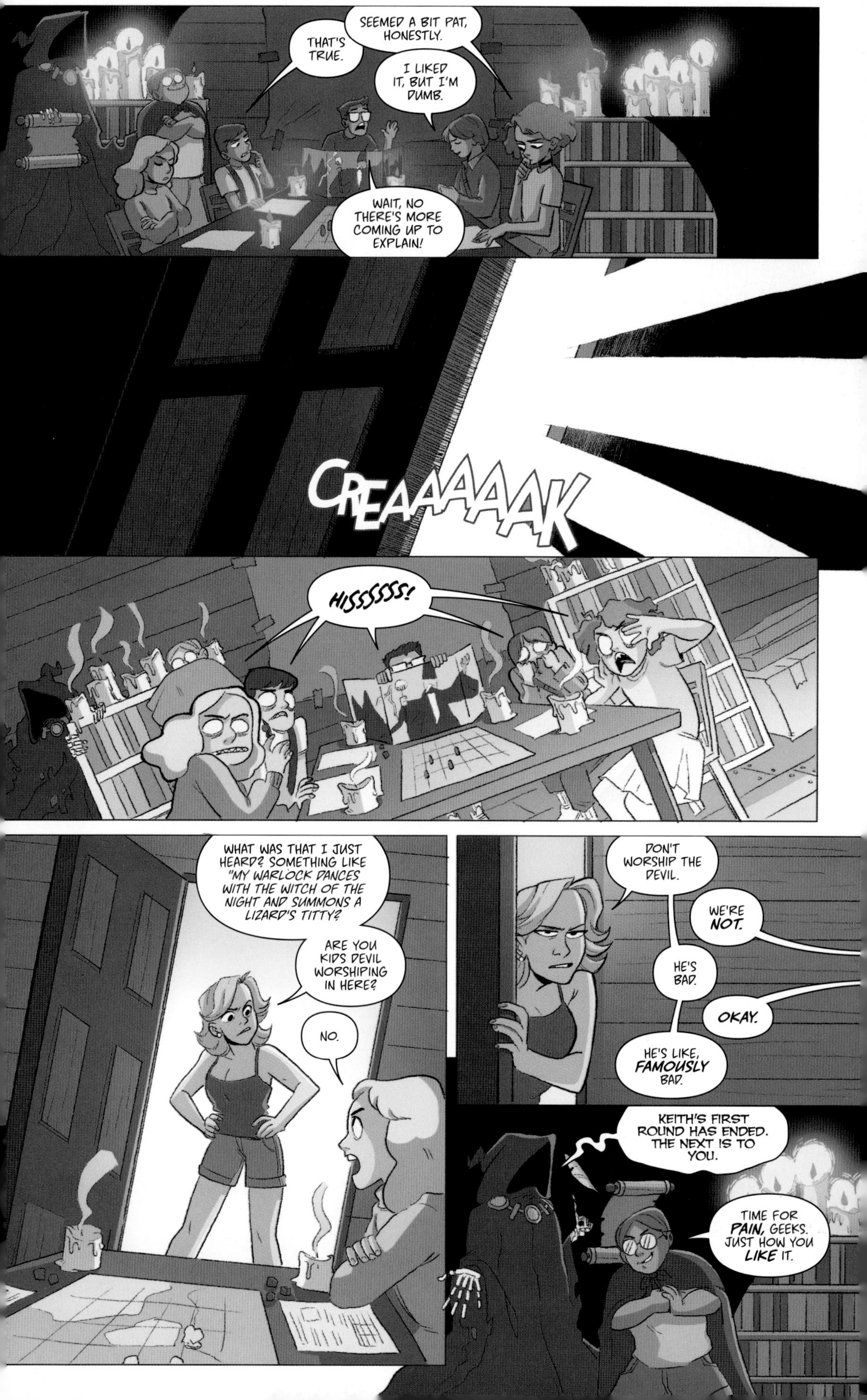

THAT'S TRUE.
SEEMED A BIT PAT, HONESTLY.
I LIKED IT, BUT I'M DUMB.
WAIT, NO THERE'S MORE COMING UP TO EXPLAIN!
CREAAAAAK
HISSSSSS!
WHAT WAS THAT I JUST HEARD? SOMETHING LIKE "MY WARLOCK DANCES WITH THE WITCH OF THE NIGHT AND SUMMONS A LIZARD'S TITTY?
ARE YOU KIDS DEVIL WORSHIPING IN HERE?
NO.
DON'T WORSHIP THE DEVIL.
WE'RE NOT.
HE'S BAD.
OKAY.
HE'S LIKE, FAMOUSLY BAD.
KEITH'S FIRST ROUND HAS ENDED. THE NEXT IS TO YOU.
TIME FOR PAIN, GEEKS. JUST HOW YOU LIKE IT.

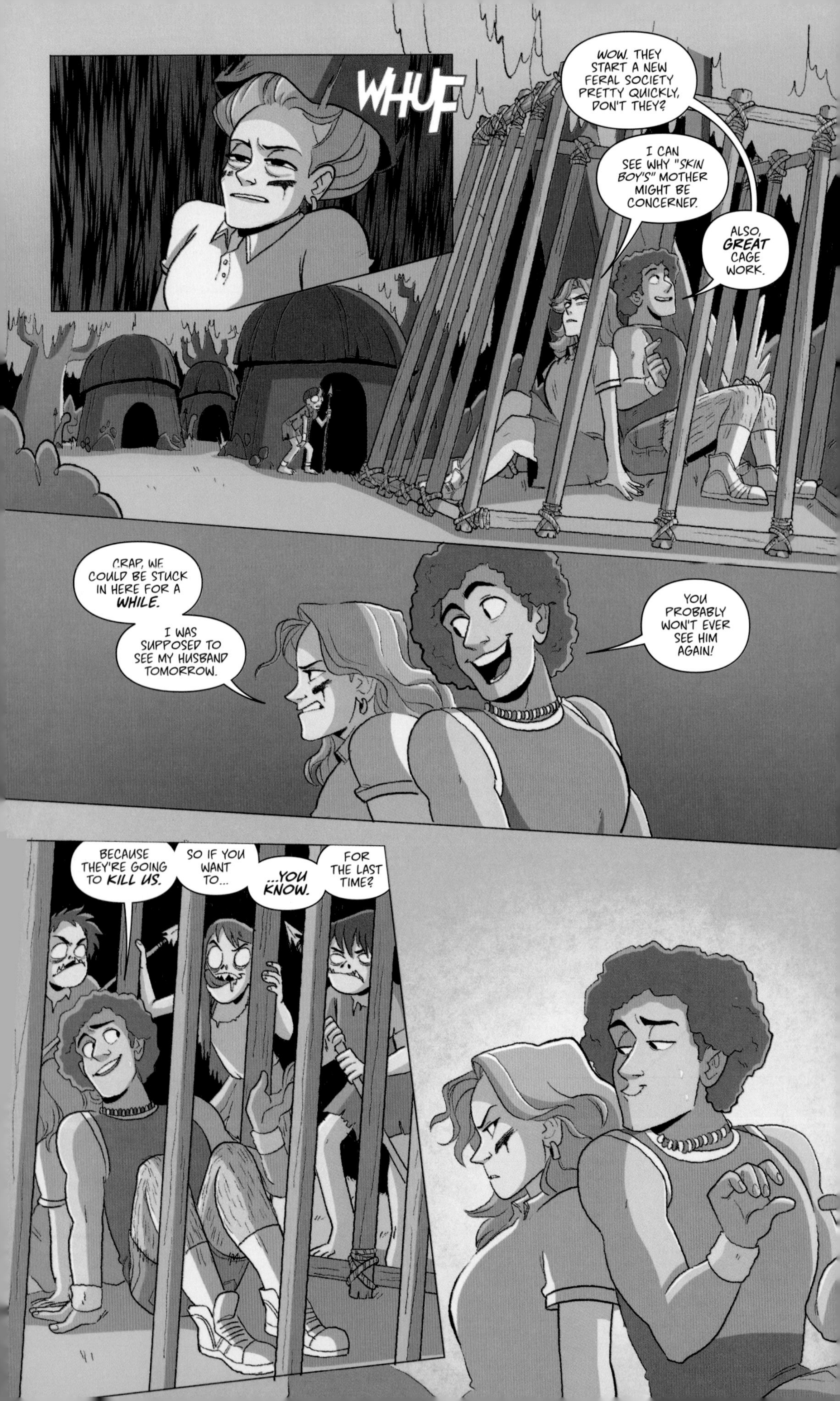
WHUF
WOW. THEY START A NEW FERAL SOCIETY PRETTY QUICKLY, DON'T THEY?
I CAN SEE WHY "SKIN BOY'S" MOTHER MIGHT BE CONCERNED.
ALSO, GREAT CAGE WORK.
CRAP, WE COULD BE STUCK IN HERE FOR A WHILE.
I WAS SUPPOSED TO SEE MY HUSBAND TOMORROW.
YOU PROBABLY WON'T EVER SEE HIM AGAIN!
BECAUSE THEY'RE GOING TO KILL US.
SO IF YOU WANT TO...
...YOU KNOW.
FOR THE LAST TIME?

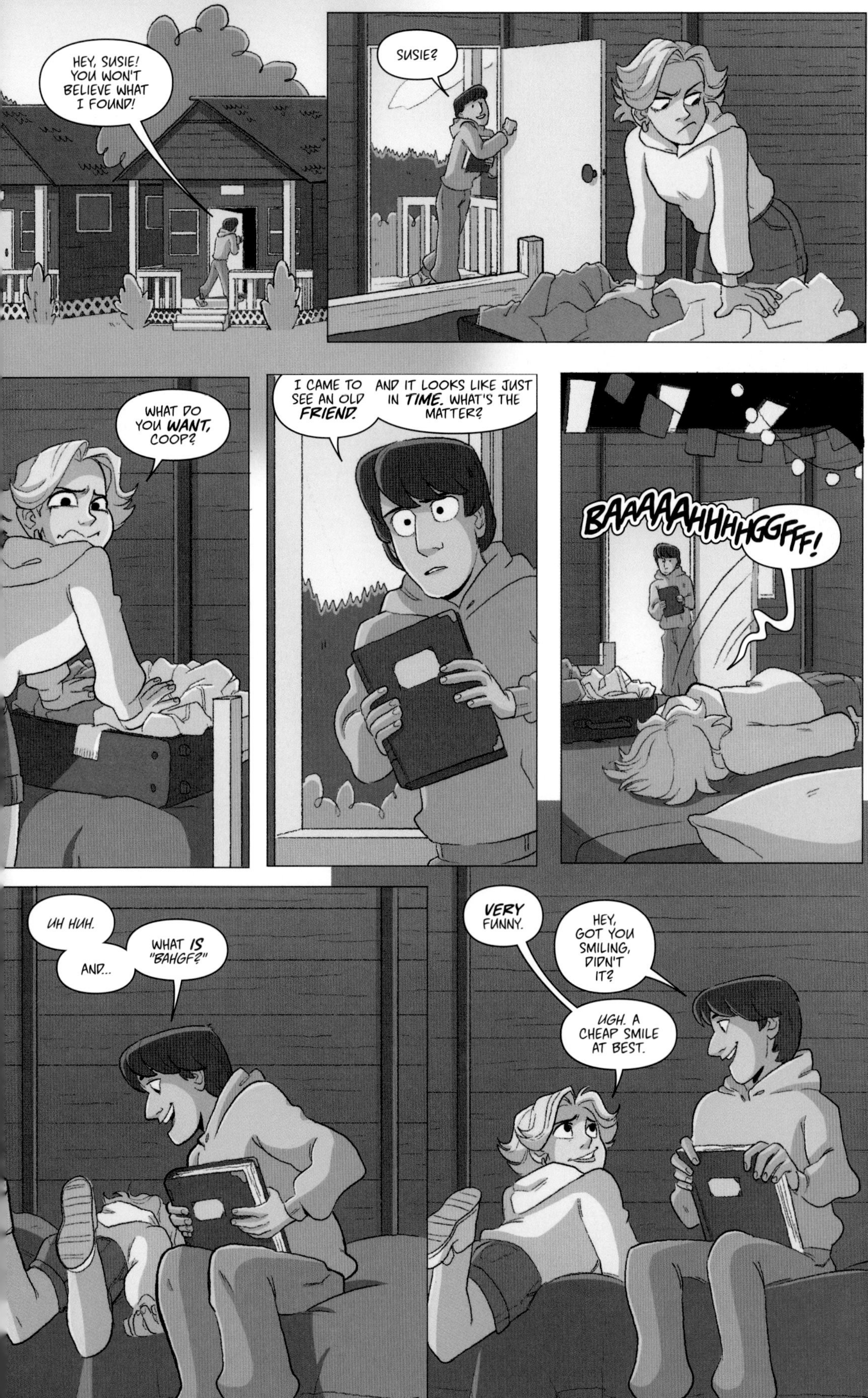
HEY, SUSIE! YOU WON'T BELIEVE WHAT I FOUND!
SUSIE?
WHAT DO YOU WANT, COOP?
I CAME TO SEE AN OLD FRIEND.
AND IT LOOKS LIKE JUST IN TIME. WHAT'S THE MATTER?
BAAAAAHHHHGGFFF!
UH HUH.
AND...
WHAT IS "BAHGF?"
VERY FUNNY.
HEY, GOT YOU SMILING, DIDN'T IT?
UGH. A CHEAP SMILE AT BEST.

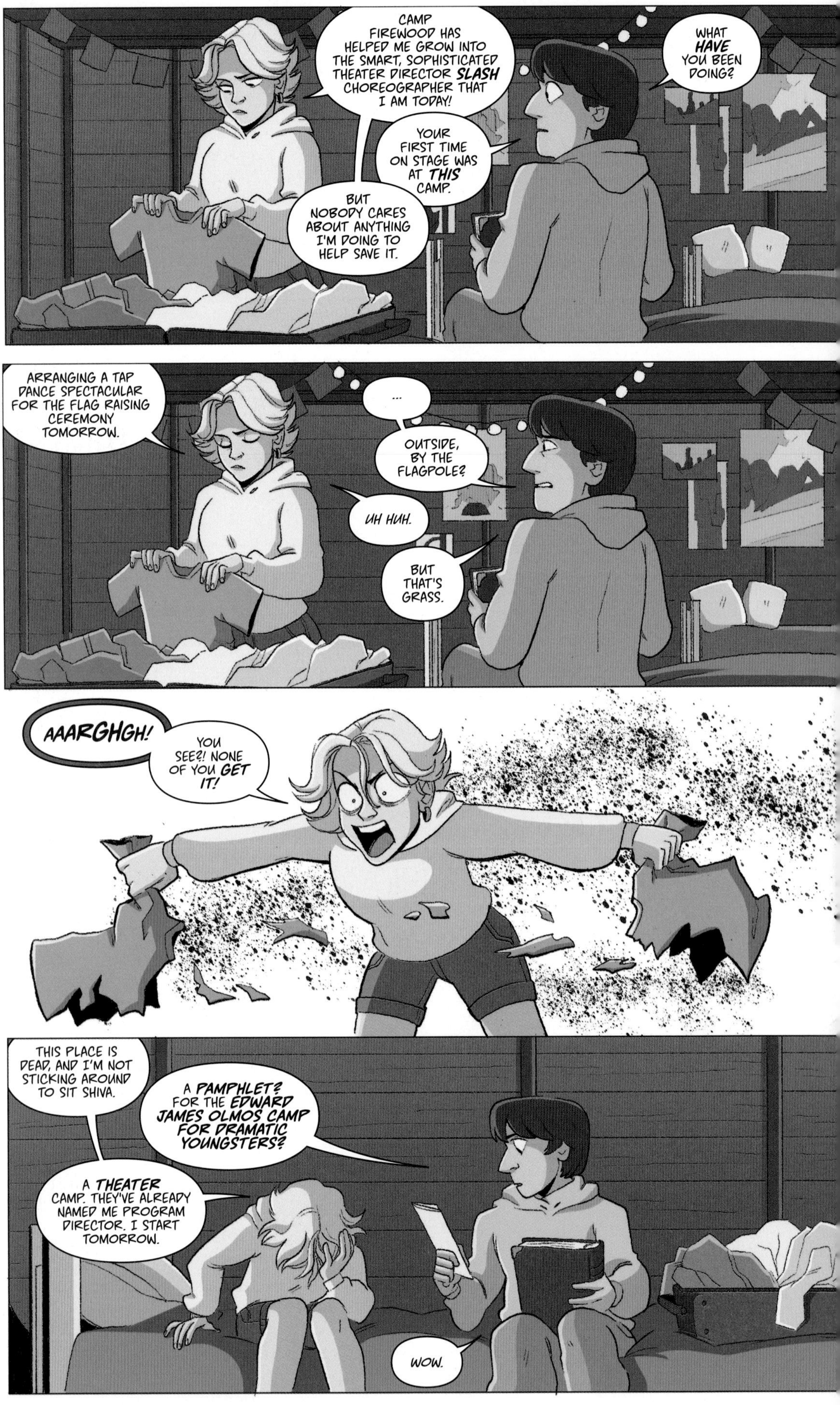
CAMP FIREWOOD HAS HELPED ME GROW INTO THE SMART, SOPHISTICATED THEATER DIRECTOR SLASH CHOREOGRAPHER THAT I AM TODAY!
BUT NOBODY CARES ABOUT ANYTHING I'M DOING TO HELP SAVE IT.
YOUR FIRST TIME ON STAGE WAS AT THIS CAMP.
WHAT HAVE YOU BEEN DOING?
ARRANGING A TAP DANCE SPECTACULAR FOR THE FLAG RAISING CEREMONY TOMORROW.
...
OUTSIDE, BY THE FLAGPOLE?
UH HUH.
BUT THAT'S GRASS.
AAARGHGH!
YOU SEE?! NONE OF YOU GET IT!
THIS PLACE IS DEAD, AND I'M NOT STICKING AROUND TO SIT SHIVA.
A PAMPHLET? FOR THE EDWARD JAMES OLMOS CAMP FOR DRAMATIC YOUNGSTERS?
A THEATER CAMP. THEY'VE ALREADY NAMED ME PROGRAM DIRECTOR. I START TOMORROW.
WOW.

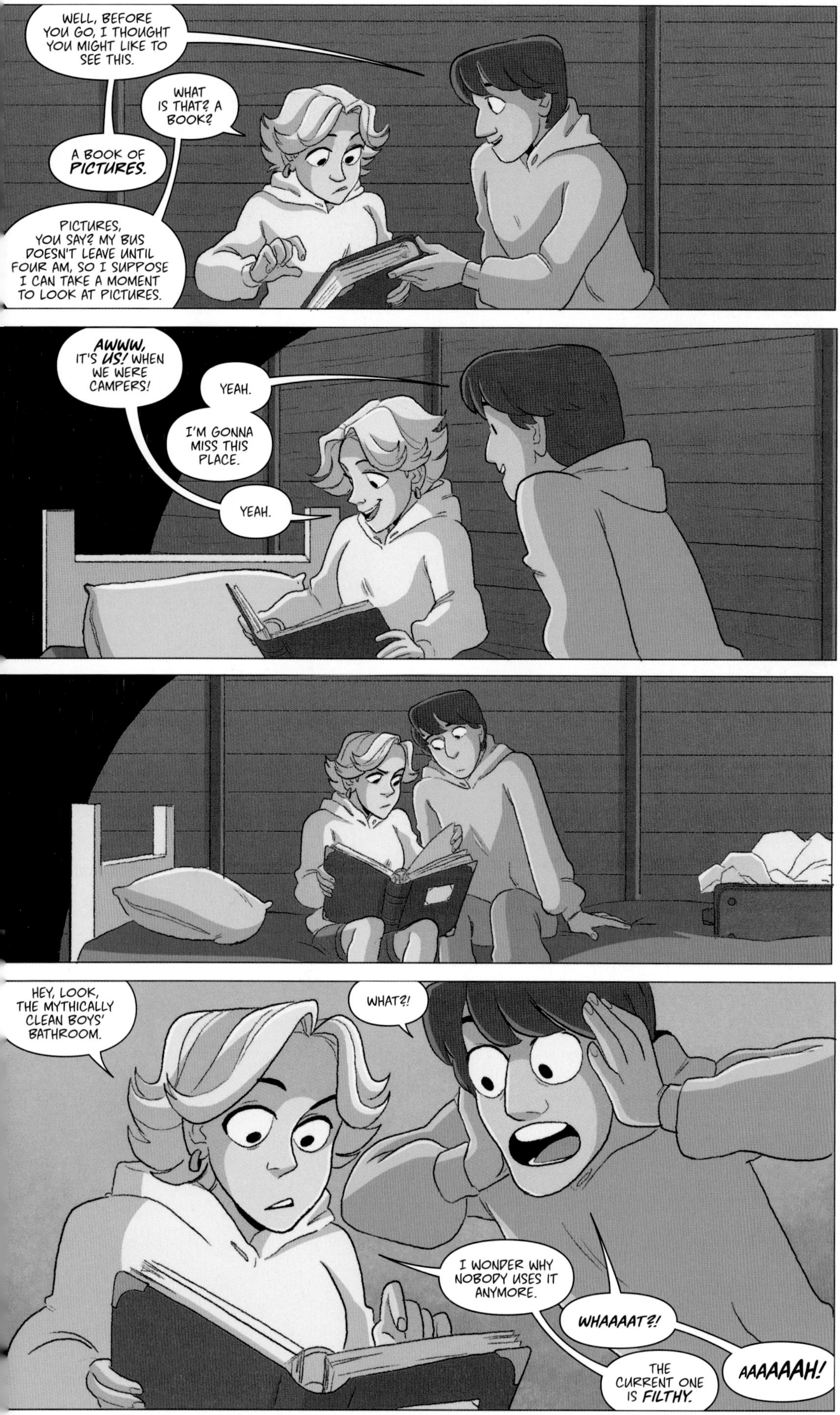
WELL, BEFORE YOU GO, I THOUGHT YOU MIGHT LIKE TO SEE THIS.
WHAT IS THAT? A BOOK?
A BOOK OF *PICTURES.*
PICTURES, YOU SAY? MY BUS DOESN'T LEAVE UNTIL FOUR AM, SO I SUPPOSE I CAN TAKE A MOMENT TO LOOK AT PICTURES.
AWWW, IT'S *US!* WHEN WE WERE CAMPERS!
YEAH.
I'M GONNA MISS THIS PLACE.
YEAH.
HEY, LOOK, THE MYTHICALLY CLEAN BOYS' BATHROOM.
WHAT?!
I WONDER WHY NOBODY USES IT ANYMORE.
WHAAAAT?!
THE CURRENT ONE IS *FILTHY.*
AAAAAAH!

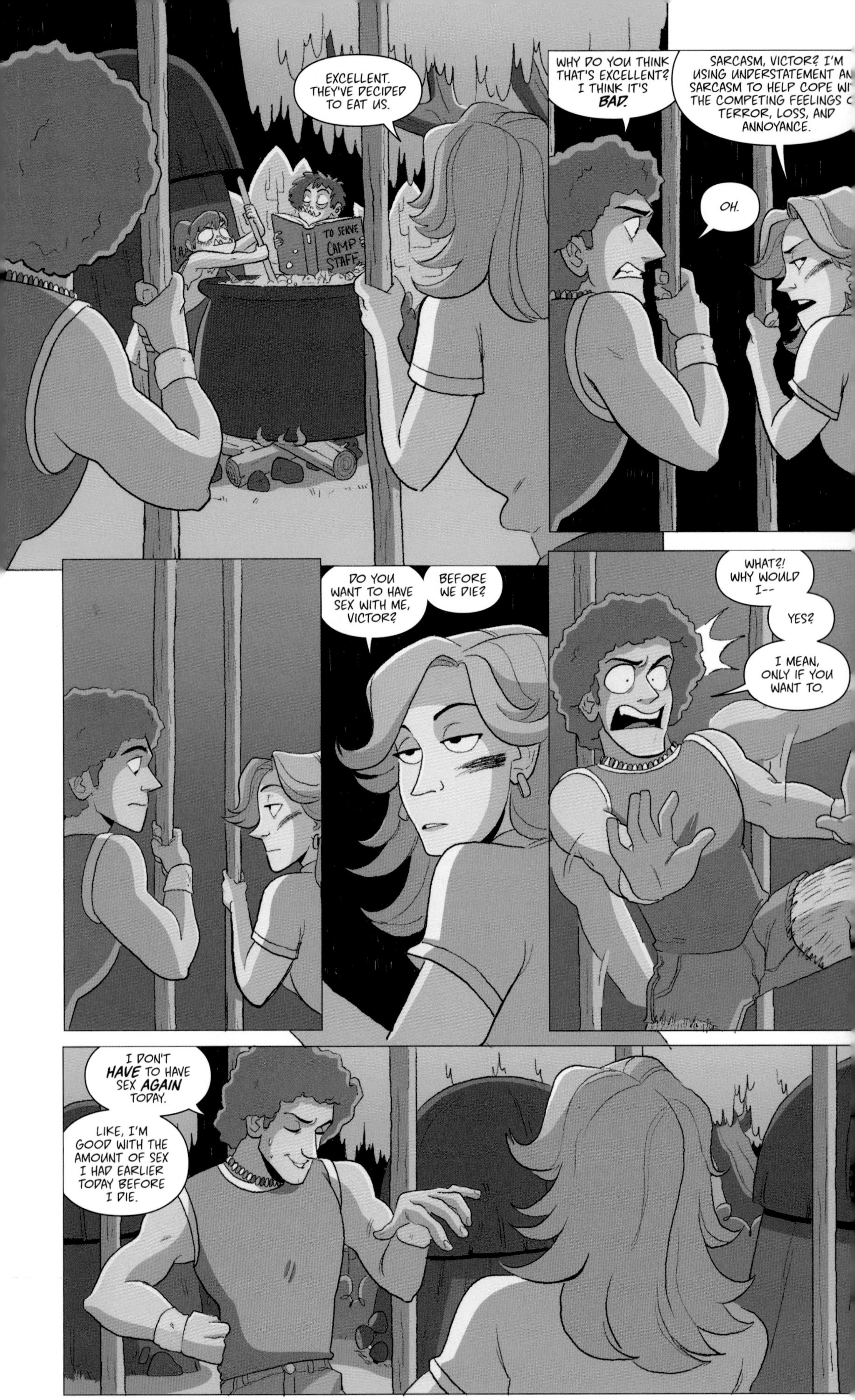
EXCELLENT. THEY'VE DECIDED TO EAT US.
TO SERVE CAMP STAFF
WHY DO YOU THINK THAT'S EXCELLENT? I THINK IT'S **BAD.**
SARCASM, VICTOR? I'M USING UNDERSTATEMENT AN SARCASM TO HELP COPE WI THE COMPETING FEELINGS C TERROR, LOSS, AND ANNOYANCE.
OH.
DO YOU WANT TO HAVE SEX WITH ME, VICTOR?
BEFORE WE DIE?
WHAT?! WHY WOULD I--
YES?
I MEAN, ONLY IF YOU WANT TO.
I DON'T **HAVE** TO HAVE SEX **AGAIN** TODAY.
LIKE, I'M GOOD WITH THE AMOUNT OF SEX I HAD EARLIER TODAY BEFORE I DIE.

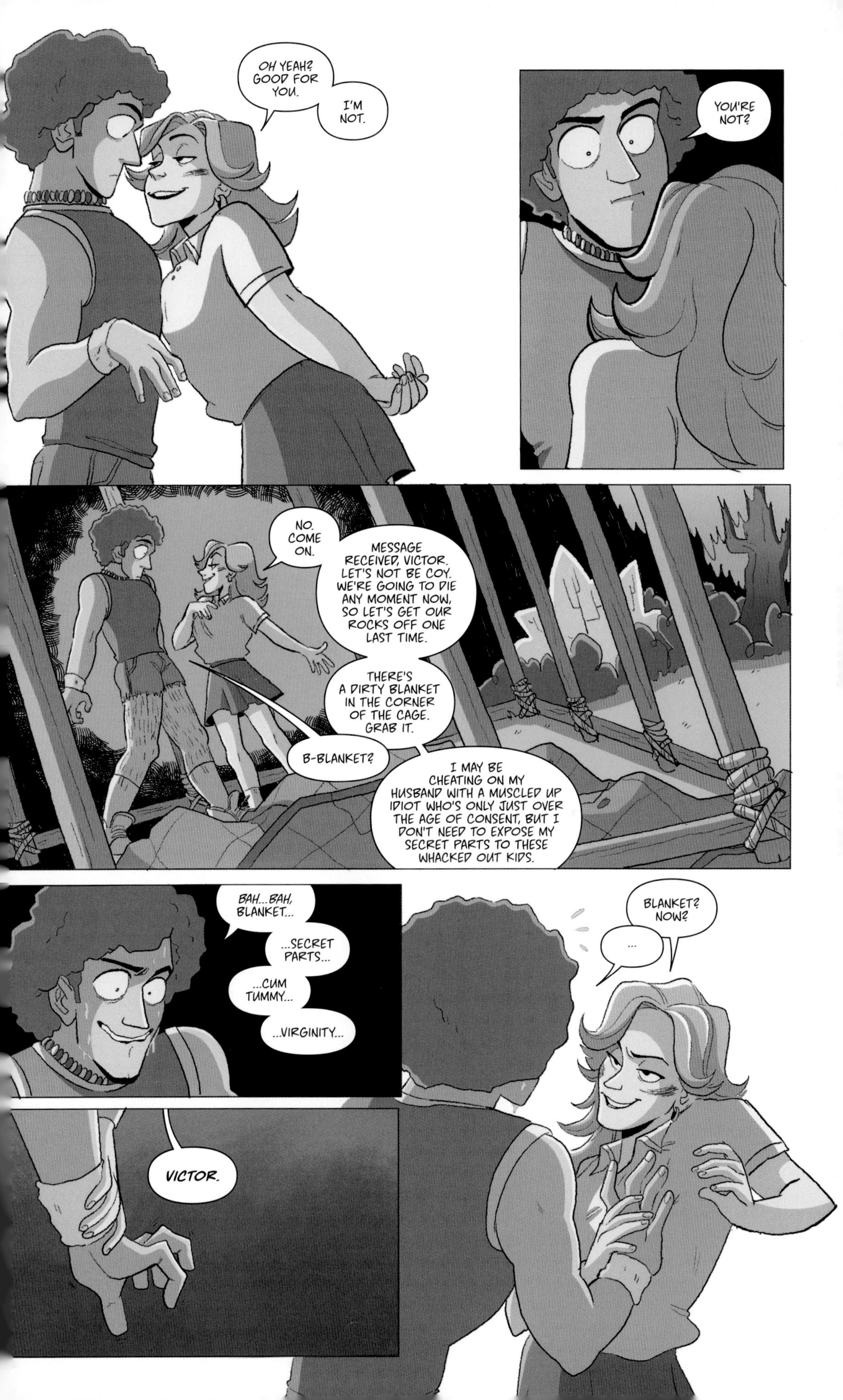
OH YEAH? GOOD FOR YOU.
I'M NOT.
YOU'RE NOT?
NO. COME ON.
MESSAGE RECEIVED, VICTOR. LET'S NOT BE COY. WE'RE GOING TO DIE ANY MOMENT NOW, SO LET'S GET OUR ROCKS OFF ONE LAST TIME.
THERE'S A DIRTY BLANKET IN THE CORNER OF THE CAGE. GRAB IT.
B-BLANKET?
I MAY BE CHEATING ON MY HUSBAND WITH A MUSCLED UP IDIOT WHO'S ONLY JUST OVER THE AGE OF CONSENT, BUT I DON'T NEED TO EXPOSE MY SECRET PARTS TO THESE WHACKED OUT KIDS.
BAH...BAH, BLANKET...
...SECRET PARTS...
...CUM TUMMY...
...VIRGINITY...
BLANKET? NOW?
...
VICTOR.

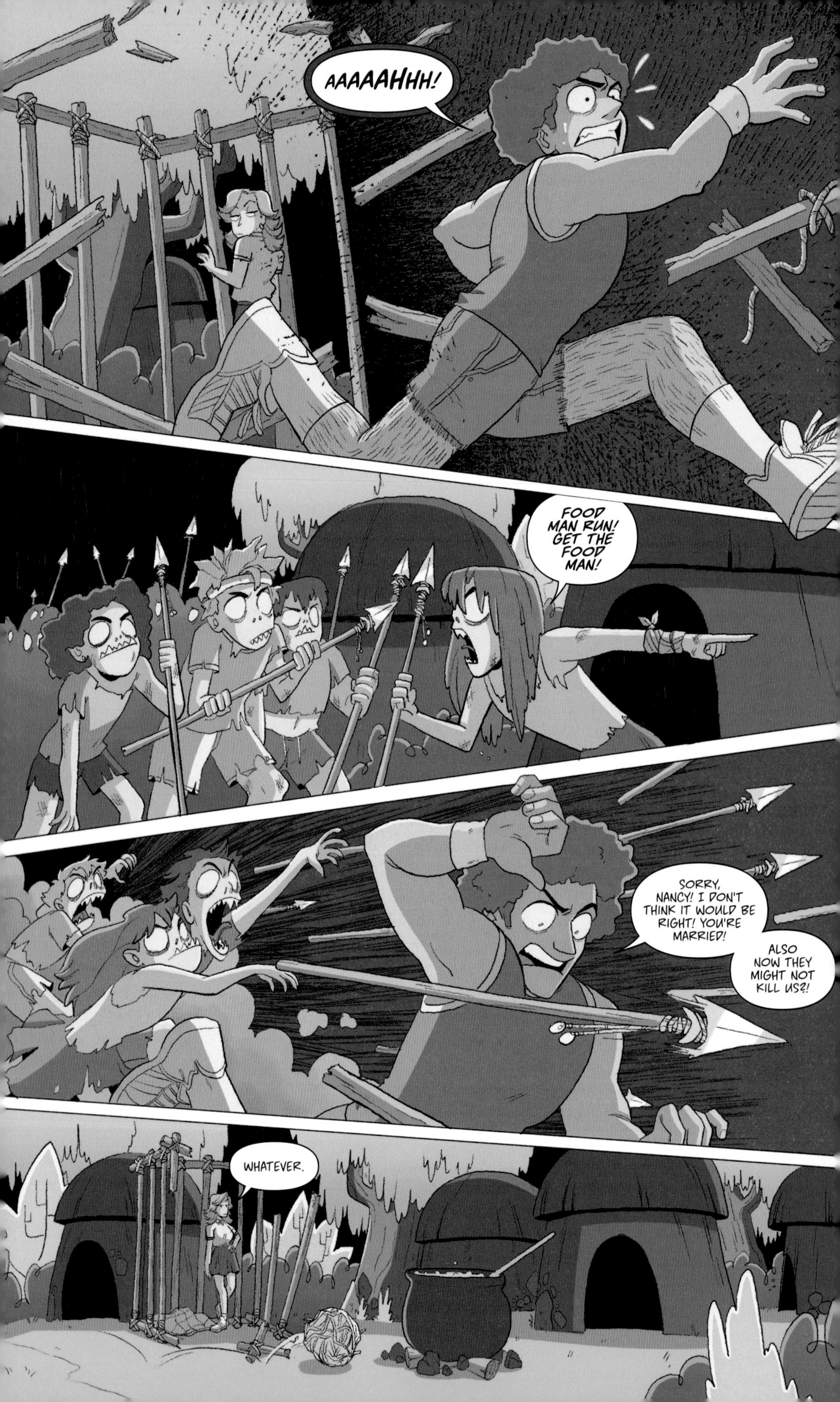
AAAAAHHH!
FOOD MAN RUN! GET THE FOOD MAN!
SORRY, NANCY! I DON'T THINK IT WOULD BE RIGHT! YOU'RE MARRIED!
ALSO NOW THEY MIGHT NOT KILL US?!
WHATEVER.

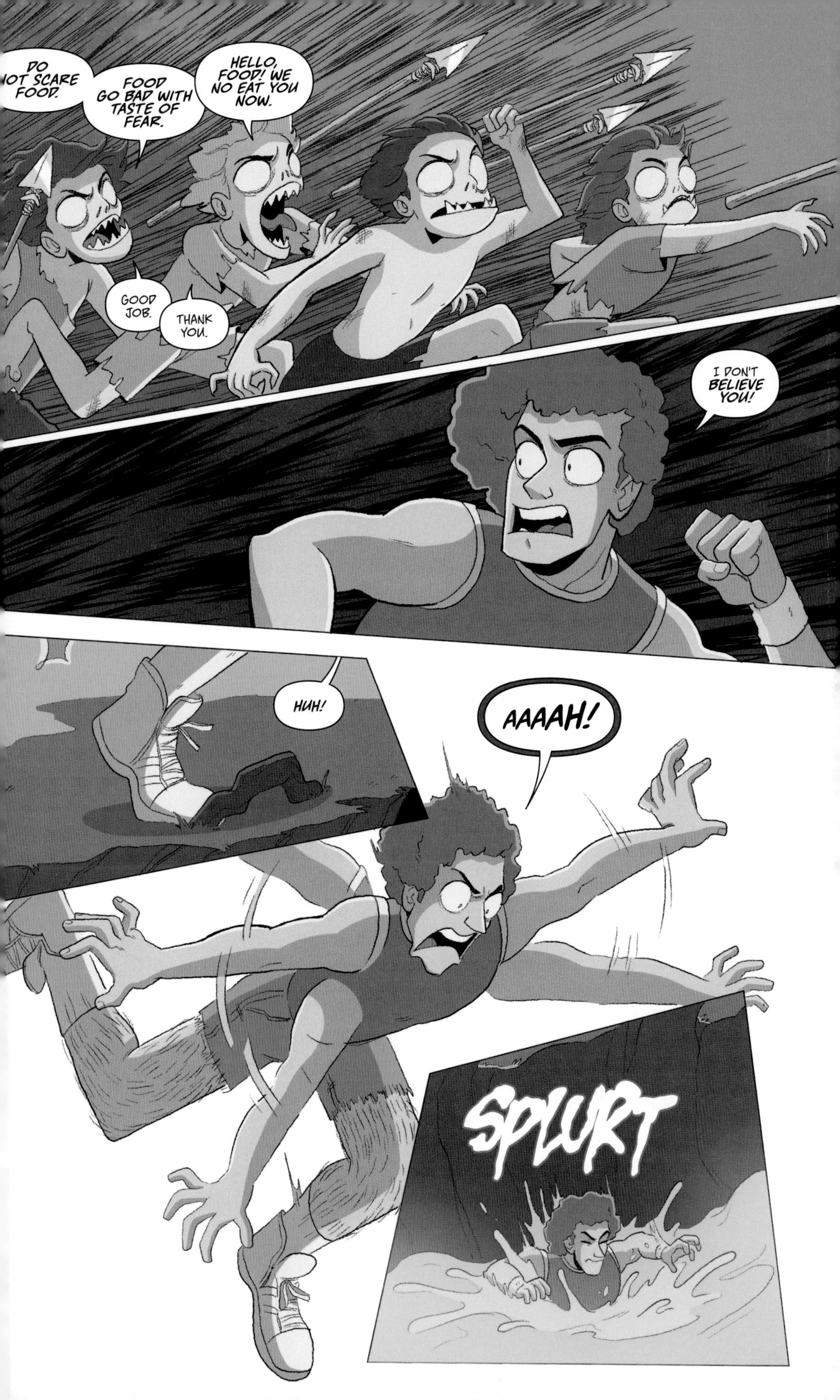
DO NOT SCARE FOOD.
FOOD GO BAD WITH TASTE OF FEAR.
HELLO, FOOD! WE NO EAT YOU NOW.
GOOD JOB.
THANK YOU.
I DON'T BELIEVE YOU!
HUH!
AAAAH!
SPLURT

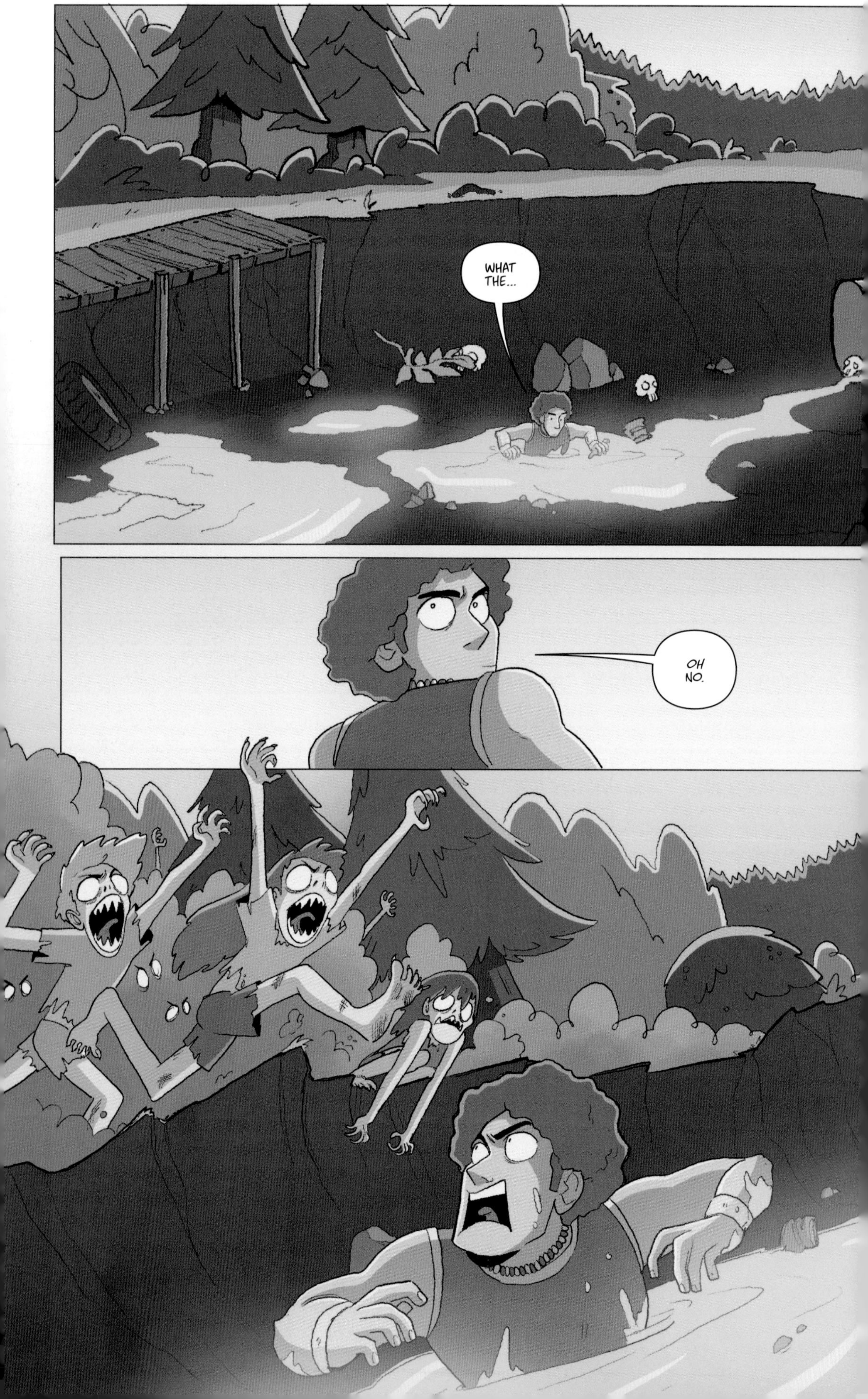
WHAT THE...
OH NO.

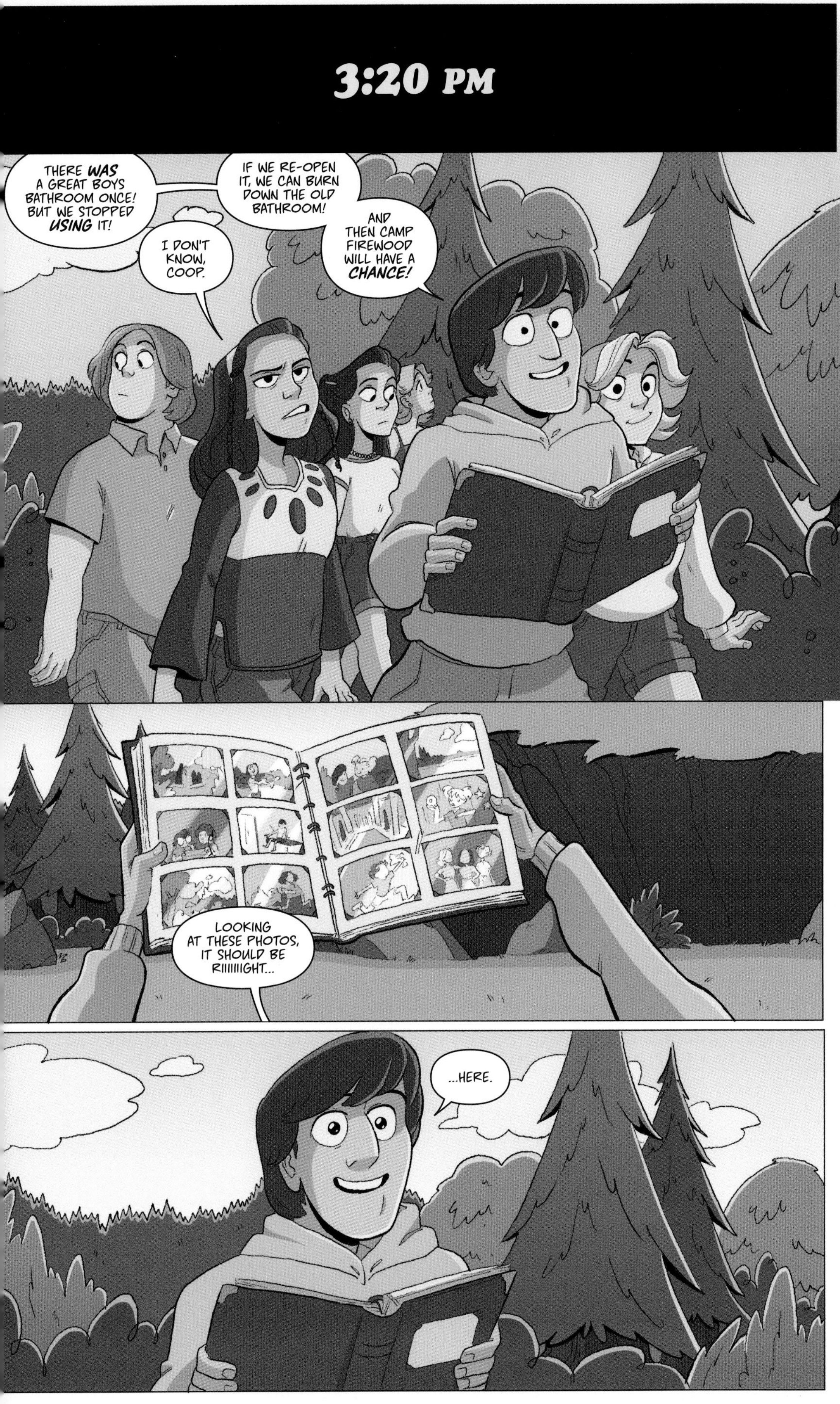
3:20 PM
THERE WAS A GREAT BOYS BATHROOM ONCE! BUT WE STOPPED USING IT!
IF WE RE-OPEN IT, WE CAN BURN DOWN THE OLD BATHROOM!
I DON'T KNOW, COOP.
AND THEN CAMP FIREWOOD WILL HAVE A CHANCE!
LOOKING AT THESE PHOTOS, IT SHOULD BE RIIIIIIGHT...
...HERE.

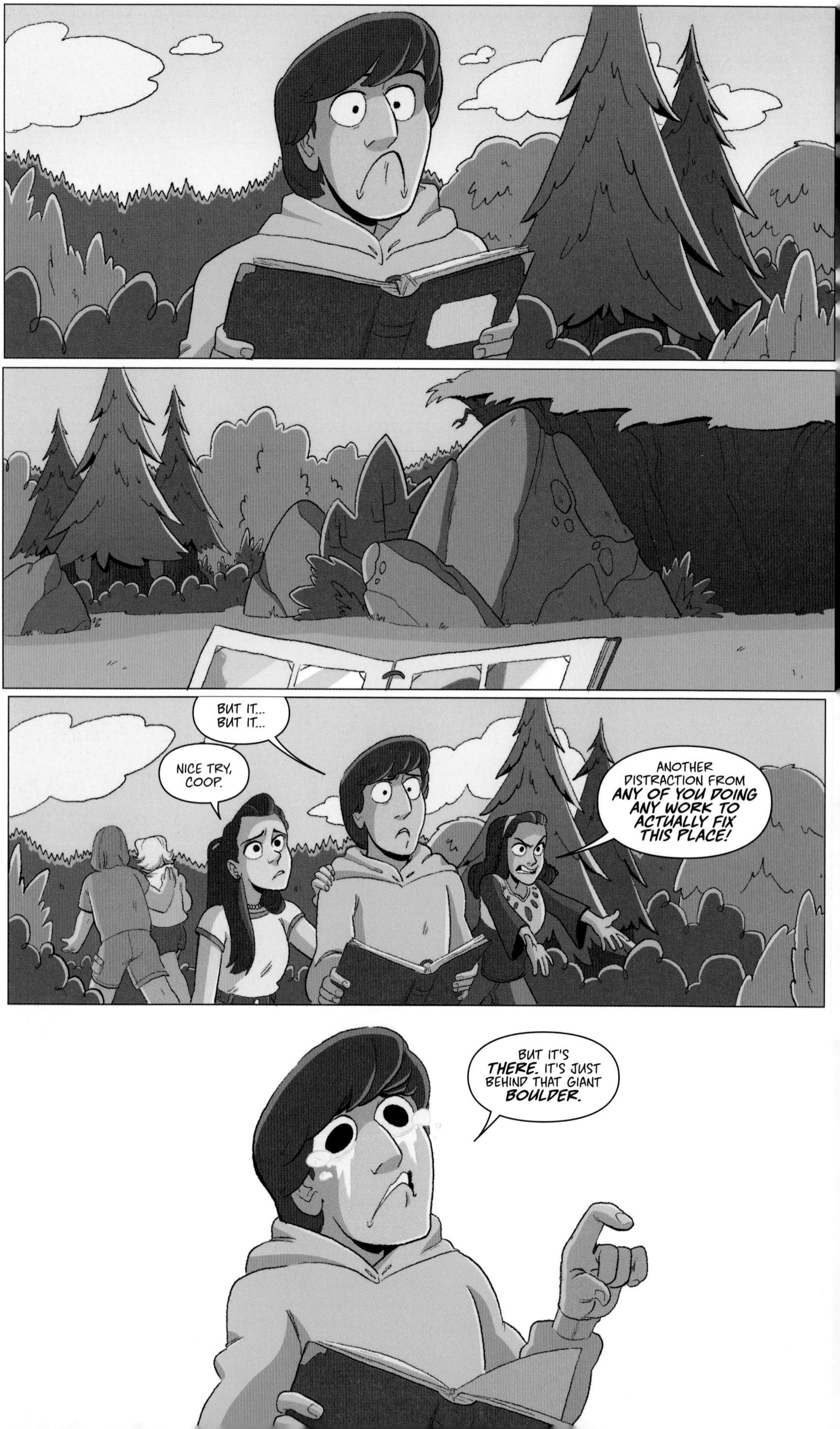
BUT IT... BUT IT...
NICE TRY, COOP.
ANOTHER DISTRACTION FROM ANY OF YOU DOING ANY WORK TO ACTUALLY FIX THIS PLACE!
BUT IT'S THERE. IT'S JUST BEHIND THAT GIANT BOULDER.

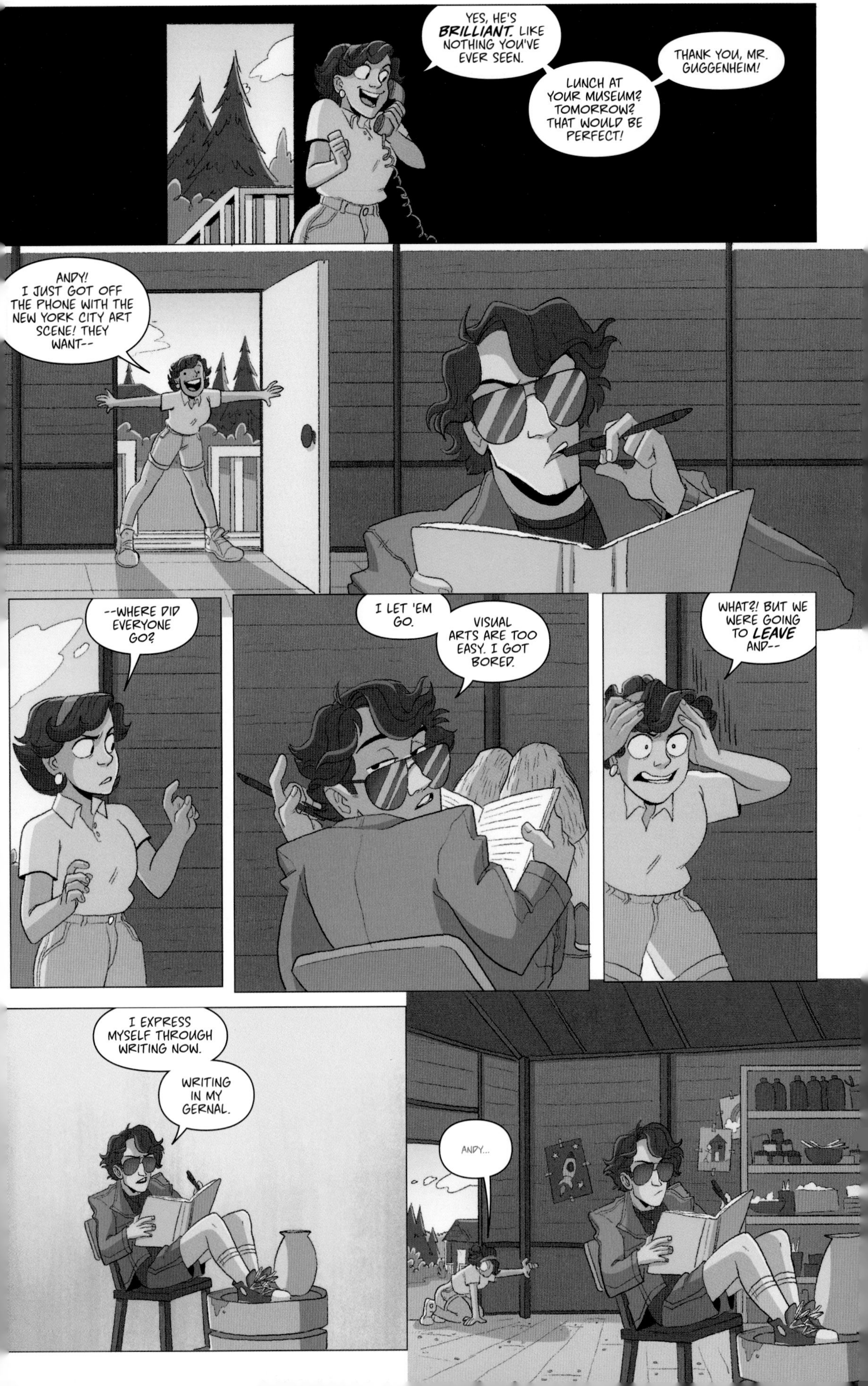

YES, HE'S BRILLIANT. LIKE NOTHING YOU'VE EVER SEEN.
LUNCH AT YOUR MUSEUM? TOMORROW? THAT WOULD BE PERFECT!
THANK YOU, MR. GUGGENHEIM!
ANDY! I JUST GOT OFF THE PHONE WITH THE NEW YORK CITY ART SCENE! THEY WANT--
--WHERE DID EVERYONE GO?
I LET 'EM GO.
VISUAL ARTS ARE TOO EASY. I GOT BORED.
WHAT?! BUT WE WERE GOING TO LEAVE AND--
I EXPRESS MYSELF THROUGH WRITING NOW.
WRITING IN MY GERNAL.
ANDY...

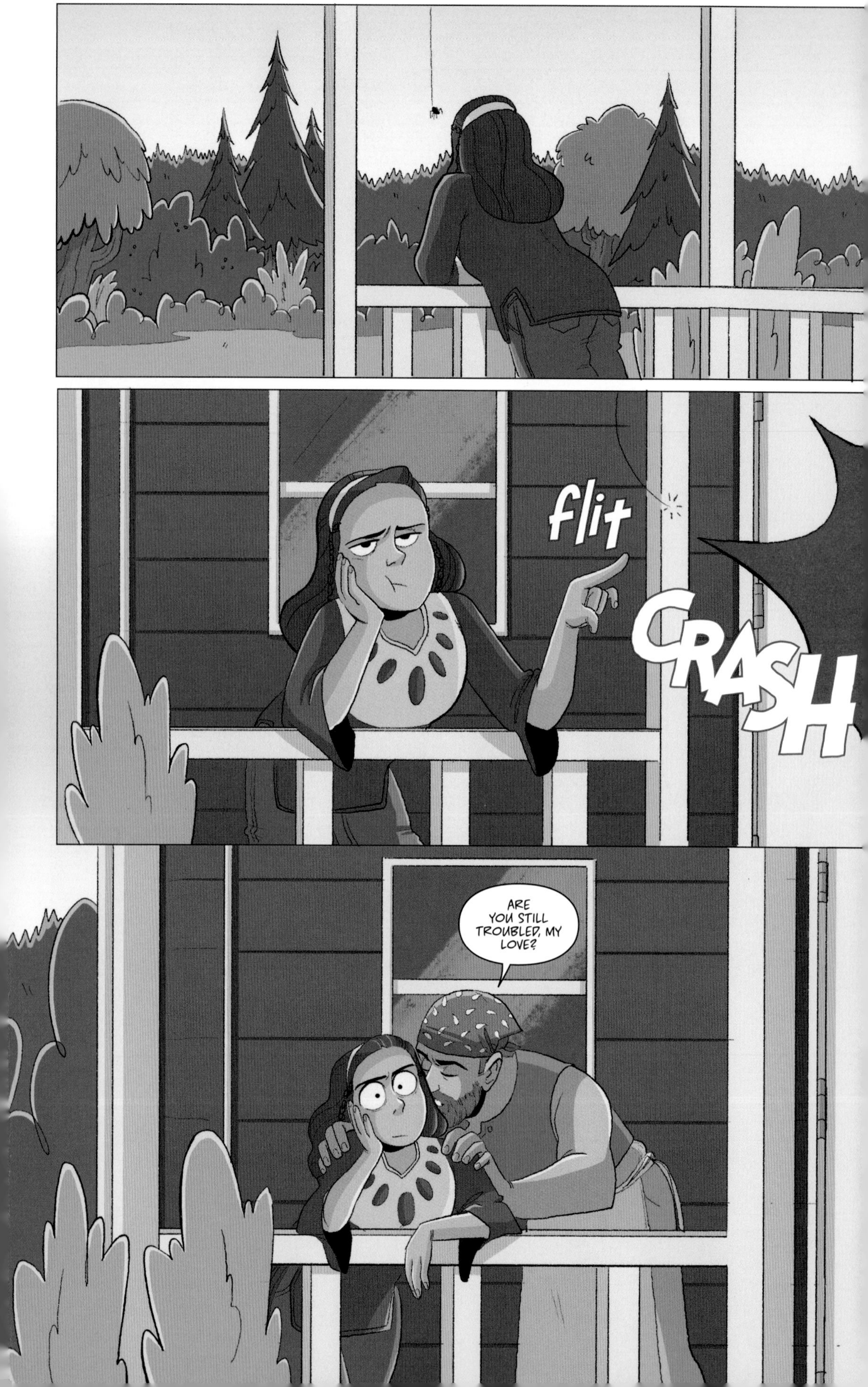
flit
CRASH
ARE YOU STILL TROUBLED, MY LOVE?

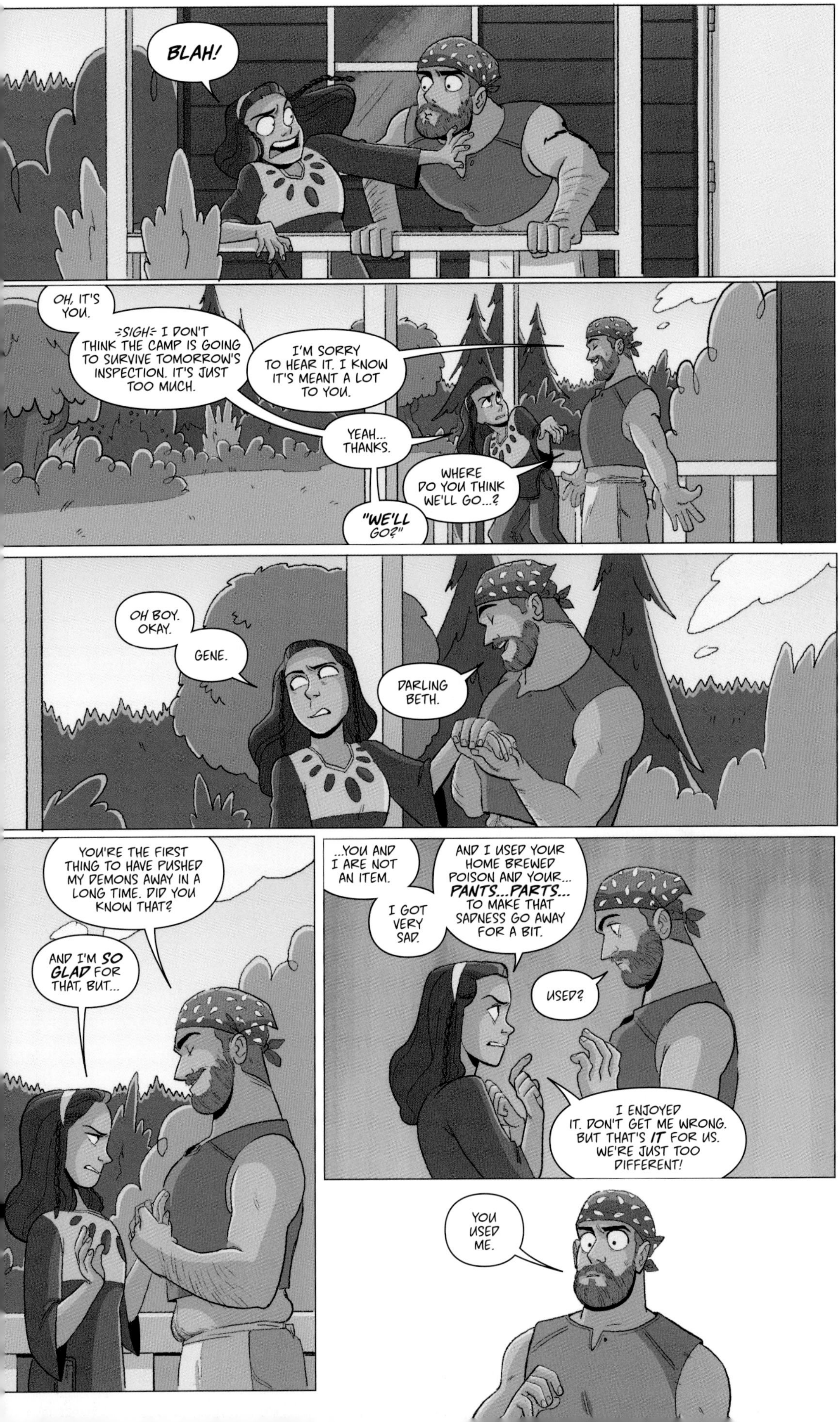
BLAH!
OH, IT'S YOU.
=SIGH= I DON'T THINK THE CAMP IS GOING TO SURVIVE TOMORROW'S INSPECTION. IT'S JUST TOO MUCH.
I'M SORRY TO HEAR IT. I KNOW IT'S MEANT A LOT TO YOU.
YEAH... THANKS.
WHERE DO YOU THINK WE'LL GO...?
"WE'LL GO?"
OH BOY. OKAY.
GENE.
DARLING BETH.
YOU'RE THE FIRST THING TO HAVE PUSHED MY DEMONS AWAY IN A LONG TIME. DID YOU KNOW THAT?
AND I'M SO GLAD FOR THAT, BUT...
...YOU AND I ARE NOT AN ITEM.
I GOT VERY SAD.
AND I USED YOUR HOME BREWED POISON AND YOUR... PANTS...PARTS... TO MAKE THAT SADNESS GO AWAY FOR A BIT.
USED?
I ENJOYED IT. DON'T GET ME WRONG. BUT THAT'S IT FOR US. WE'RE JUST TOO DIFFERENT!
YOU USED ME.

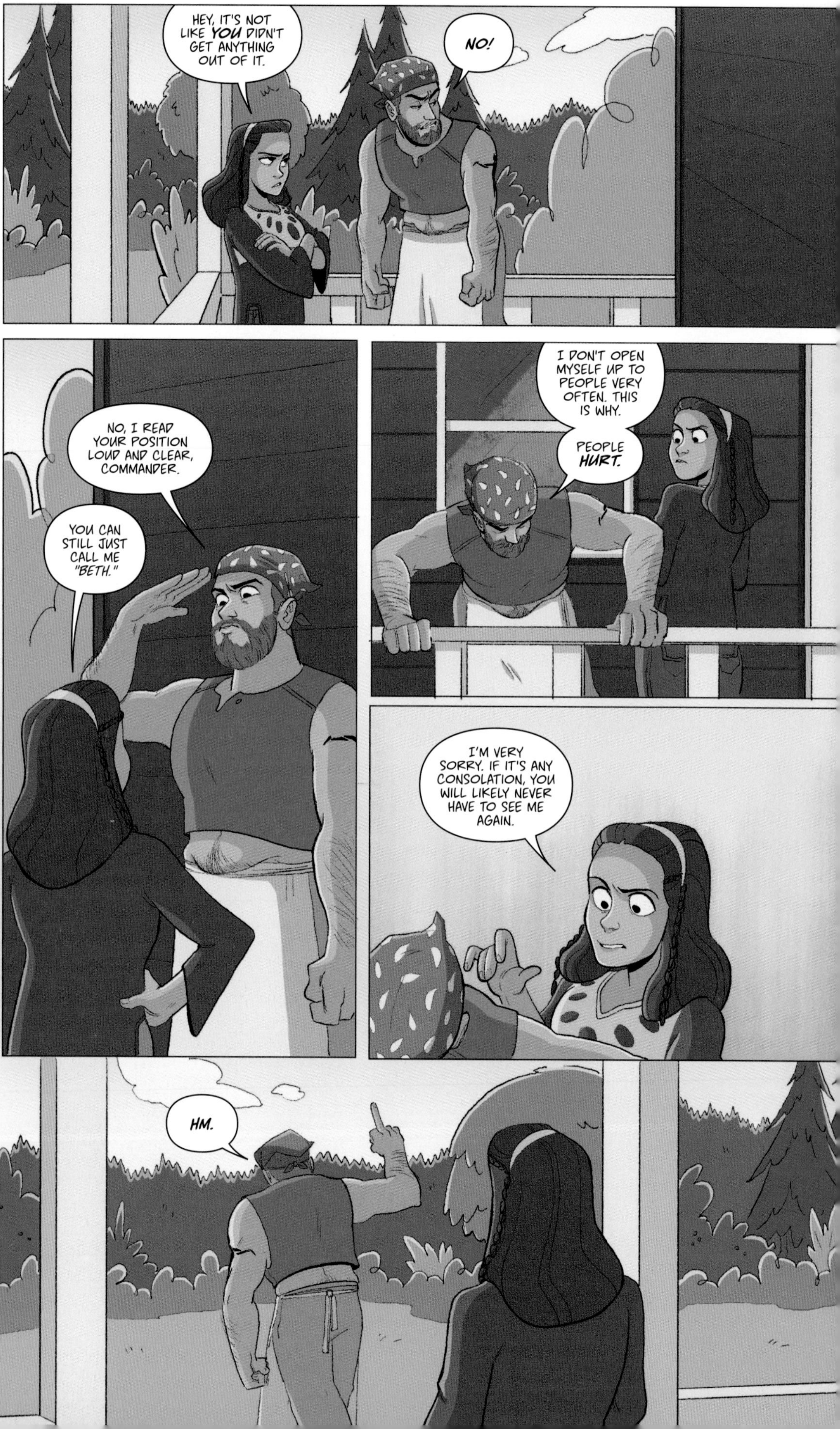
HEY, IT'S NOT LIKE YOU DIDN'T GET ANYTHING OUT OF IT.
NO!
NO, I READ YOUR POSITION LOUD AND CLEAR, COMMANDER.
YOU CAN STILL JUST CALL ME "BETH."
I DON'T OPEN MYSELF UP TO PEOPLE VERY OFTEN. THIS IS WHY.
PEOPLE HURT.
I'M VERY SORRY. IF IT'S ANY CONSOLATION, YOU WILL LIKELY NEVER HAVE TO SEE ME AGAIN.
HM.

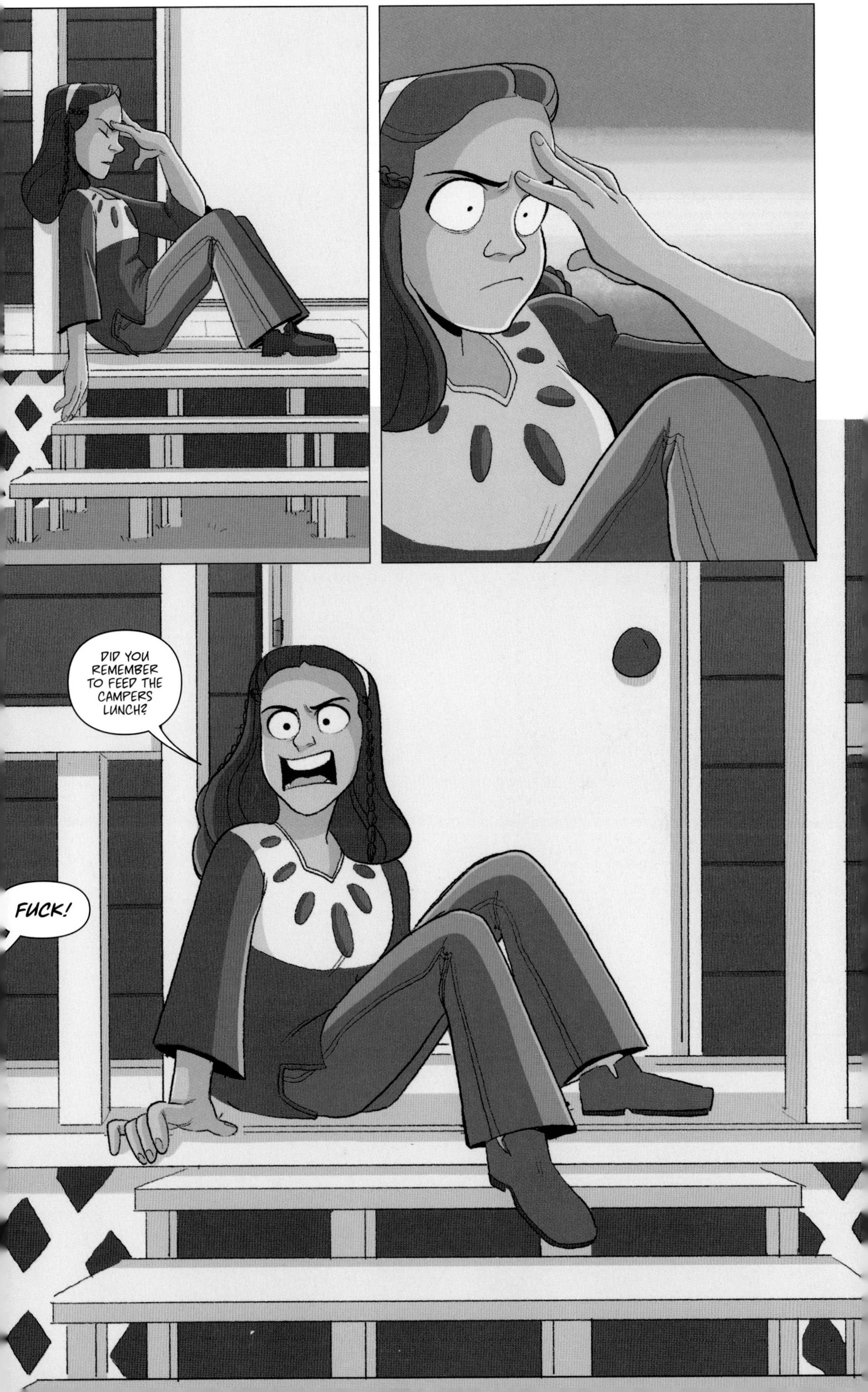
DID YOU REMEMBER TO FEED THE CAMPERS LUNCH?
FUCK!

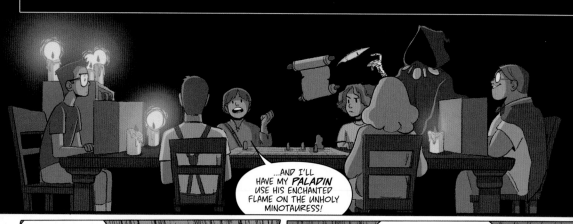

...AND I'LL HAVE MY *PALADIN* USE HIS ENCHANTED FLAME ON THE UNHOLY MINOTAURESS!

THE MINOTAURESS IS IMMUNE TO YOUR HOLY FLAME. SHE LAUGHS AS IT--

JUST A MOMENT, MAESTRO.

THE LADY MINOTAUR IS NO MERE AMALGAMATION OF WOMAN AND BOVINE BEAST.

YOU HAVE PRESENTED HER TO THE PLAYERS AS UNQUESTIONABLY EVIL, OR "UNHOLY."

IF MEMORY SERVES, A PALADIN'S BLESSED FLAME WOULD NOT ONLY INDEED HARM YOUR CREATURE, BUT DO *EXTRA* DAMAGE.

WE'LL... WE'LL....JUST CHECK THE BOOK, AND--

PAGE 309 OF THE MONSTER MANUAL.

THWACK

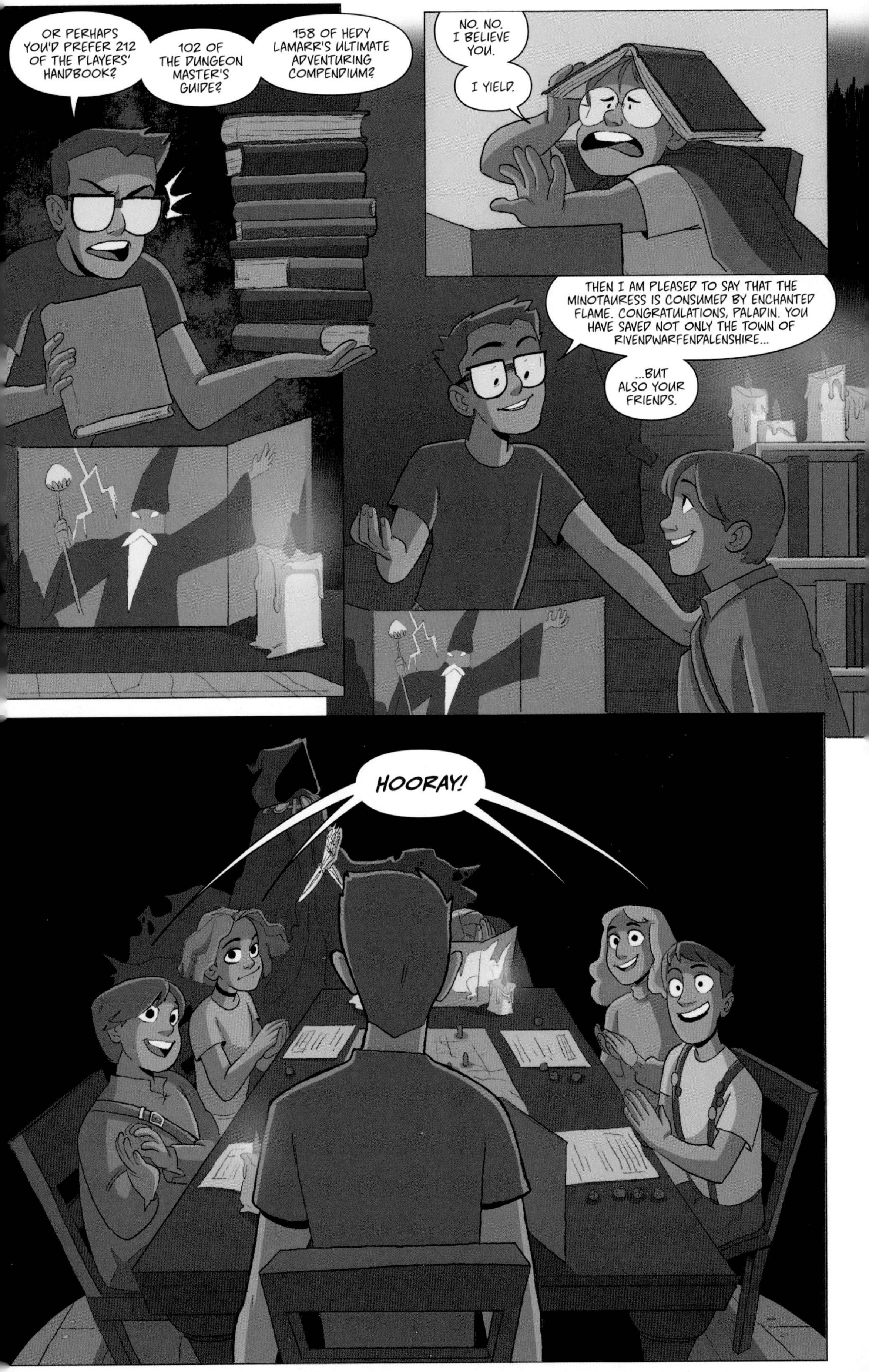
OR PERHAPS YOU'D PREFER 212 OF THE PLAYERS' HANDBOOK?
102 OF THE DUNGEON MASTER'S GUIDE?
158 OF HEDY LAMARR'S ULTIMATE ADVENTURING COMPENDIUM?
NO. NO. I BELIEVE YOU.
I YIELD.
THEN I AM PLEASED TO SAY THAT THE MINOTAURESS IS CONSUMED BY ENCHANTED FLAME. CONGRATULATIONS, PALADIN. YOU HAVE SAVED NOT ONLY THE TOWN OF RIVENDWARFENDALENSHIRE...
...BUT ALSO YOUR FRIENDS.
HOORAY!

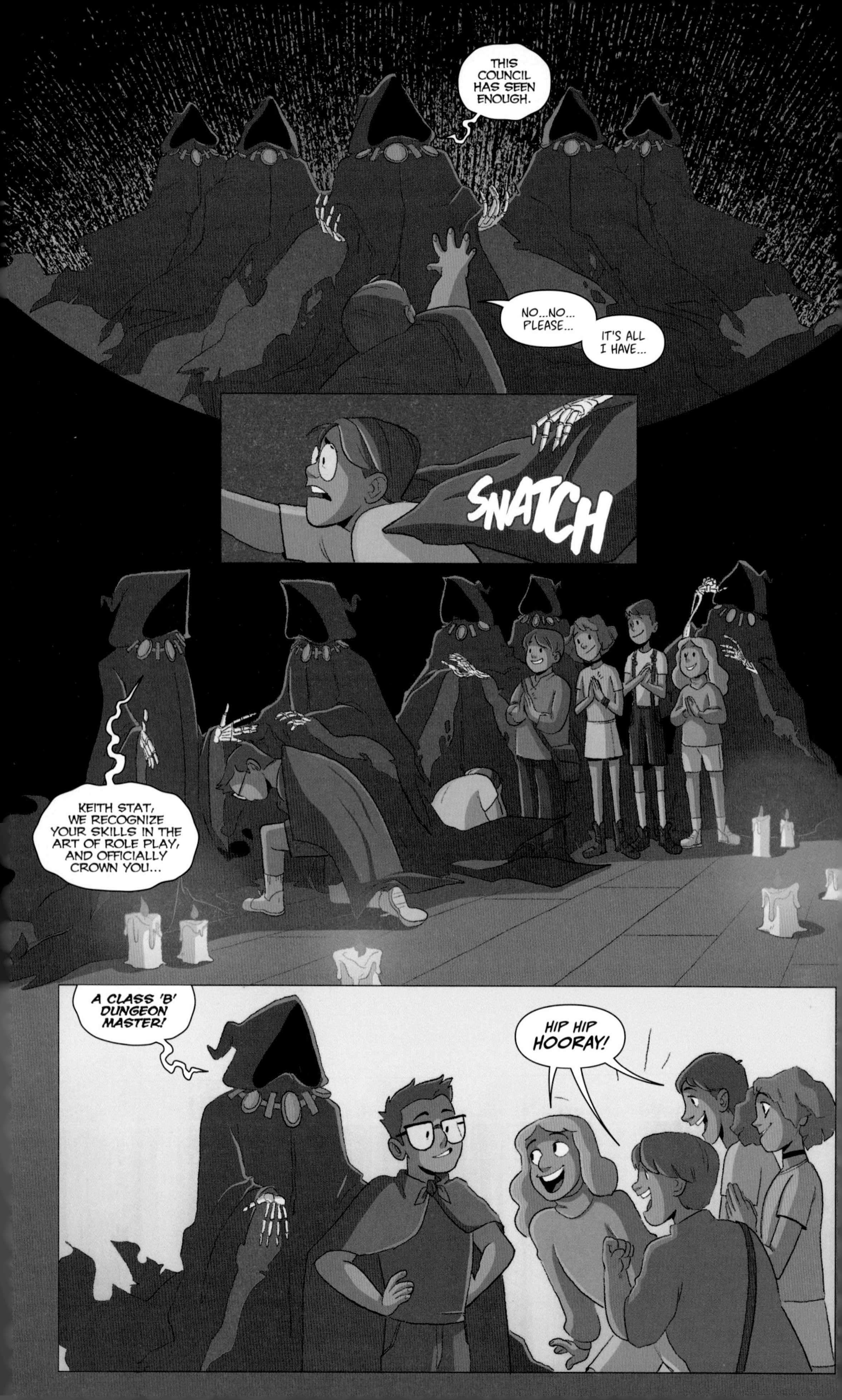

THIS COUNCIL HAS SEEN ENOUGH.
NO...NO... PLEASE...
IT'S ALL I HAVE...
SNATCH
KEITH STAT, WE RECOGNIZE YOUR SKILLS IN THE ART OF ROLE PLAY, AND OFFICIALLY CROWN YOU...
A CLASS 'B' DUNGEON MASTER!
HIP HIP HOORAY!

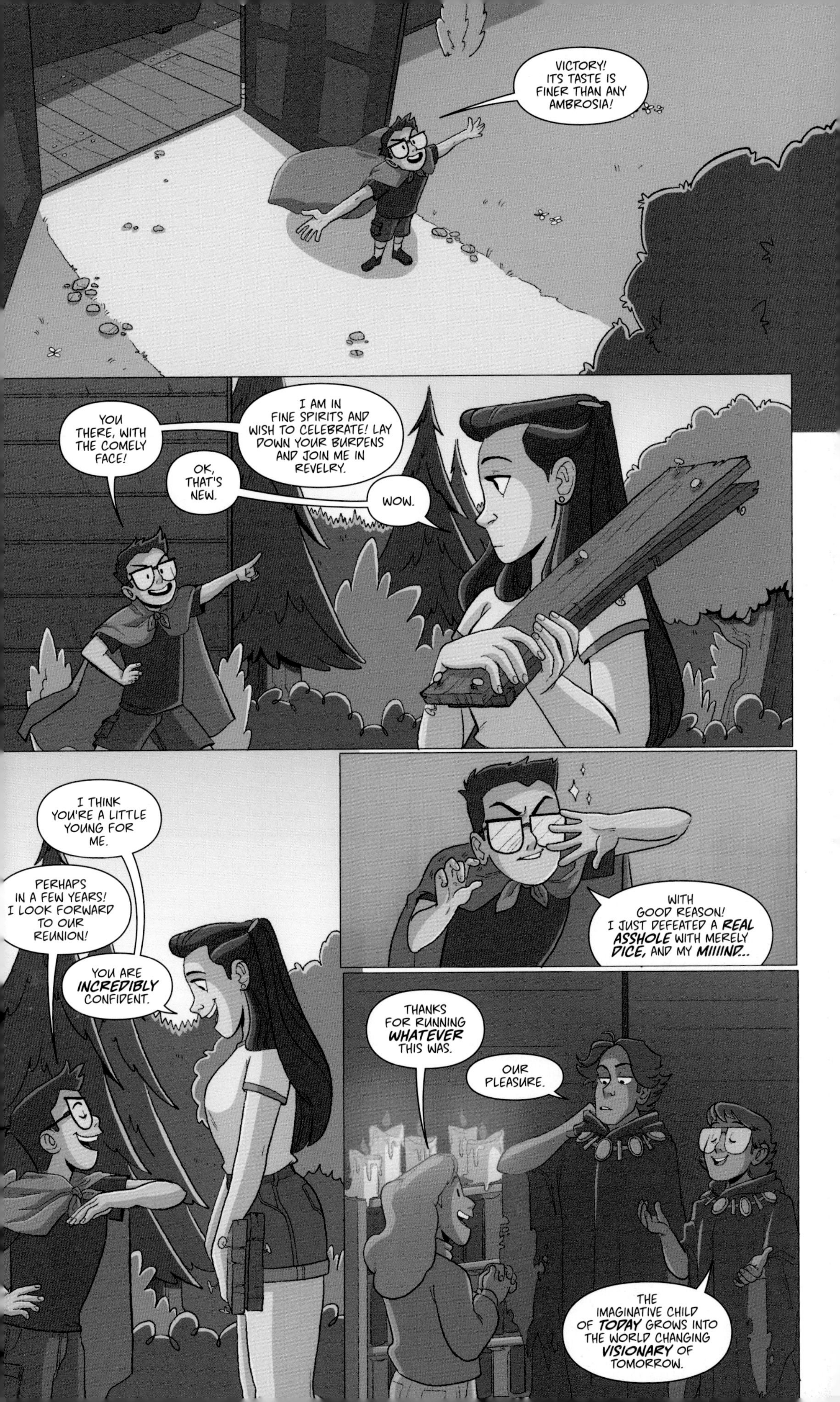
VICTORY! ITS TASTE IS FINER THAN ANY AMBROSIA!
YOU THERE, WITH THE COMELY FACE!
I AM IN FINE SPIRITS AND WISH TO CELEBRATE! LAY DOWN YOUR BURDENS AND JOIN ME IN REVELRY.
OK, THAT'S NEW.
WOW.
I THINK YOU'RE A LITTLE YOUNG FOR ME.
PERHAPS IN A FEW YEARS! I LOOK FORWARD TO OUR REUNION!
YOU ARE INCREDIBLY CONFIDENT.
WITH GOOD REASON! I JUST DEFEATED A REAL ASSHOLE WITH MERELY DICE, AND MY MIIIIND...
THANKS FOR RUNNING WHATEVER THIS WAS.
OUR PLEASURE.
THE IMAGINATIVE CHILD OF TODAY GROWS INTO THE WORLD CHANGING VISIONARY OF TOMORROW.

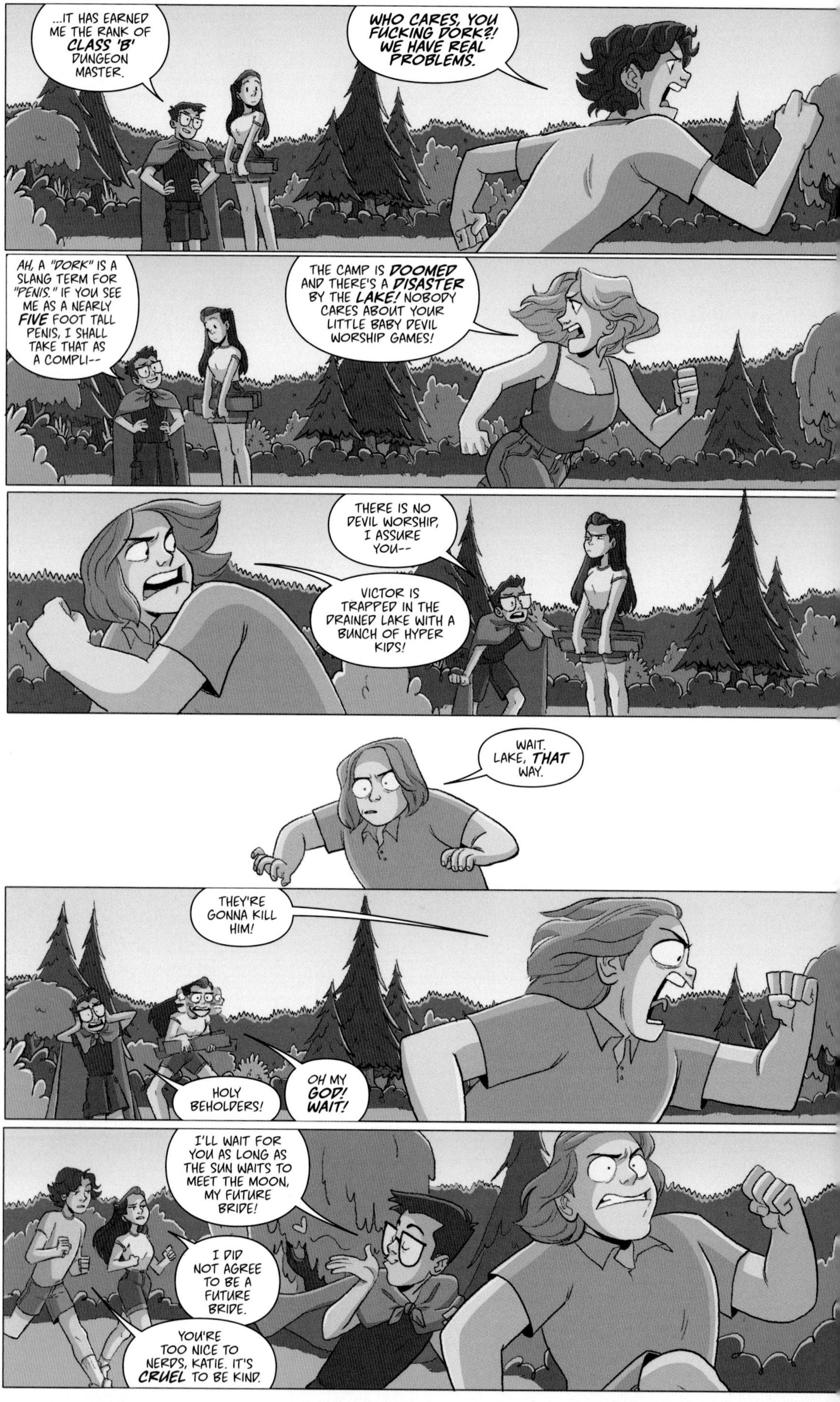
...IT HAS EARNED ME THE RANK OF CLASS 'B' DUNGEON MASTER.
WHO CARES, YOU FUCKING DORK?! WE HAVE REAL PROBLEMS.
AH, A "DORK" IS A SLANG TERM FOR "PENIS." IF YOU SEE ME AS A NEARLY FIVE FOOT TALL PENIS, I SHALL TAKE THAT AS A COMPLI--
THE CAMP IS DOOMED AND THERE'S A DISASTER BY THE LAKE! NOBODY CARES ABOUT YOUR LITTLE BABY DEVIL WORSHIP GAMES!
THERE IS NO DEVIL WORSHIP, I ASSURE YOU--
VICTOR IS TRAPPED IN THE DRAINED LAKE WITH A BUNCH OF HYPER KIDS!
WAIT. LAKE, THAT WAY.
THEY'RE GONNA KILL HIM!
HOLY BEHOLDERS!
OH MY GOD! WAIT!
I'LL WAIT FOR YOU AS LONG AS THE SUN WAITS TO MEET THE MOON, MY FUTURE BRIDE!
I DID NOT AGREE TO BE A FUTURE BRIDE.
YOU'RE TOO NICE TO NERDS, KATIE. IT'S CRUEL TO BE KIND.

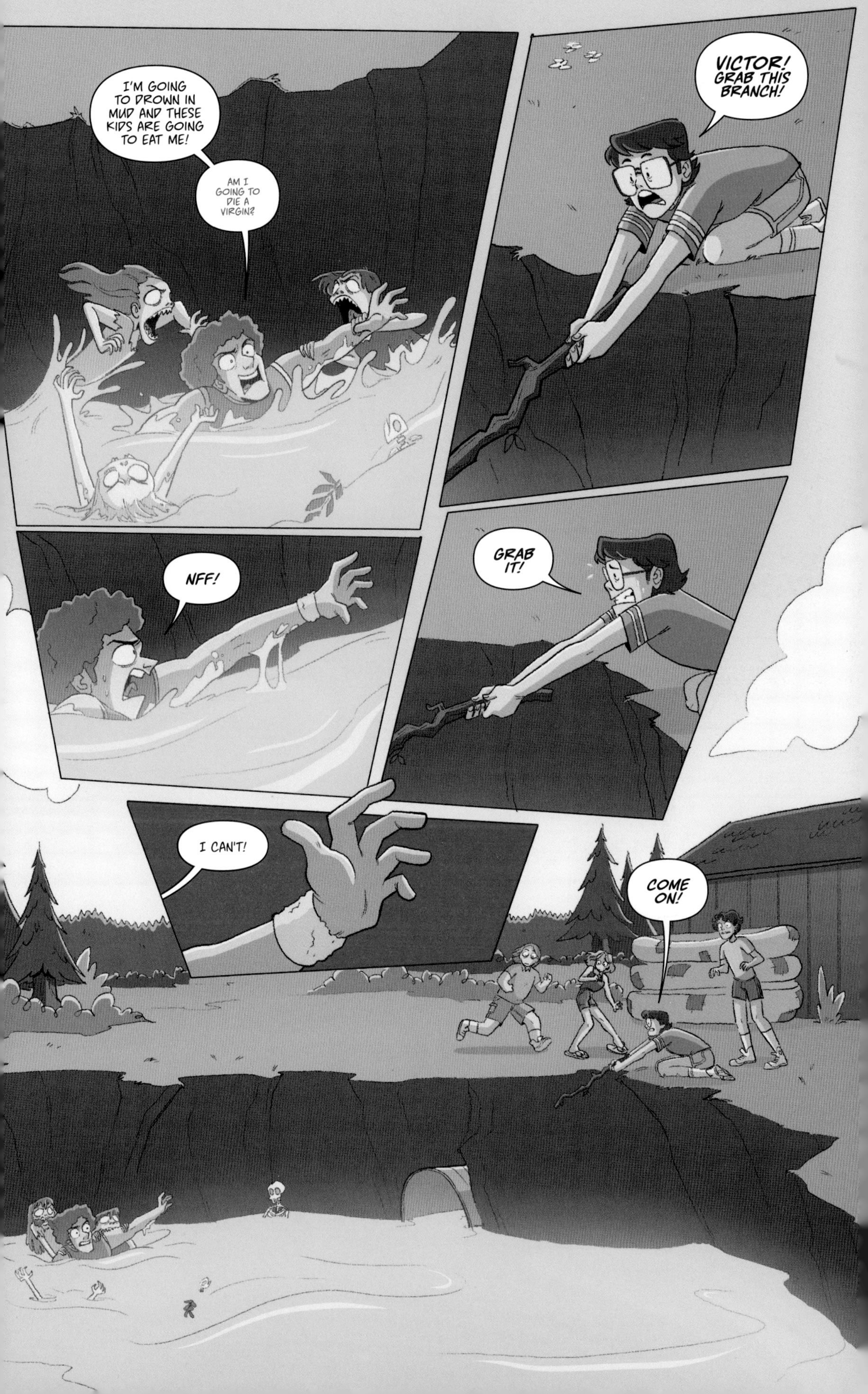

I'M GOING TO DROWN IN MUD AND THESE KIDS ARE GOING TO EAT ME!
AM I GOING TO DIE A VIRGIN?
VICTOR! GRAB THIS BRANCH!
NFF!
GRAB IT!
I CAN'T!
COME ON!

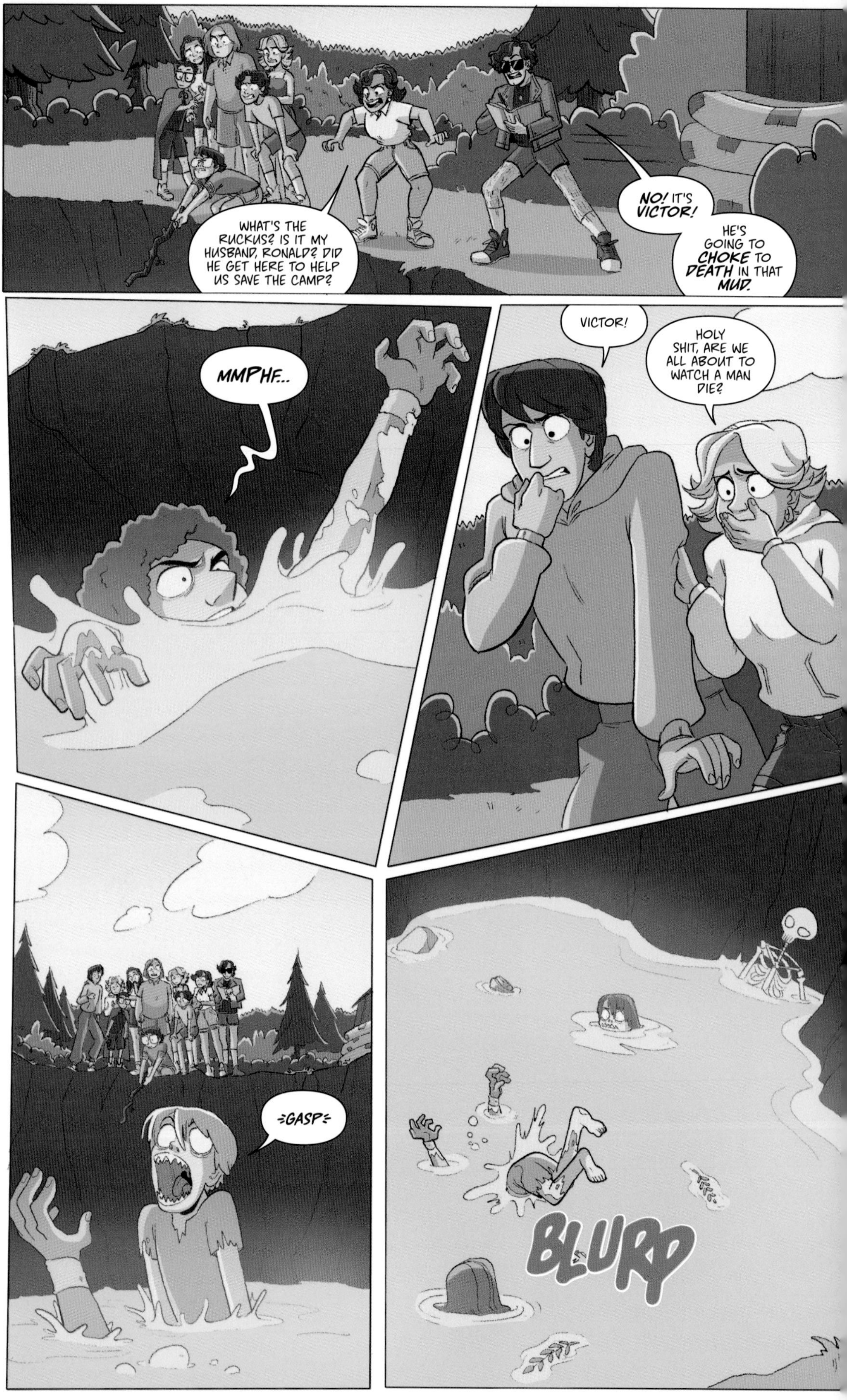
WHAT'S THE RUCKUS? IS IT MY HUSBAND, RONALD? DID HE GET HERE TO HELP US SAVE THE CAMP?
NO! IT'S VICTOR!
HE'S GOING TO CHOKE TO DEATH IN THAT MUD.
MMPHF...
VICTOR!
HOLY SHIT, ARE WE ALL ABOUT TO WATCH A MAN DIE?
=GASP=
BLURP

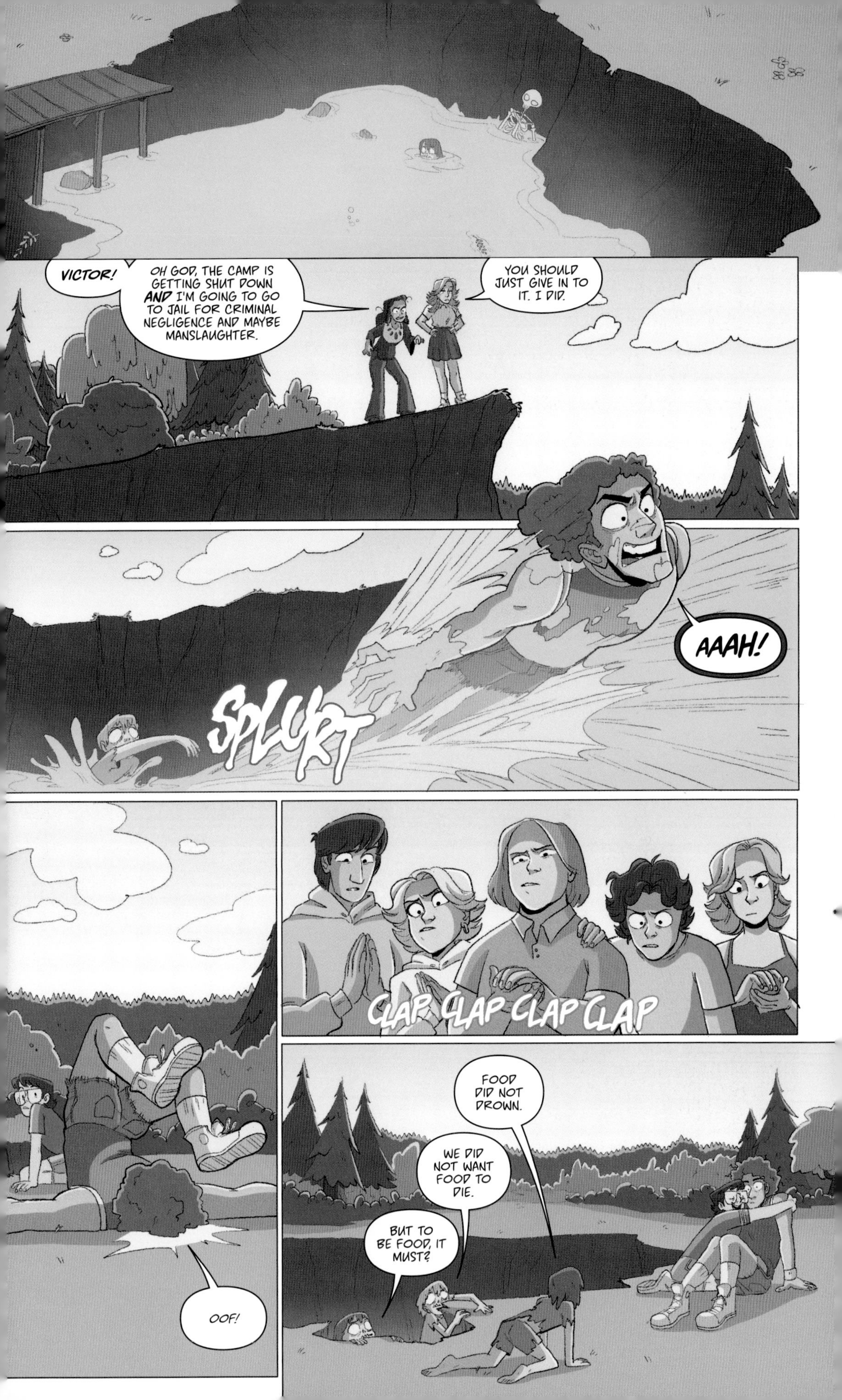

VICTOR!
OH GOD, THE CAMP IS GETTING SHUT DOWN AND I'M GOING TO GO TO JAIL FOR CRIMINAL NEGLIGENCE AND MAYBE MANSLAUGHTER.
YOU SHOULD JUST GIVE IN TO IT. I DID.
AAAH!
SPLURT
CLAP CLAP CLAP CLAP
OOF!
FOOD DID NOT DROWN.
WE DID NOT WANT FOOD TO DIE.
BUT TO BE FOOD, IT MUST?

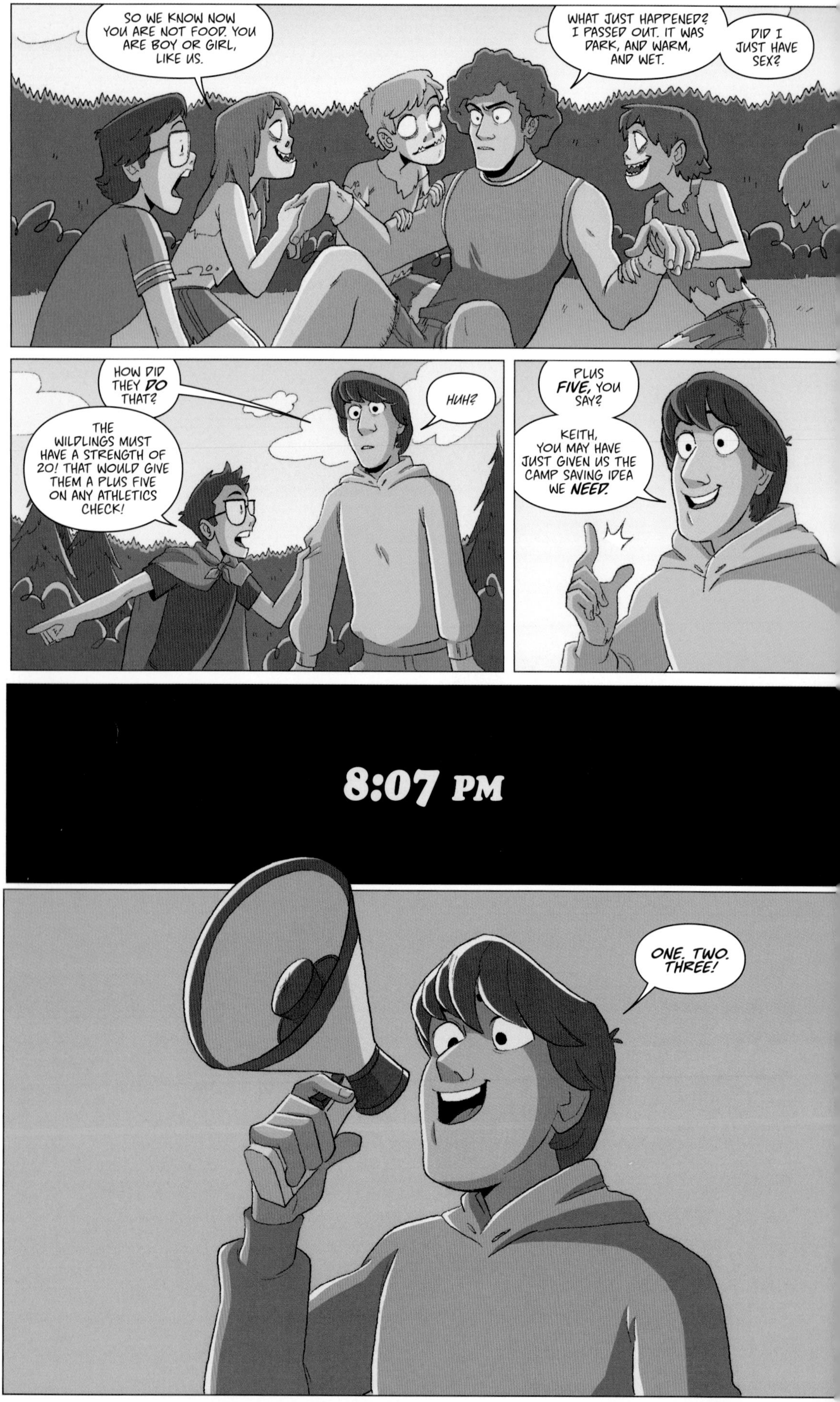
SO WE KNOW NOW YOU ARE NOT FOOD. YOU ARE BOY OR GIRL, LIKE US.
WHAT JUST HAPPENED? I PASSED OUT. IT WAS DARK, AND WARM, AND WET.
DID I JUST HAVE SEX?
HOW DID THEY DO THAT?
HUH?
THE WILDLINGS MUST HAVE A STRENGTH OF 20! THAT WOULD GIVE THEM A PLUS FIVE ON ANY ATHLETICS CHECK!
PLUS FIVE, YOU SAY?
KEITH, YOU MAY HAVE JUST GIVEN US THE CAMP SAVING IDEA WE NEED.
8:07 PM
ONE. TWO. THREE!

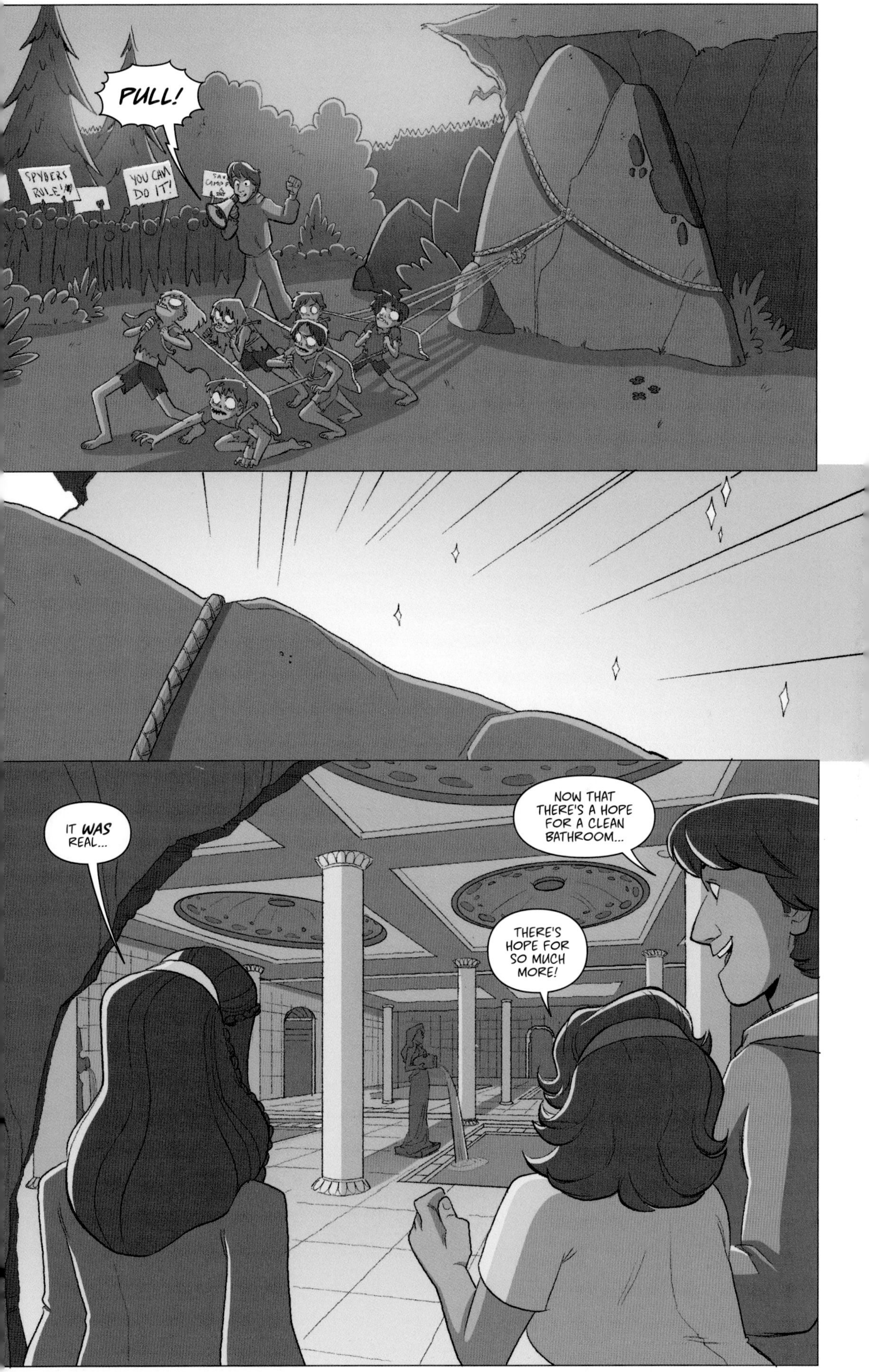
PULL!
SPYDERS RULE!
YOU CAN DO IT!
IT WAS REAL...
NOW THAT THERE'S A HOPE FOR A CLEAN BATHROOM...
THERE'S HOPE FOR SO MUCH MORE!

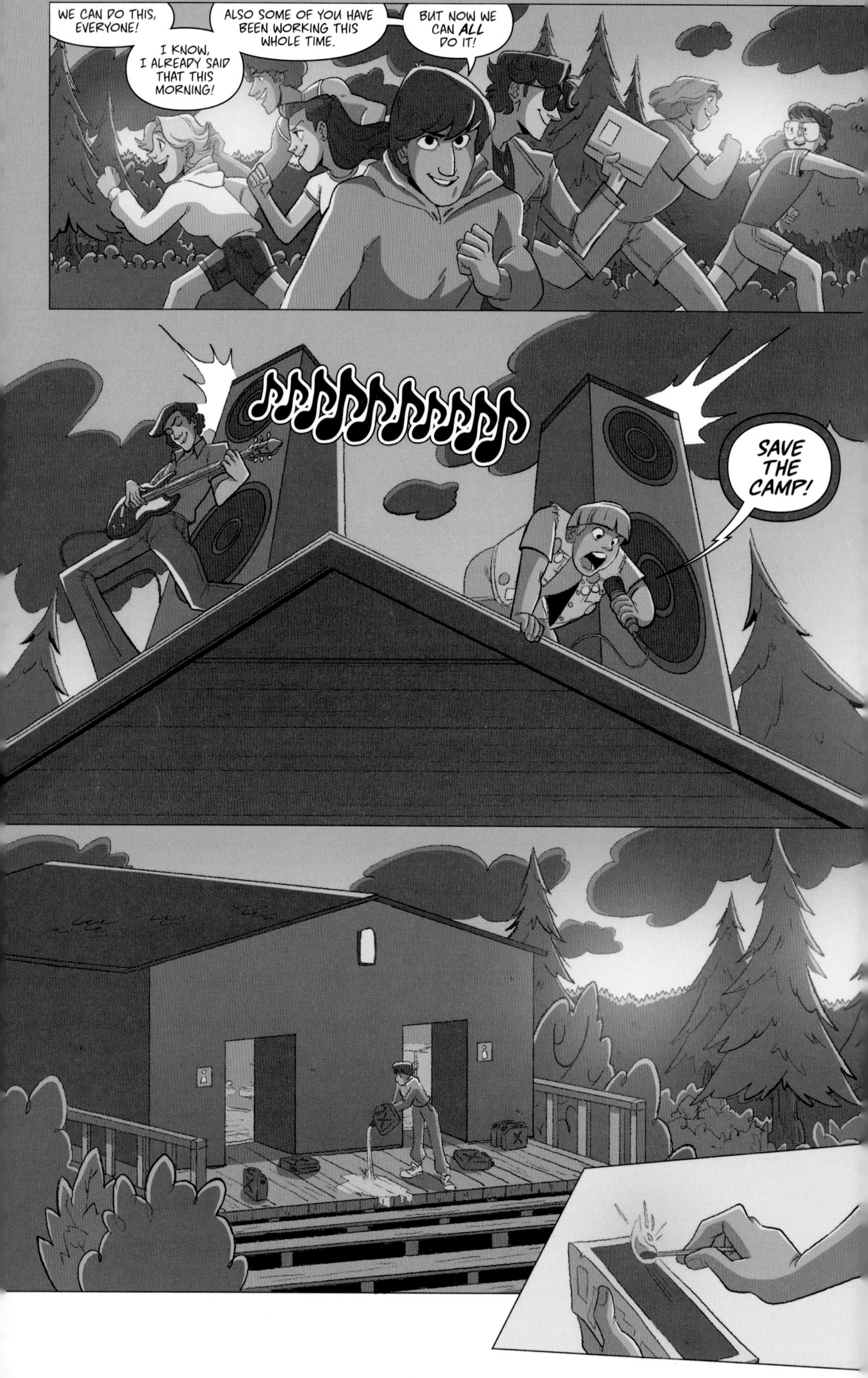
WE CAN DO THIS, EVERYONE!
I KNOW, I ALREADY SAID THAT THIS MORNING!
ALSO SOME OF YOU HAVE BEEN WORKING THIS WHOLE TIME.
BUT NOW WE CAN ALL DO IT!
SAVE THE CAMP!

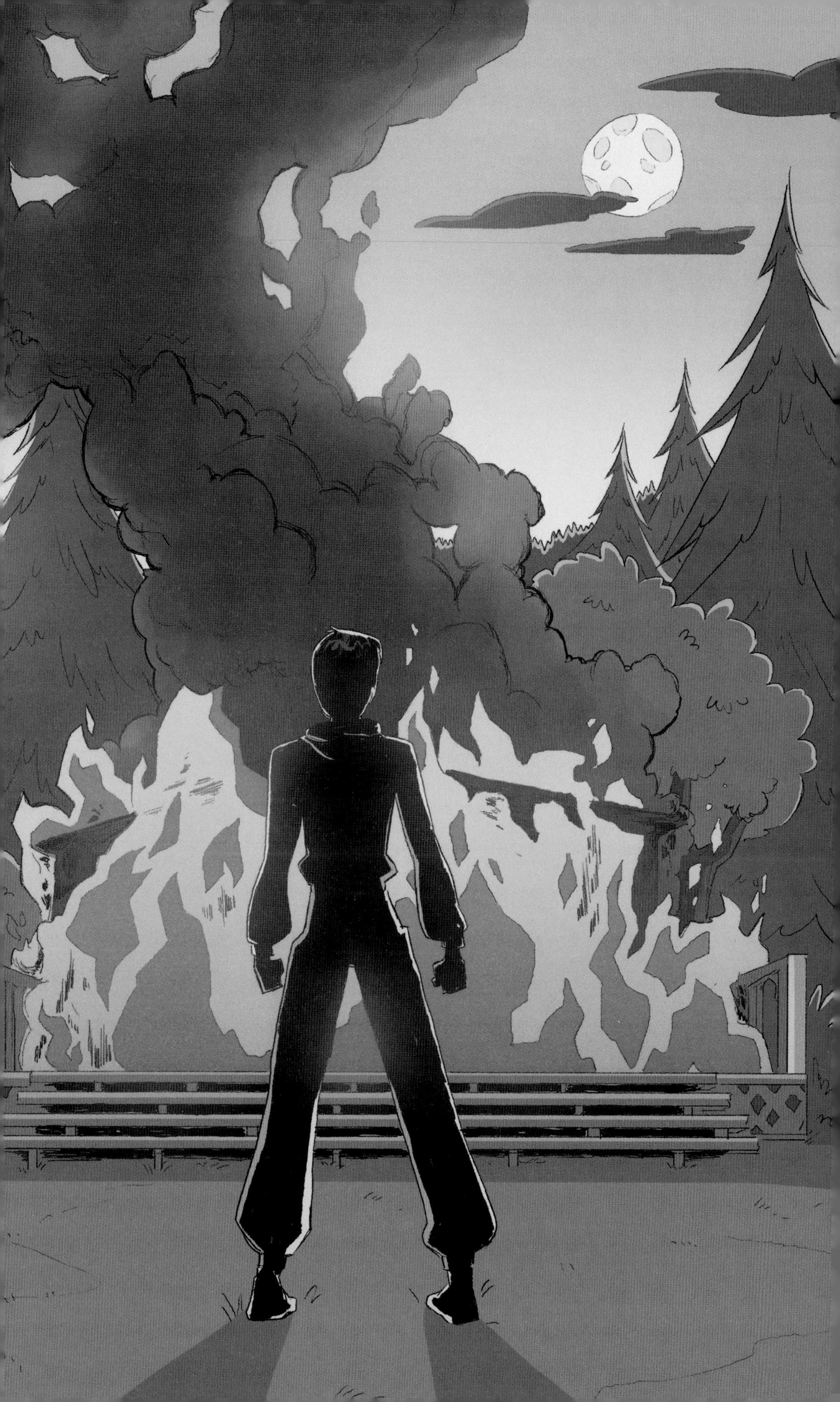

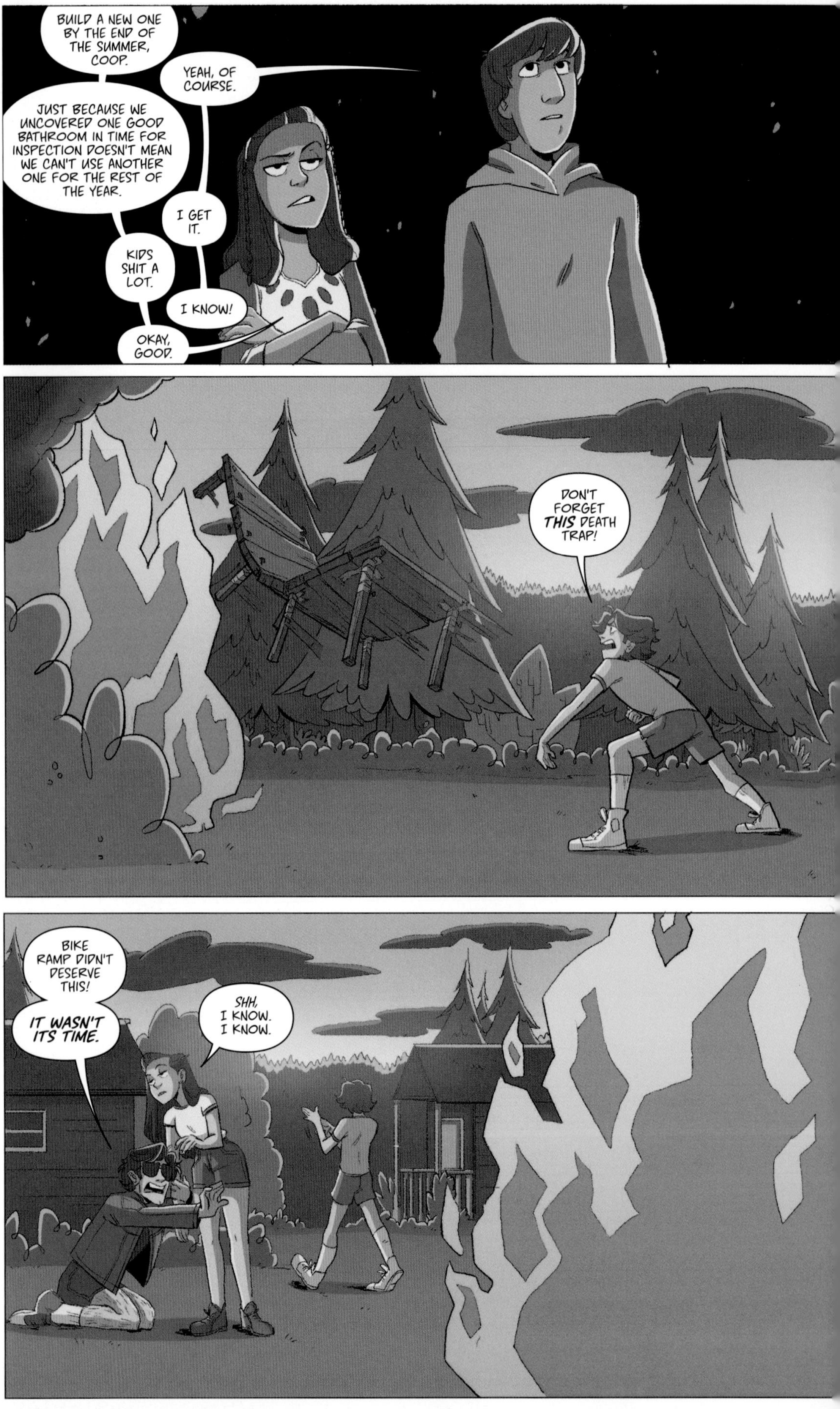
BUILD A NEW ONE BY THE END OF THE SUMMER, COOP.
YEAH, OF COURSE.
JUST BECAUSE WE UNCOVERED ONE GOOD BATHROOM IN TIME FOR INSPECTION DOESN'T MEAN WE CAN'T USE ANOTHER ONE FOR THE REST OF THE YEAR.
I GET IT.
KIDS SHIT A LOT.
I KNOW!
OKAY, GOOD.
DON'T FORGET THIS DEATH TRAP!
BIKE RAMP DIDN'T DESERVE THIS!
IT WASN'T ITS TIME.
SHH, I KNOW. I KNOW.

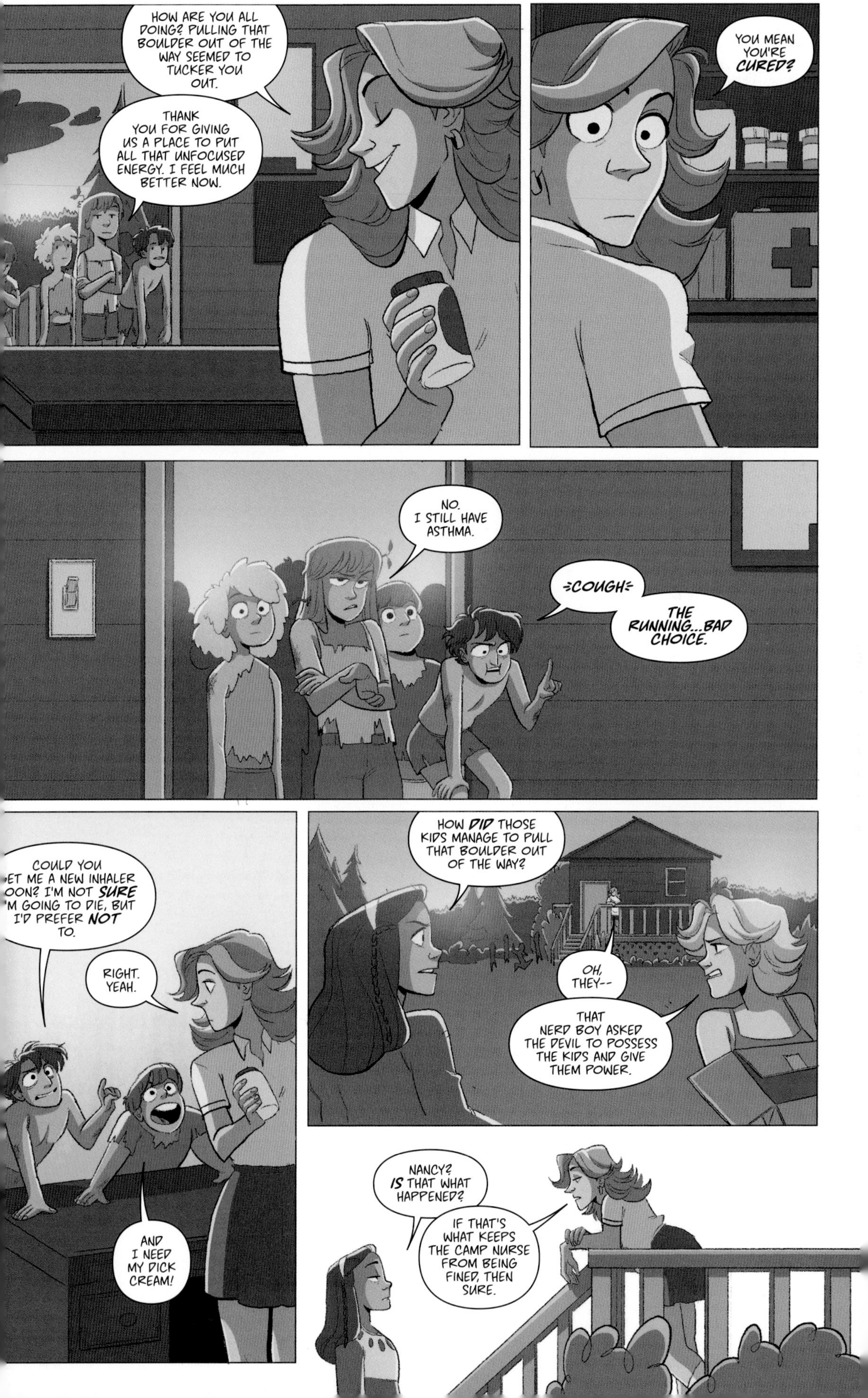

HOW ARE YOU ALL DOING? PULLING THAT BOULDER OUT OF THE WAY SEEMED TO TUCKER YOU OUT.
THANK YOU FOR GIVING US A PLACE TO PUT ALL THAT UNFOCUSED ENERGY. I FEEL MUCH BETTER NOW.
YOU MEAN YOU'RE *CURED?*
NO. I STILL HAVE ASTHMA.
COUGH
THE RUNNING...BAD CHOICE.
COULD YOU ET ME A NEW INHALER OON? I'M NOT *SURE* 'M GOING TO DIE, BUT I'D PREFER *NOT* TO.
RIGHT. YEAH.
AND I NEED MY DICK CREAM!
HOW *DID* THOSE KIDS MANAGE TO PULL THAT BOULDER OUT OF THE WAY?
OH, THEY--
THAT NERD BOY ASKED THE DEVIL TO POSSESS THE KIDS AND GIVE THEM POWER.
NANCY? *IS* THAT WHAT HAPPENED?
IF THAT'S WHAT KEEPS THE CAMP NURSE FROM BEING FINED, THEN SURE.

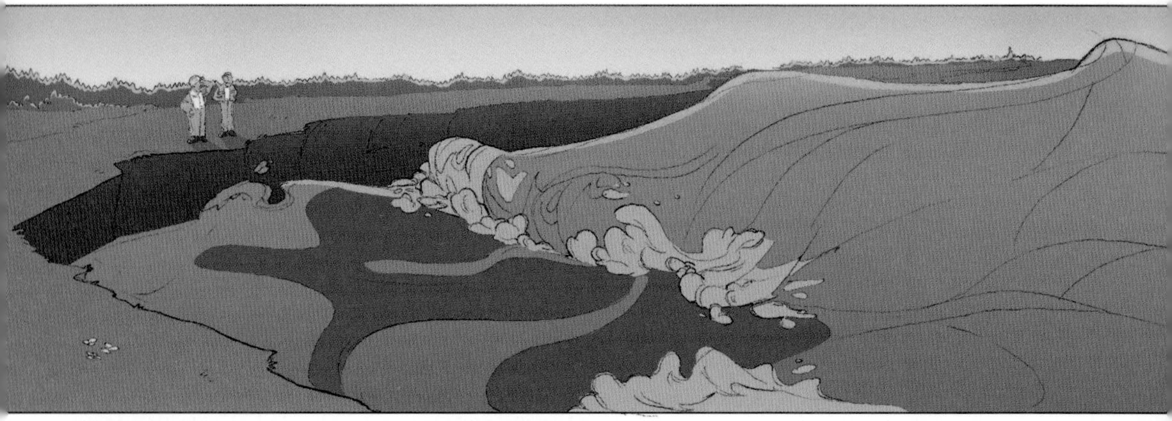
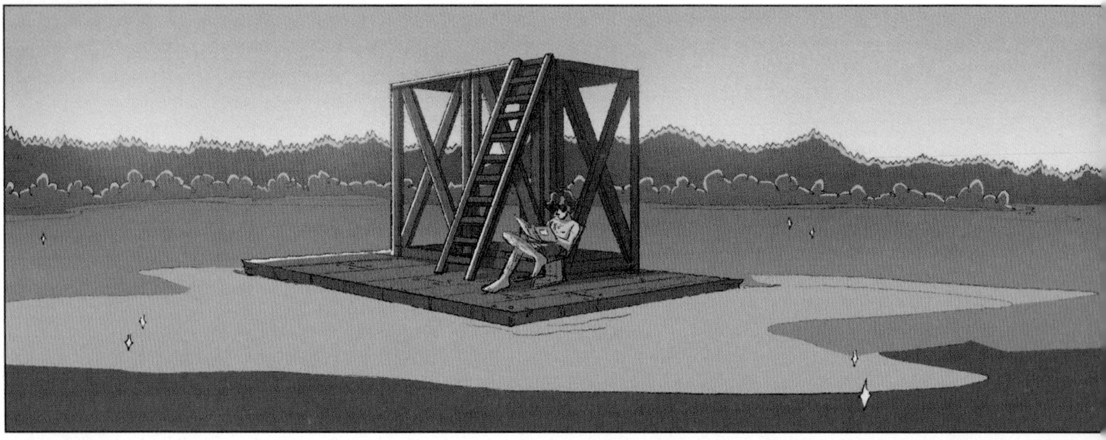
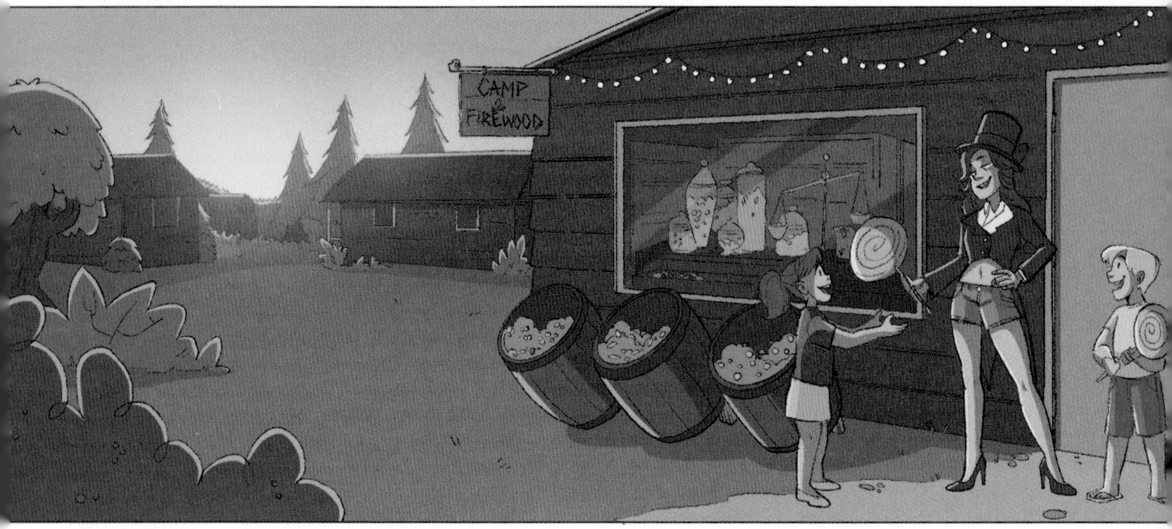
CAMP FIREWOOD
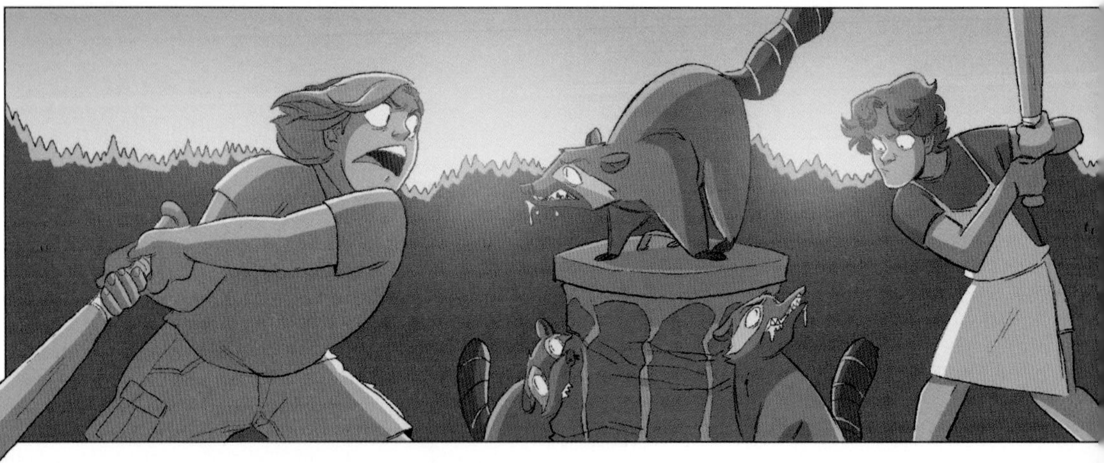

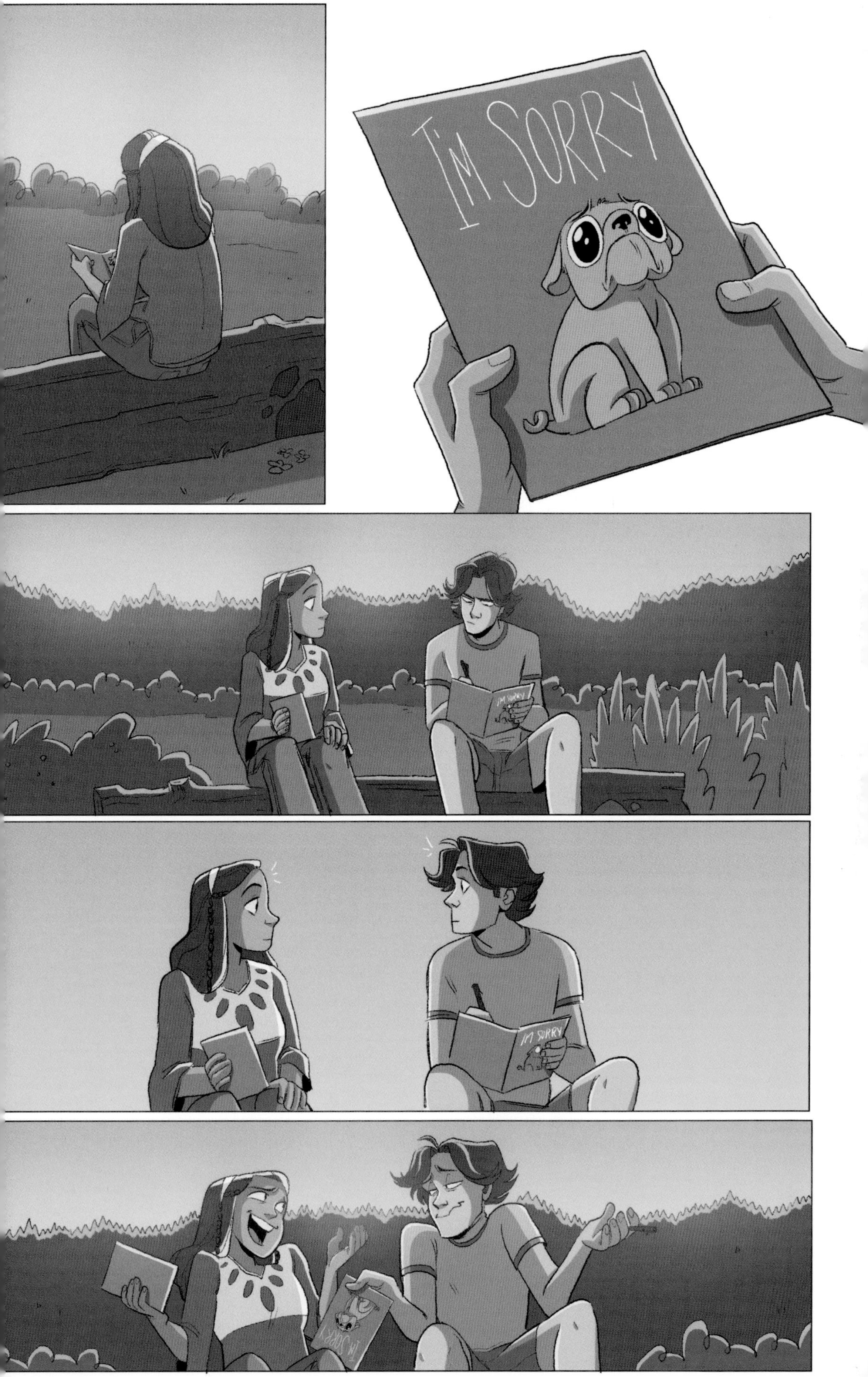
I'M SORRY

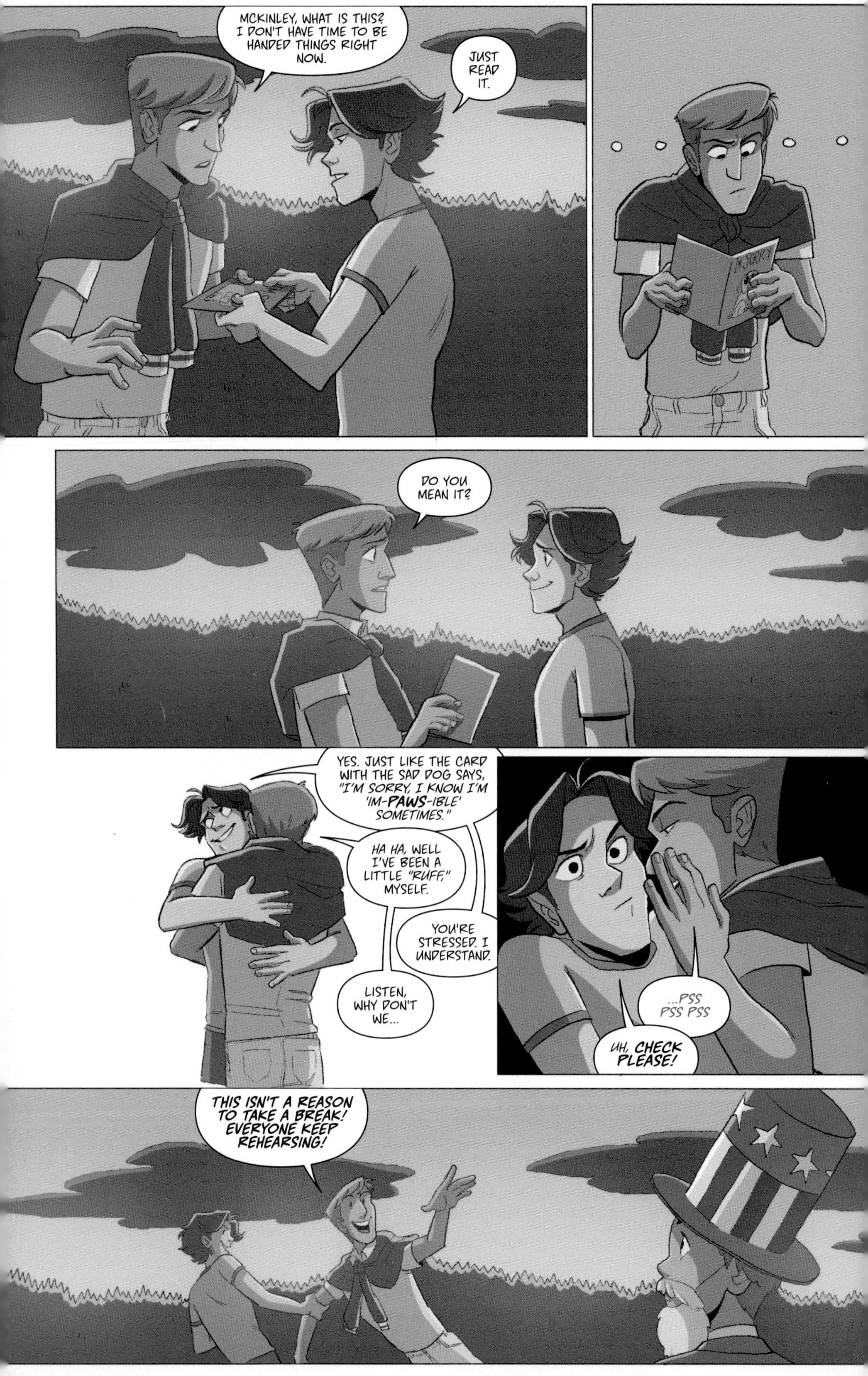
MCKINLEY, WHAT IS THIS? I DON'T HAVE TIME TO BE HANDED THINGS RIGHT NOW.
JUST READ IT.
I'M SORRY
DO YOU MEAN IT?
YES. JUST LIKE THE CARD WITH THE SAD DOG SAYS, "I'M SORRY, I KNOW I'M 'IM-PAWS-IBLE' SOMETIMES."
HA HA, WELL I'VE BEEN A LITTLE "RUFF," MYSELF.
YOU'RE STRESSED. I UNDERSTAND.
LISTEN, WHY DON'T WE...
...PSS PSS PSS
UH, CHECK PLEASE!
THIS ISN'T A REASON TO TAKE A BREAK! EVERYONE KEEP REHEARSING!

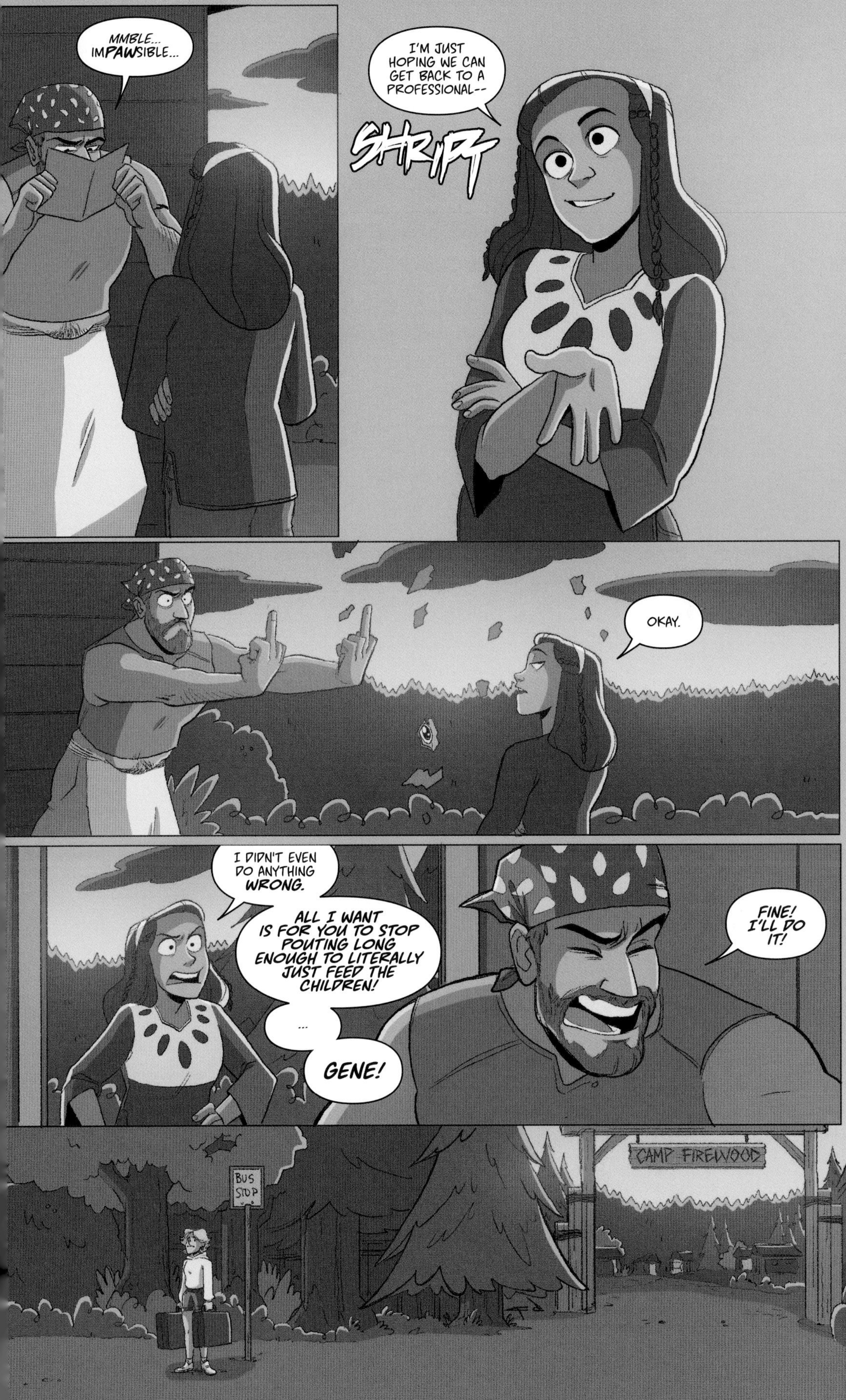

MMBLE... IMPAWSIBLE...
I'M JUST HOPING WE CAN GET BACK TO A PROFESSIONAL--
SHRIP
OKAY.
I DIDN'T EVEN DO ANYTHING WRONG.
ALL I WANT IS FOR YOU TO STOP POUTING LONG ENOUGH TO LITERALLY JUST FEED THE CHILDREN!
...
GENE!
FINE! I'LL DO IT!
BUS STOP
CAMP FIREWOOD

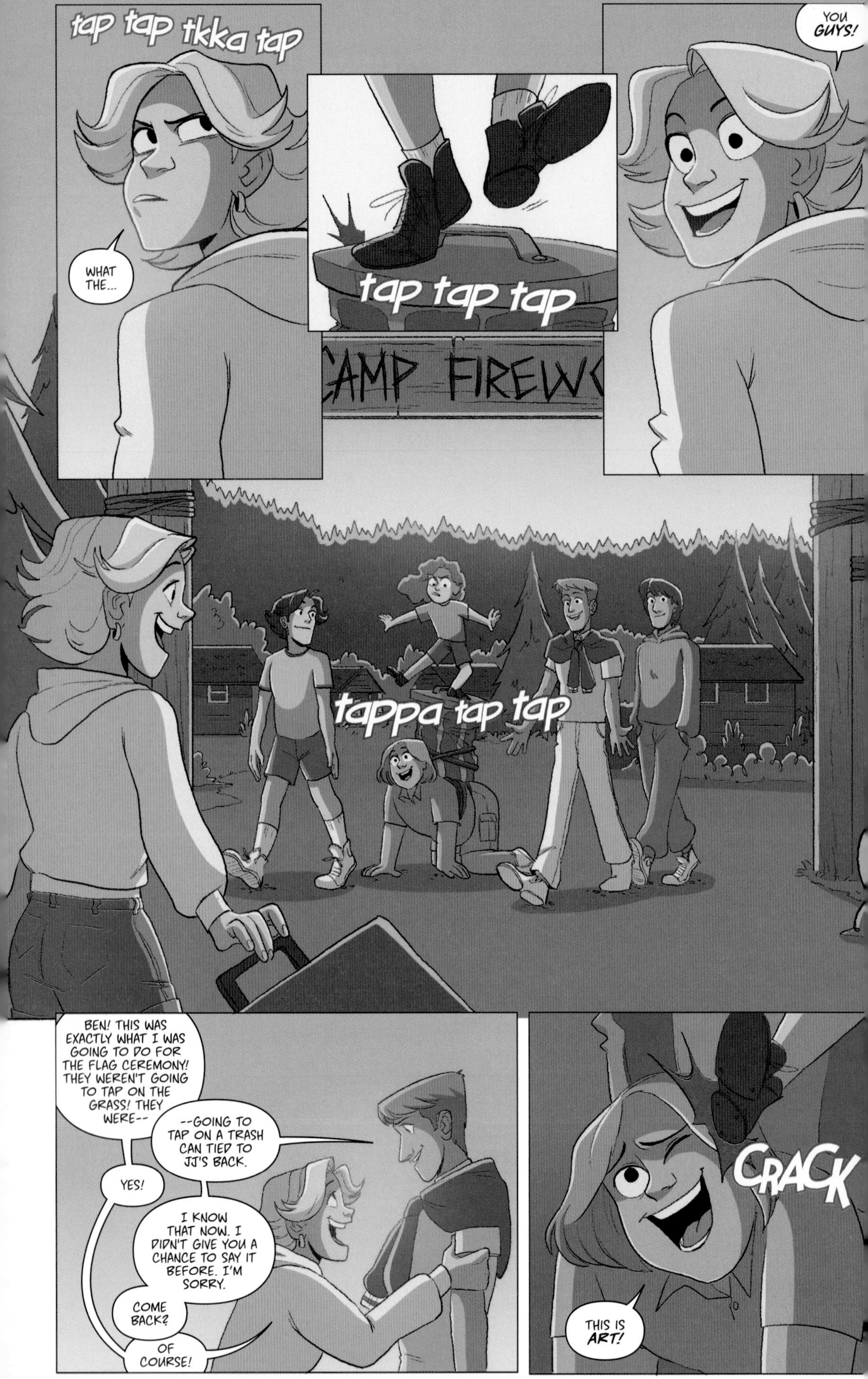
tap tap tkka tap
WHAT THE...
tap tap tap
CAMP FIREWO
YOU GUYS!
tappa tap tap
BEN! THIS WAS EXACTLY WHAT I WAS GOING TO DO FOR THE FLAG CEREMONY! THEY WEREN'T GOING TO TAP ON THE GRASS! THEY WERE--
--GOING TO TAP ON A TRASH CAN TIED TO JJ'S BACK.
YES!
I KNOW THAT NOW. I DIDN'T GIVE YOU A CHANCE TO SAY IT BEFORE. I'M SORRY.
COME BACK?
OF COURSE!
CRACK
THIS IS ART!

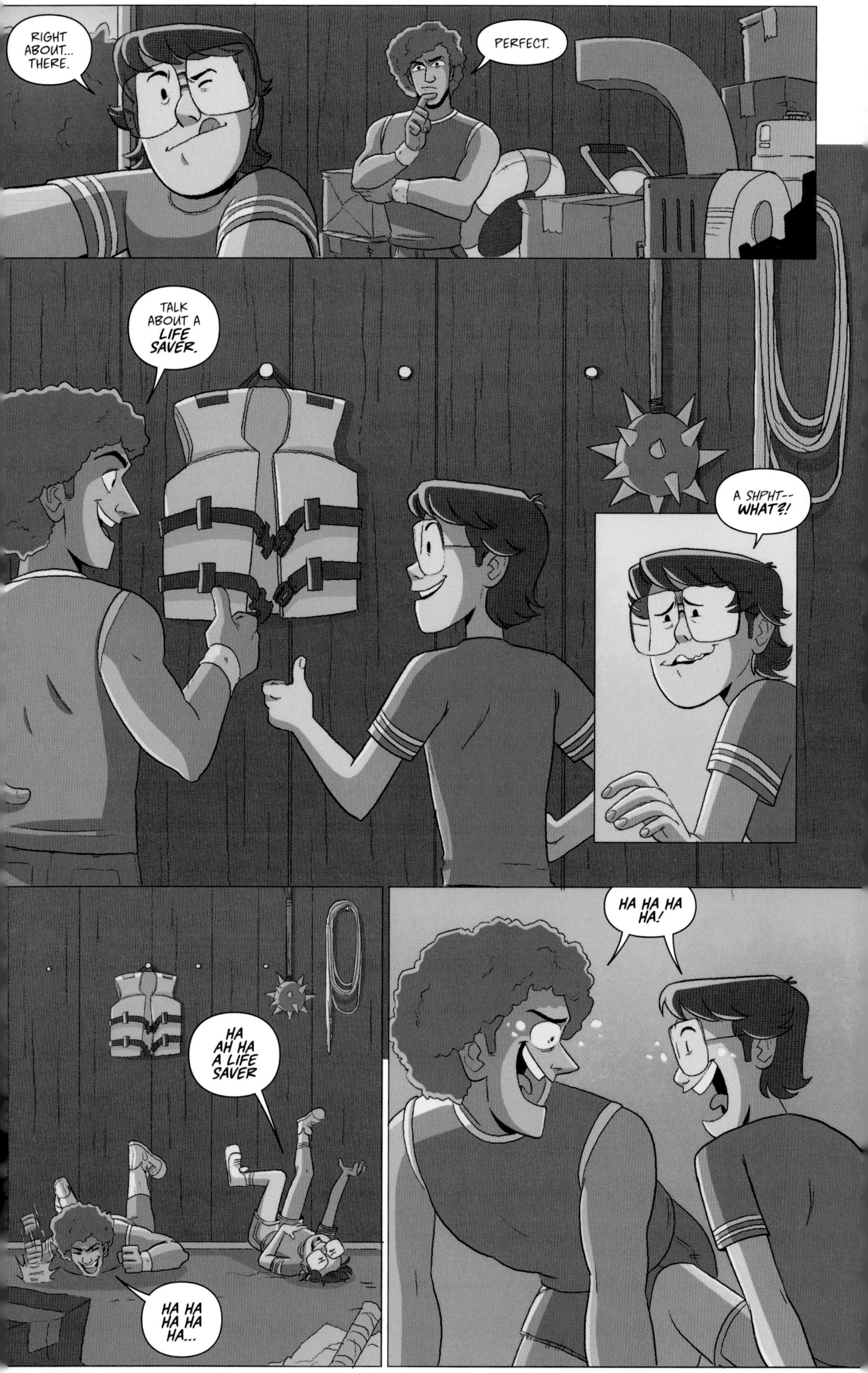
RIGHT ABOUT... THERE.
PERFECT.
TALK ABOUT A LIFE SAVER.
A SHPHT-- WHAT?!
HA AH HA A LIFE SAVER
HA HA HA HA HA...
HA HA HA HA!

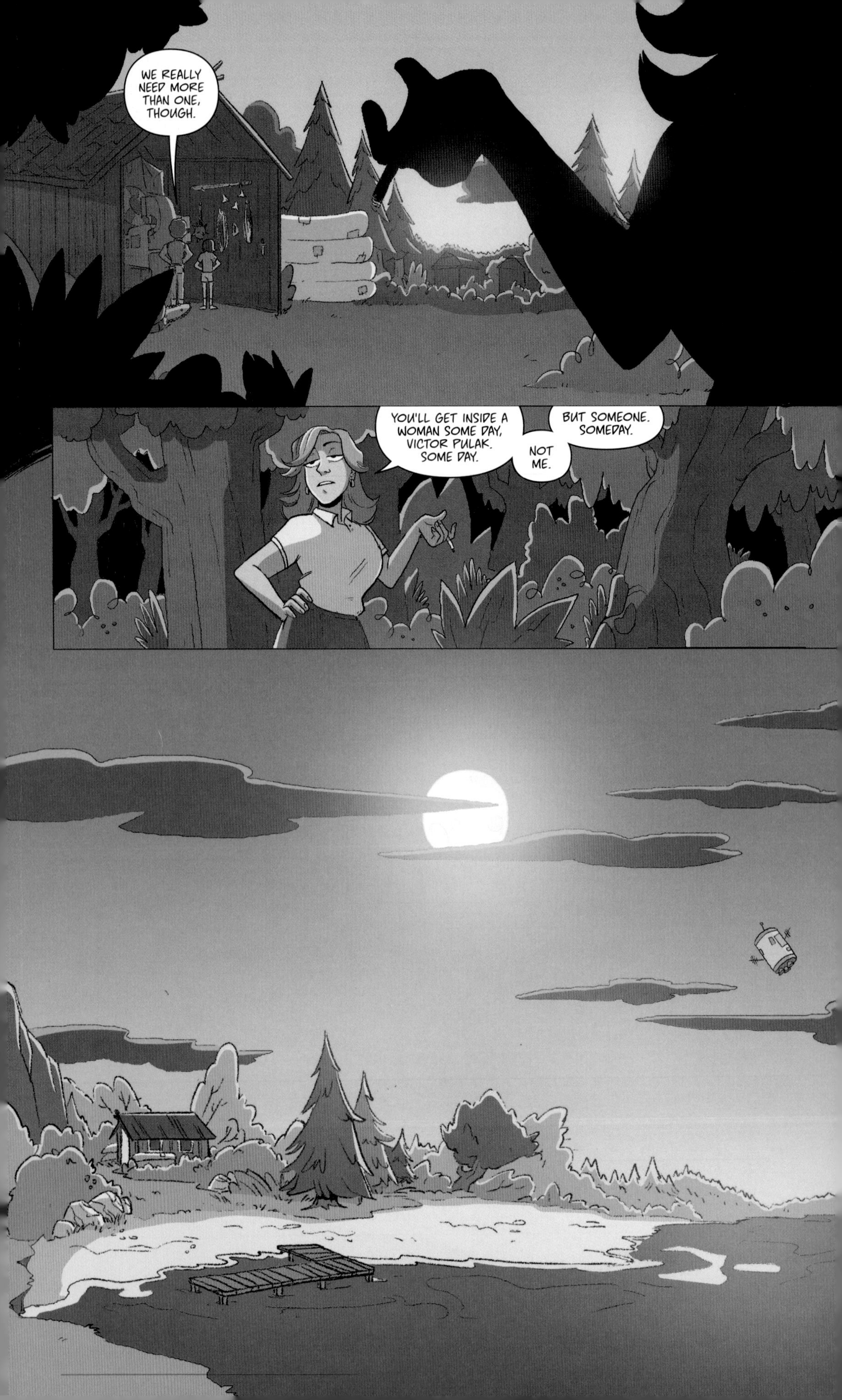

WE REALLY NEED MORE THAN ONE, THOUGH.
YOU'LL GET INSIDE A WOMAN SOME DAY, VICTOR PULAK. SOME DAY.
NOT ME.
BUT SOMEONE. SOMEDAY.

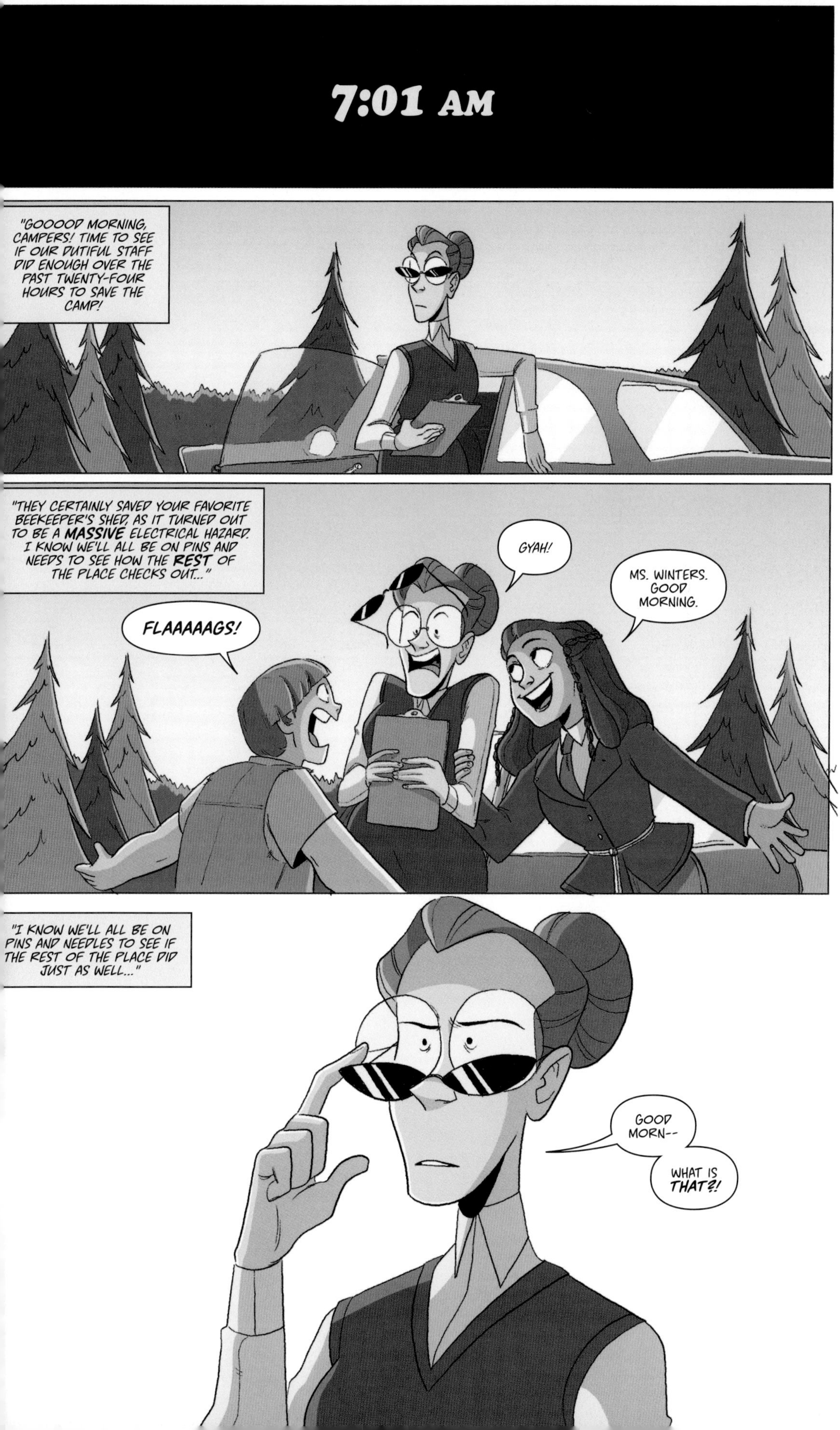
7:01 AM
"GOOOOD MORNING, CAMPERS! TIME TO SEE IF OUR DUTIFUL STAFF DID ENOUGH OVER THE PAST TWENTY-FOUR HOURS TO SAVE THE CAMP!
"THEY CERTAINLY SAVED YOUR FAVORITE BEEKEEPER'S SHED, AS IT TURNED OUT TO BE A MASSIVE ELECTRICAL HAZARD. I KNOW WE'LL ALL BE ON PINS AND NEEDS TO SEE HOW THE REST OF THE PLACE CHECKS OUT..."
FLAAAAAGS!
GYAH!
MS. WINTERS. GOOD MORNING.
"I KNOW WE'LL ALL BE ON PINS AND NEEDLES TO SEE IF THE REST OF THE PLACE DID JUST AS WELL..."
GOOD MORN--
WHAT IS THAT?!

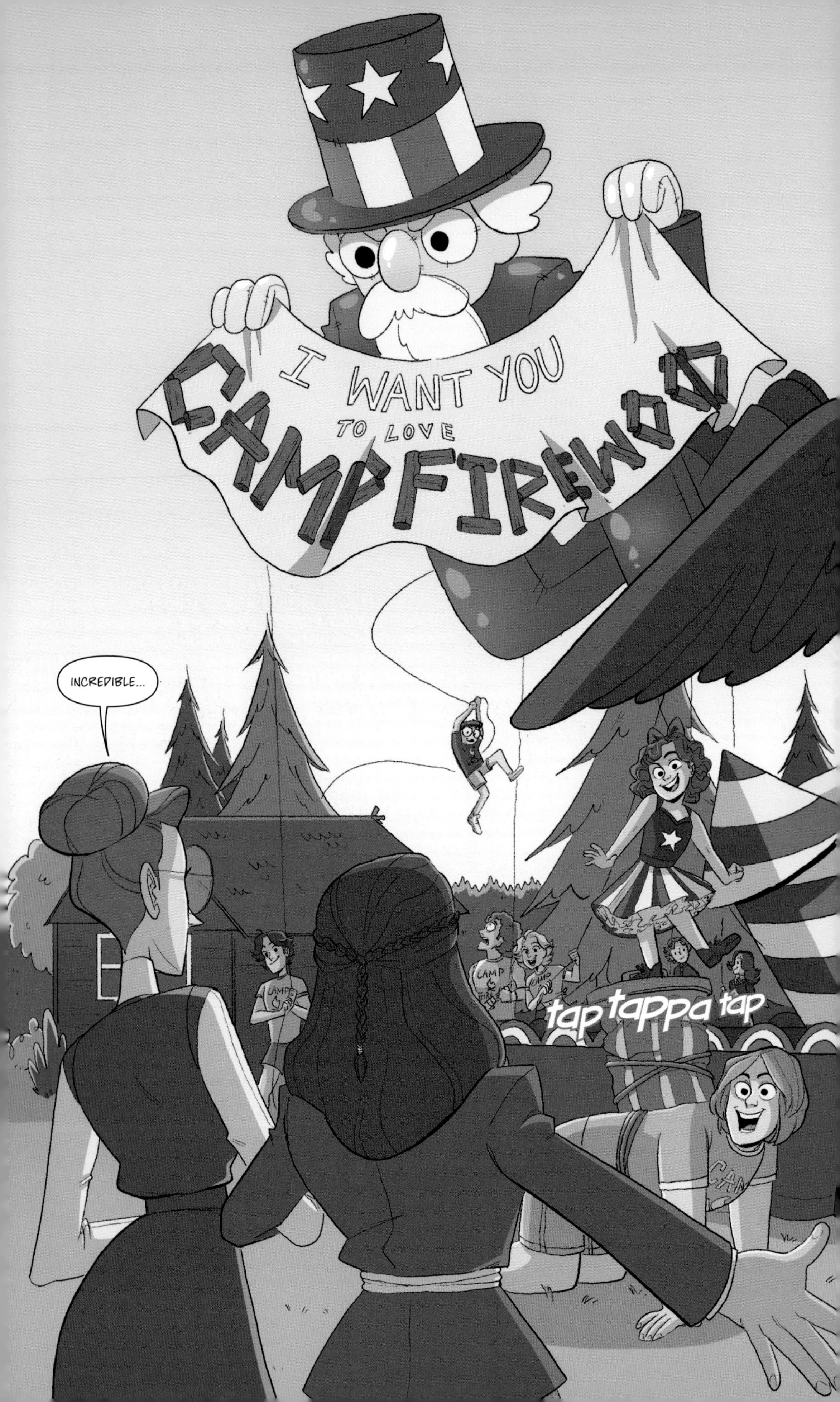
I WANT YOU
TO LOVE
CAMPFIREWOOD
INCREDIBLE...
tap tappa tap

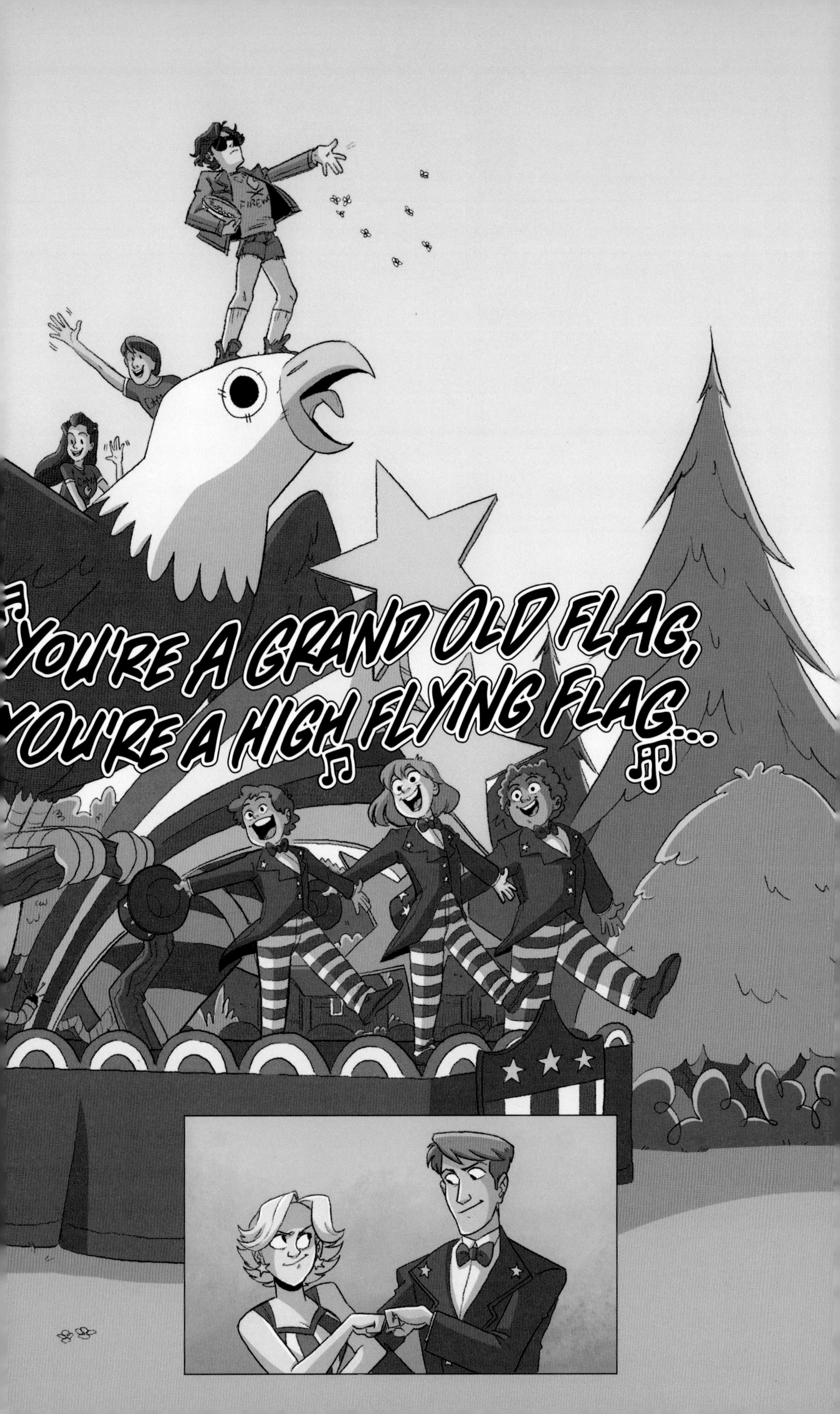
YOU'RE A GRAND OLD FLAG,
YOU'RE A HIGH FLYING FLAG...

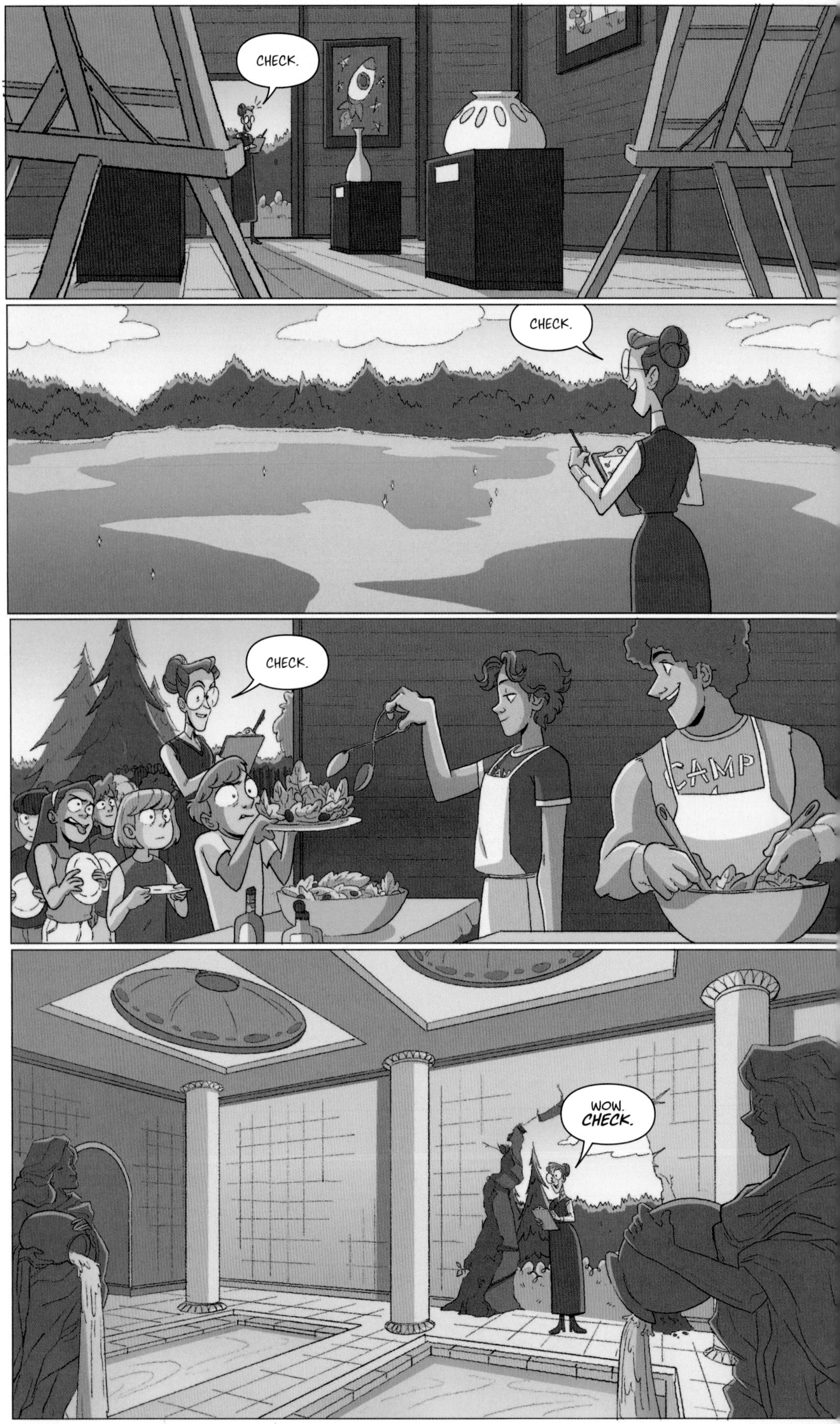
CHECK.
CHECK.
CHECK.
CAMP
WOW.
CHECK.

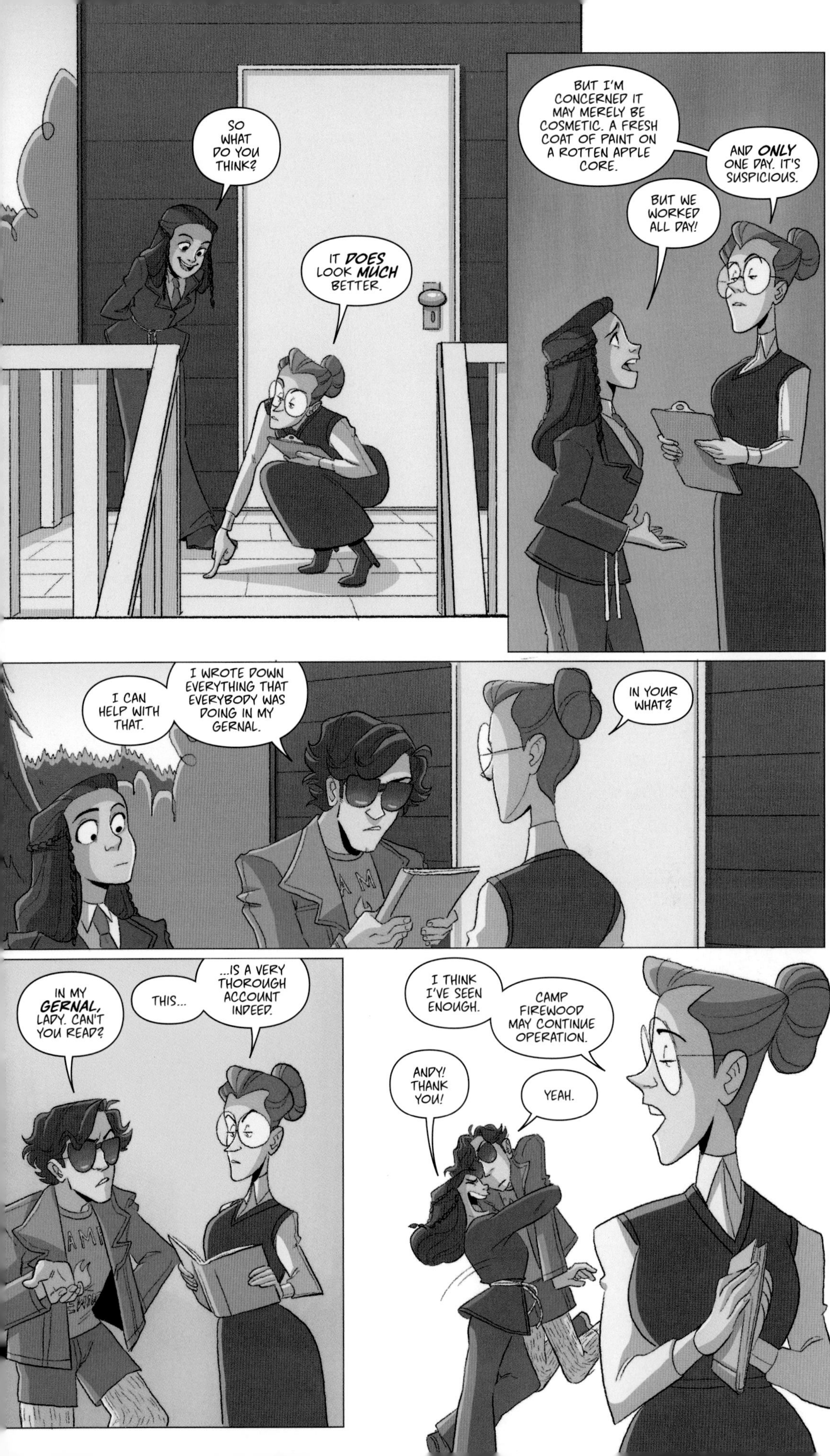

SO WHAT DO YOU THINK?
IT **DOES** LOOK **MUCH** BETTER.
BUT WE WORKED ALL DAY!
AND **ONLY** ONE DAY. IT'S SUSPICIOUS.
BUT I'M CONCERNED IT MAY MERELY BE COSMETIC. A FRESH COAT OF PAINT ON A ROTTEN APPLE CORE.
I CAN HELP WITH THAT.
I WROTE DOWN EVERYTHING THAT EVERYBODY WAS DOING IN MY GERNAL.
IN YOUR WHAT?
IN MY **GERNAL,** LADY. CAN'T YOU READ?
THIS...
...IS A VERY THOROUGH ACCOUNT INDEED.
I THINK I'VE SEEN ENOUGH.
CAMP FIREWOOD MAY CONTINUE OPERATION.
ANDY! THANK YOU!
YEAH.

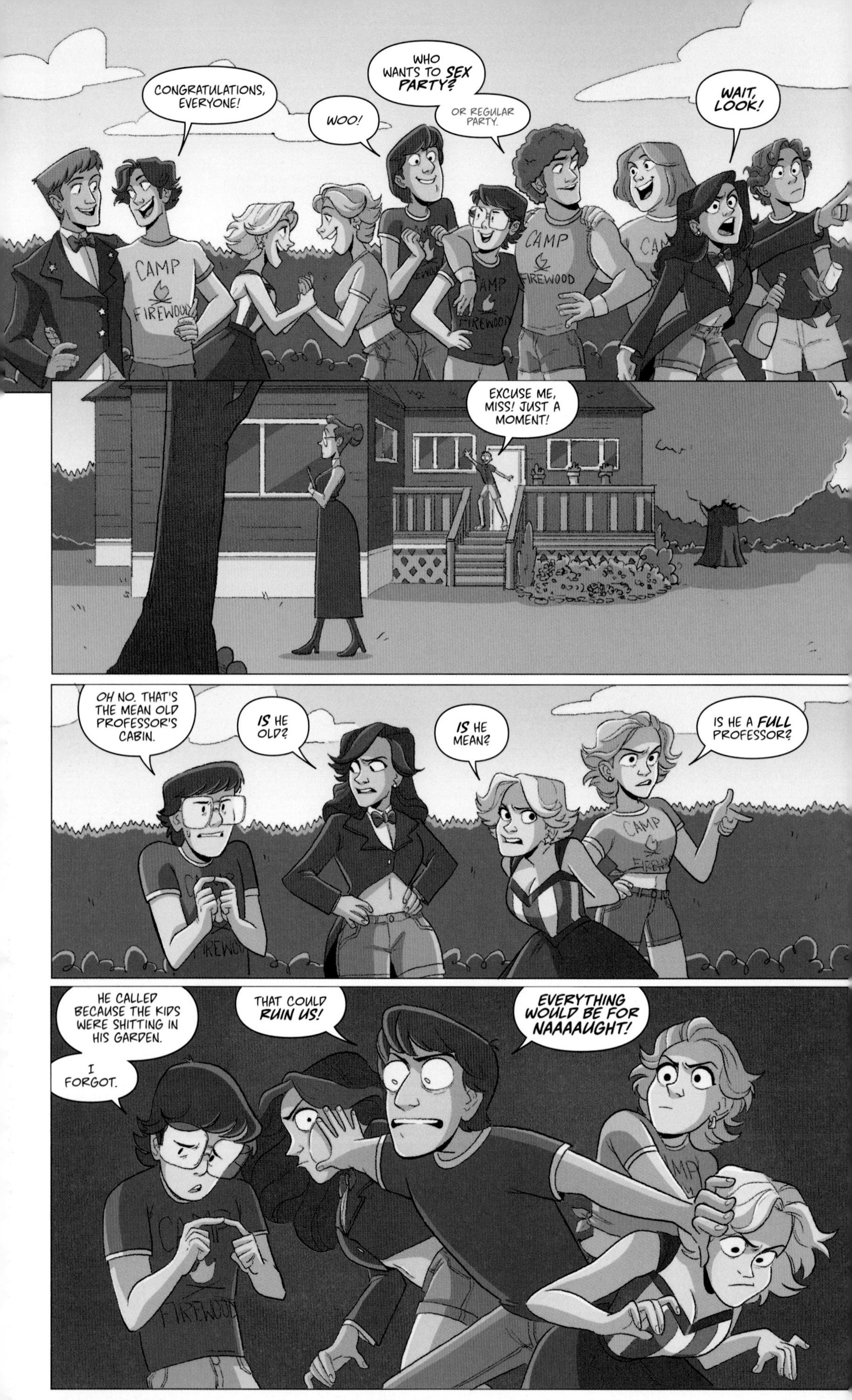
CONGRATULATIONS, EVERYONE!
WOO!
WHO WANTS TO SEX PARTY?
OR REGULAR PARTY.
WAIT, LOOK!
EXCUSE ME, MISS! JUST A MOMENT!
OH NO. THAT'S THE MEAN OLD PROFESSOR'S CABIN.
IS HE OLD?
IS HE MEAN?
IS HE A FULL PROFESSOR?
HE CALLED BECAUSE THE KIDS WERE SHITTING IN HIS GARDEN.
I FORGOT.
THAT COULD RUIN US!
EVERYTHING WOULD BE FOR NAAAAUGHT!

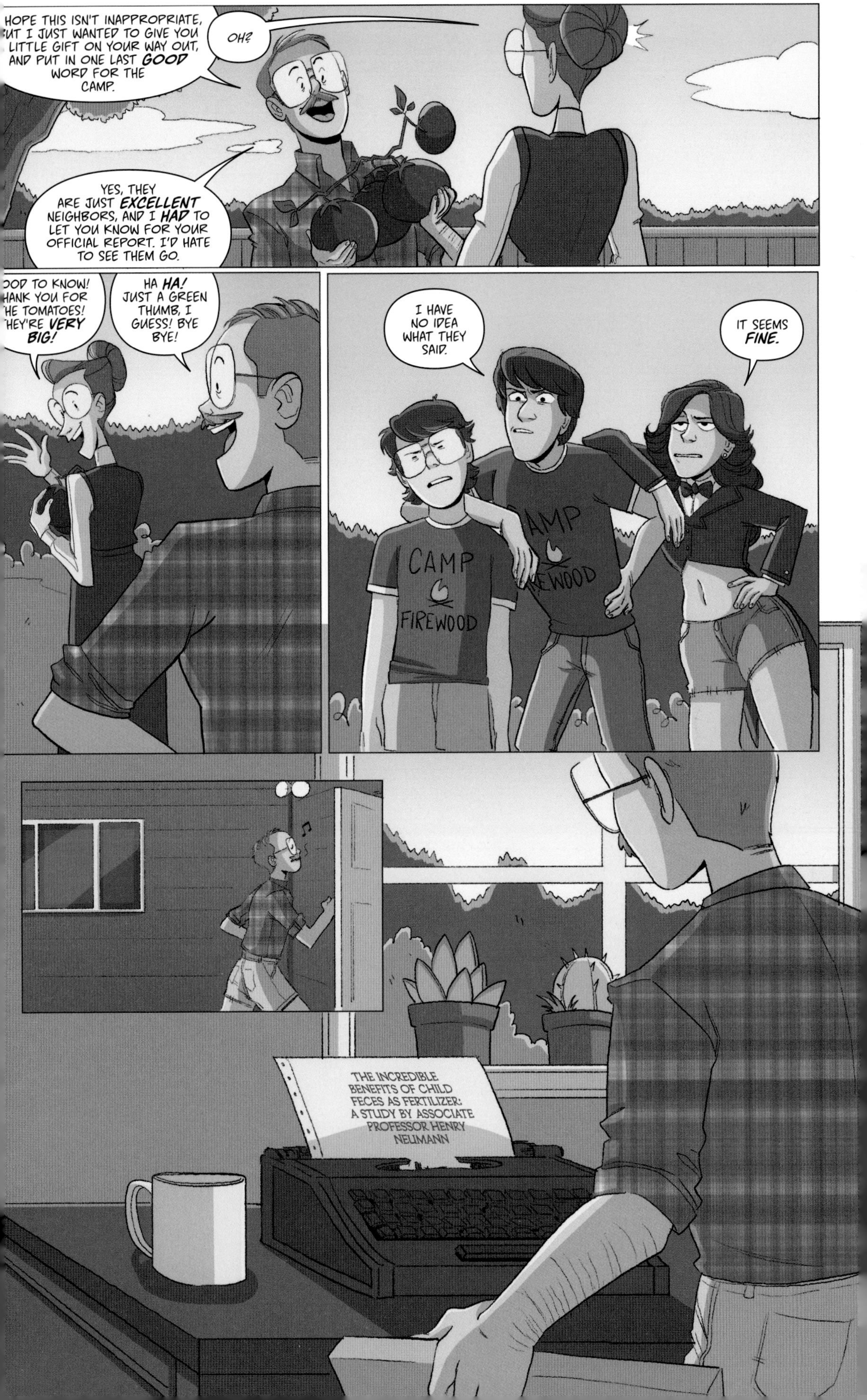

HOPE THIS ISN'T INAPPROPRIATE, UT I JUST WANTED TO GIVE YOU LITTLE GIFT ON YOUR WAY OUT, AND PUT IN ONE LAST GOOD WORD FOR THE CAMP.
OH?
YES, THEY ARE JUST EXCELLENT NEIGHBORS, AND I HAD TO LET YOU KNOW FOR YOUR OFFICIAL REPORT. I'D HATE TO SEE THEM GO.
OOD TO KNOW! HANK YOU FOR HE TOMATOES! HEY'RE VERY BIG!
HA HA! JUST A GREEN THUMB, I GUESS! BYE BYE!
I HAVE NO IDEA WHAT THEY SAID.
IT SEEMS FINE.
CAMP FIREWOOD
CAMP FIREWOOD
THE INCREDIBLE BENEFITS OF CHILD FECES AS FERTILIZER: A STUDY BY ASSOCIATE PROFESSOR HENRY NEUMANN

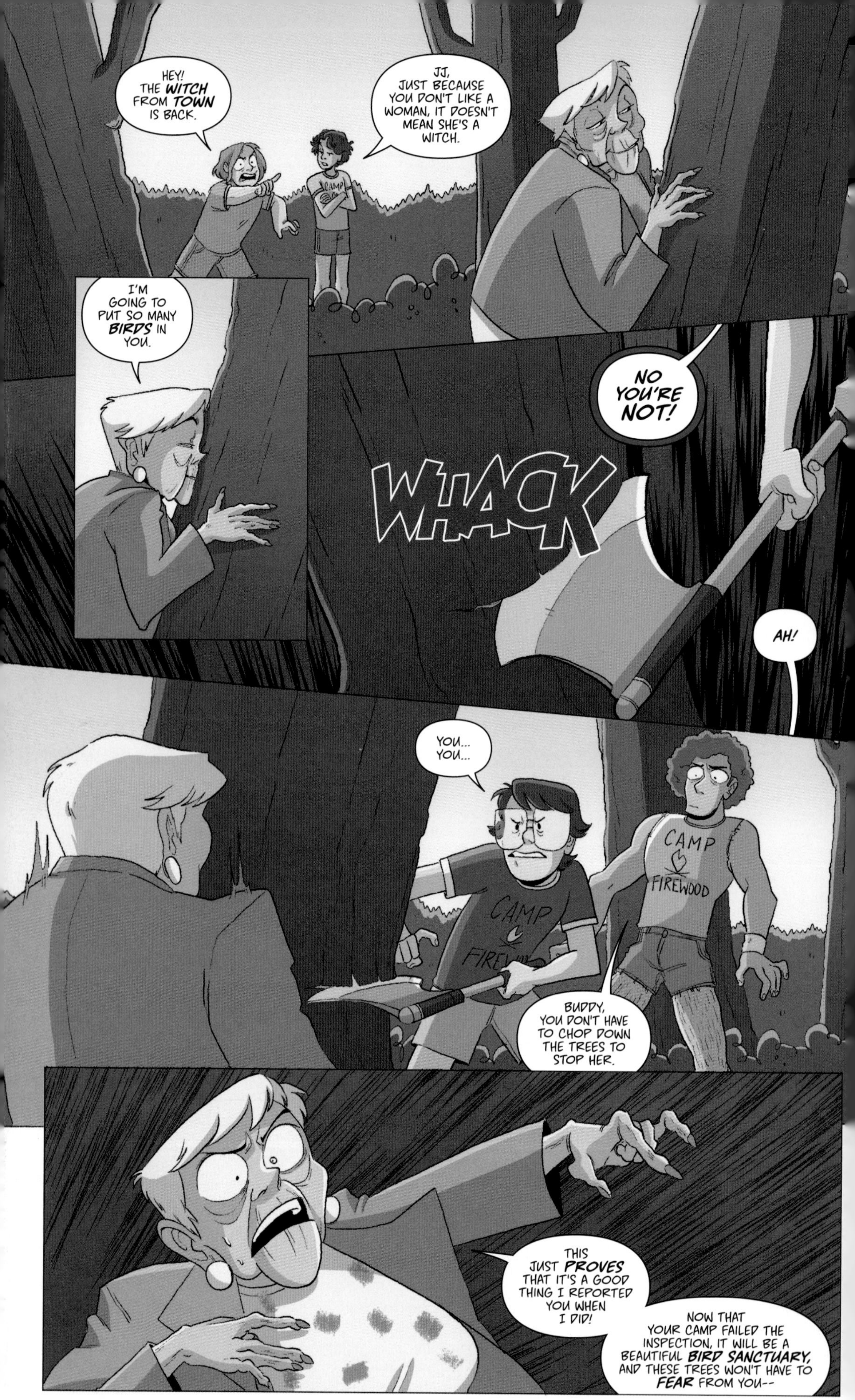
HEY! THE WITCH FROM TOWN IS BACK.
JJ, JUST BECAUSE YOU DON'T LIKE A WOMAN, IT DOESN'T MEAN SHE'S A WITCH.
CAMP
I'M GOING TO PUT SO MANY BIRDS IN YOU.
NO YOU'RE NOT!
WHACK
AH!
YOU... YOU...
CAMP FIREWOOD
CAMP FIREW
BUDDY, YOU DON'T HAVE TO CHOP DOWN THE TREES TO STOP HER.
THIS JUST PROVES THAT IT'S A GOOD THING I REPORTED YOU WHEN I DID!
NOW THAT YOUR CAMP FAILED THE INSPECTION, IT WILL BE A BEAUTIFUL BIRD SANCTUARY, AND THESE TREES WON'T HAVE TO FEAR FROM YOU--

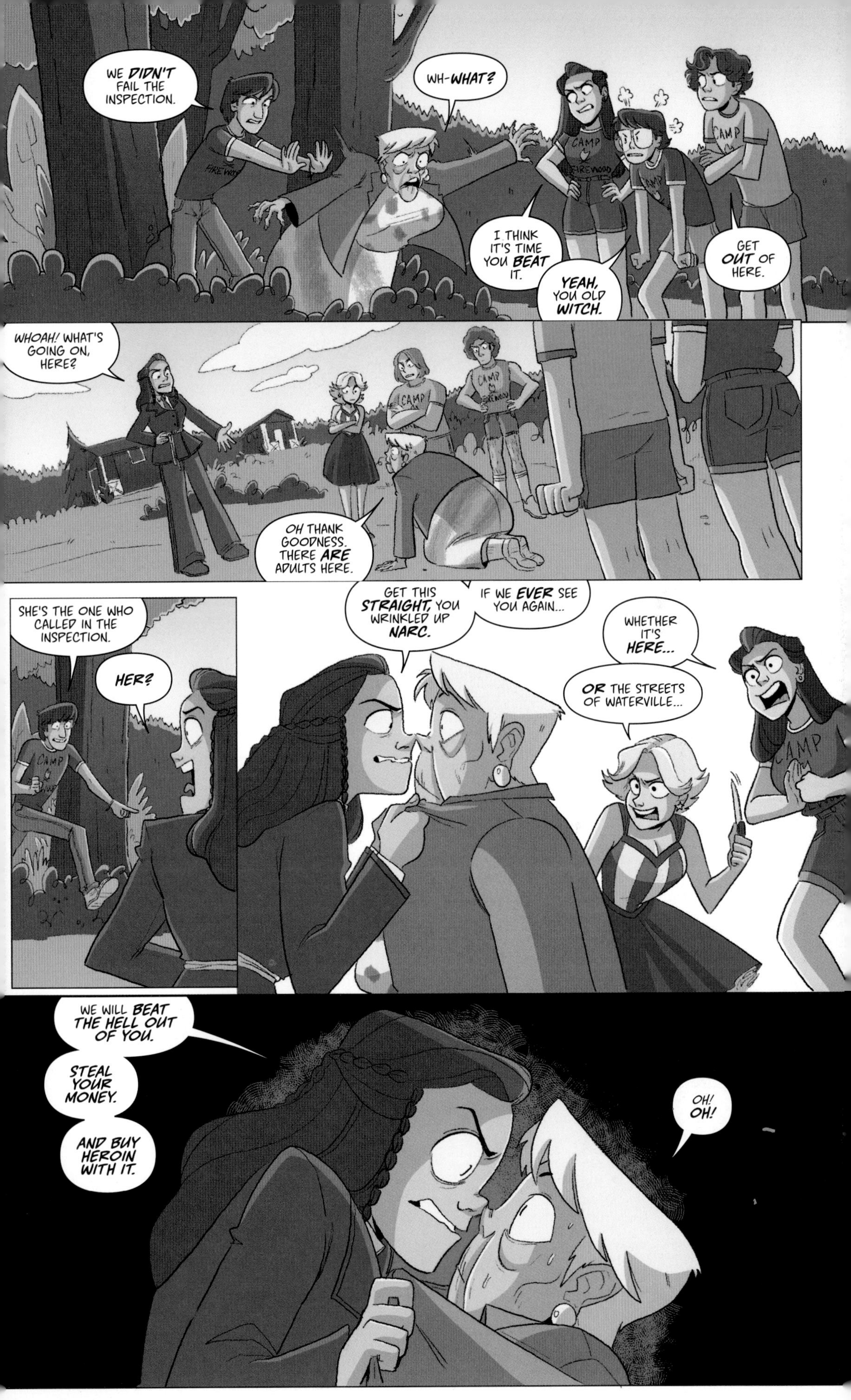
WE DIDN'T FAIL THE INSPECTION.
WH-WHAT?
I THINK IT'S TIME YOU BEAT IT.
YEAH, YOU OLD WITCH.
GET OUT OF HERE.
WHOAH! WHAT'S GOING ON, HERE?
OH THANK GOODNESS. THERE ARE ADULTS HERE.
SHE'S THE ONE WHO CALLED IN THE INSPECTION.
HER?
GET THIS STRAIGHT, YOU WRINKLED UP NARC.
IF WE EVER SEE YOU AGAIN...
WHETHER IT'S HERE...
OR THE STREETS OF WATERVILLE...
WE WILL BEAT THE HELL OUT OF YOU.
STEAL YOUR MONEY.
AND BUY HEROIN WITH IT.
OH! OH!

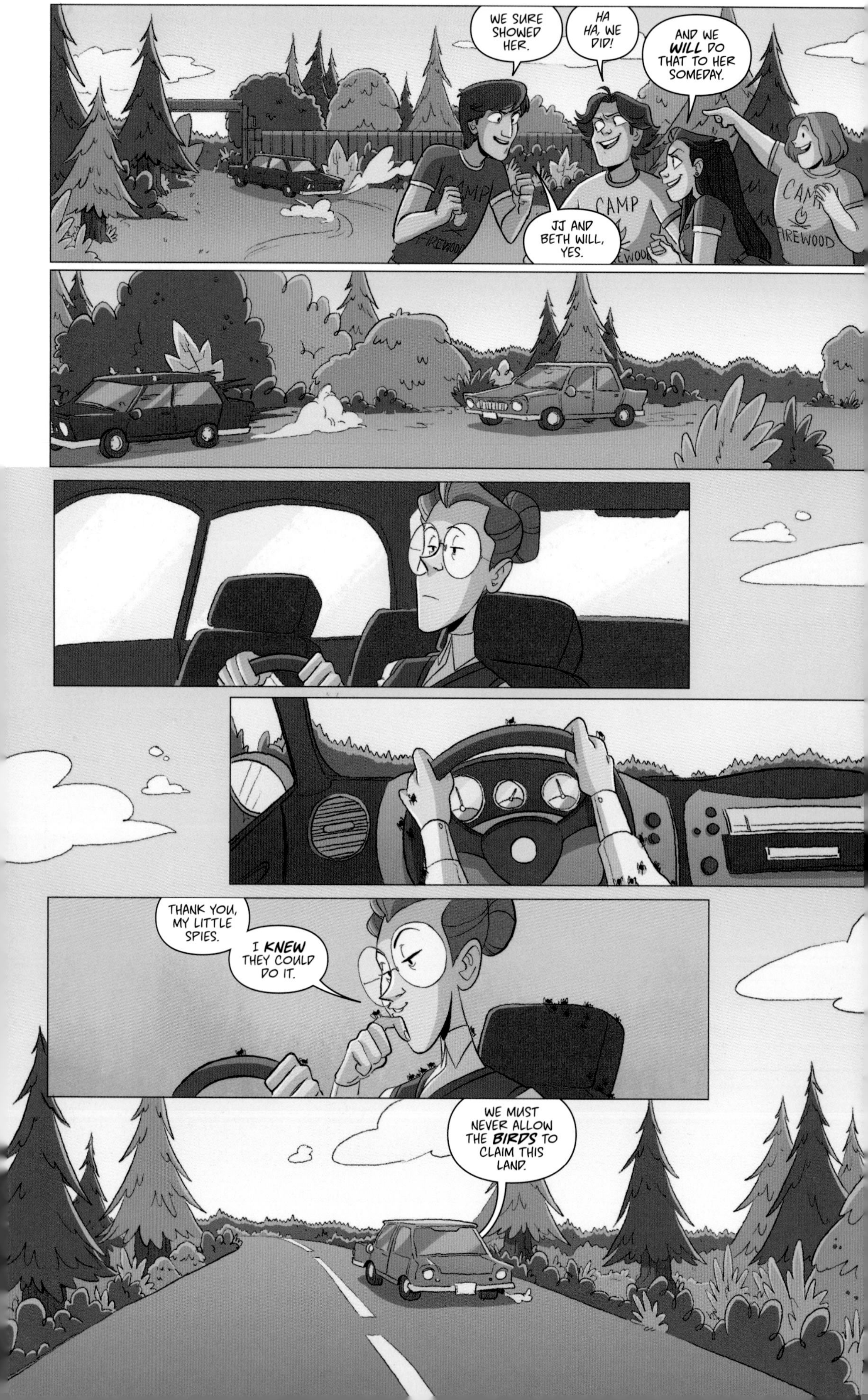
WE SURE SHOWED HER.
HA HA, WE DID!
AND WE *WILL* DO THAT TO HER SOMEDAY.
JJ AND BETH WILL, YES.
CAMP FIREWOOD
THANK YOU, MY LITTLE SPIES.
I *KNEW* THEY COULD DO IT.
WE MUST NEVER ALLOW THE *BIRDS* TO CLAIM THIS LAND.

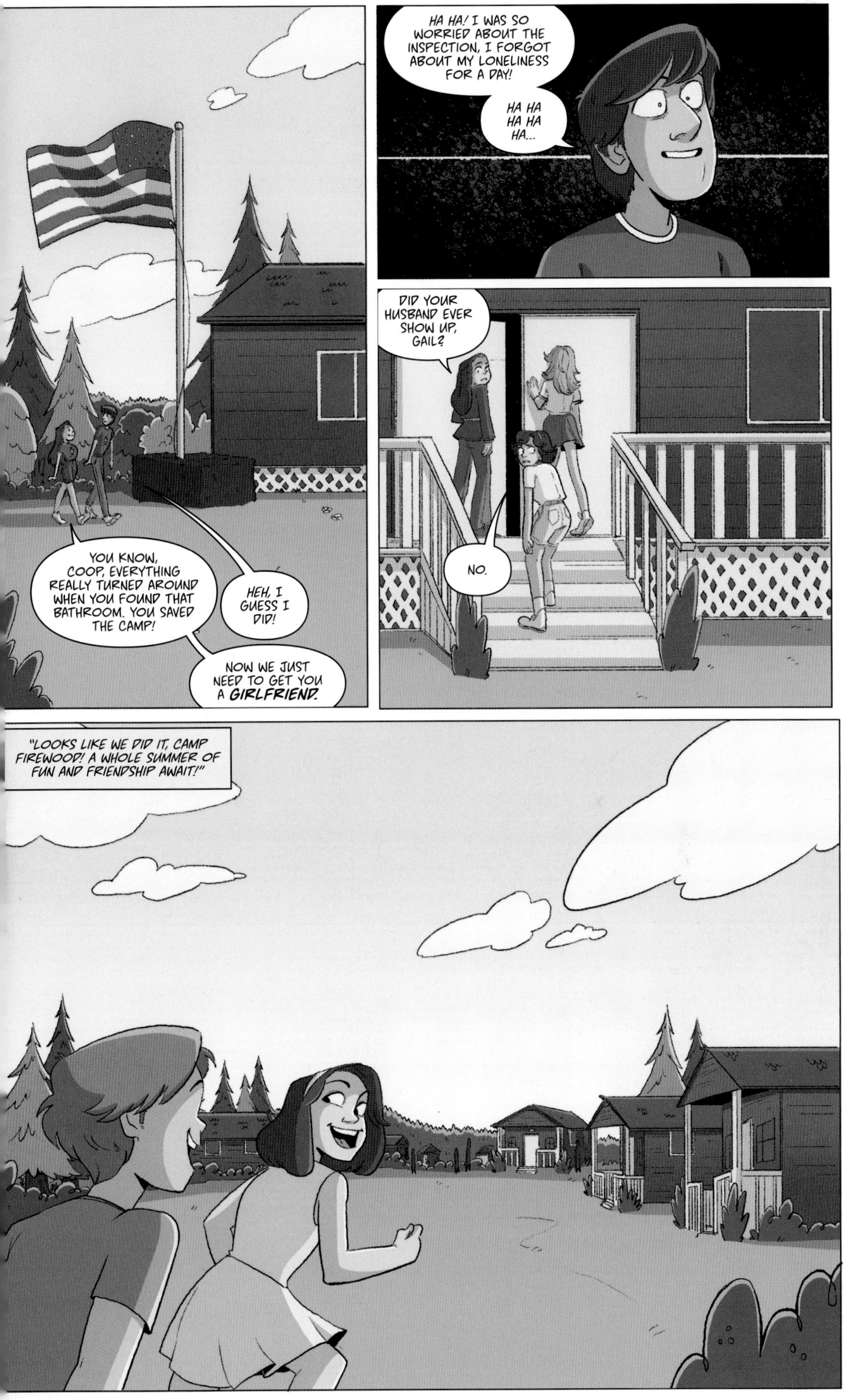
HA HA! I WAS SO WORRIED ABOUT THE INSPECTION, I FORGOT ABOUT MY LONELINESS FOR A DAY!
HA HA HA HA HA...
YOU KNOW, COOP, EVERYTHING REALLY TURNED AROUND WHEN YOU FOUND THAT BATHROOM. YOU SAVED THE CAMP!
HEH, I GUESS I DID!
NOW WE JUST NEED TO GET YOU A GIRLFRIEND.
DID YOUR HUSBAND EVER SHOW UP, GAIL?
NO.
"LOOKS LIKE WE DID IT, CAMP FIREWOOD! A WHOLE SUMMER OF FUN AND FRIENDSHIP AWAIT!"

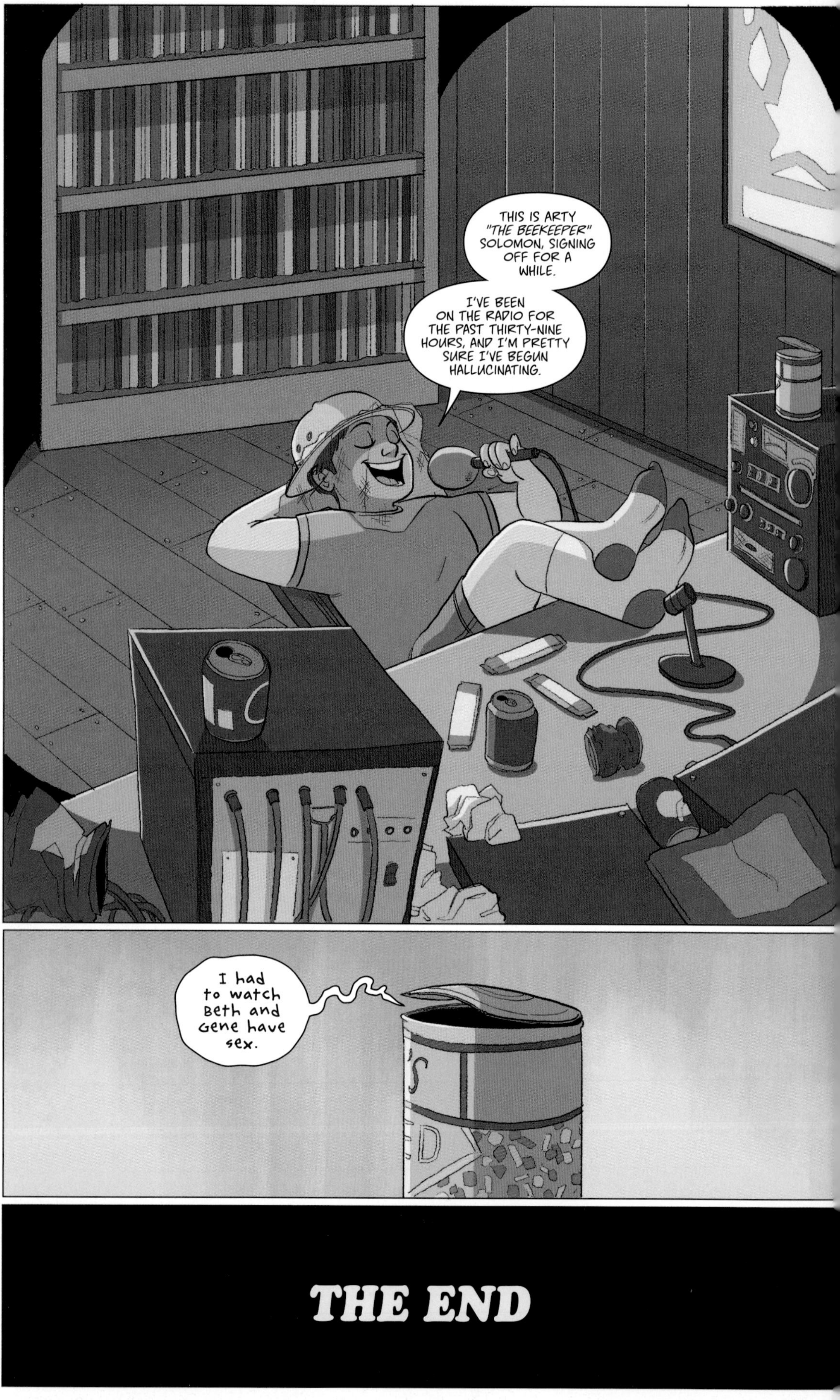
THIS IS ARTY "THE BEEKEEPER" SOLOMON, SIGNING OFF FOR A WHILE.
I'VE BEEN ON THE RADIO FOR THE PAST THIRTY-NINE HOURS, AND I'M PRETTY SURE I'VE BEGUN HALLUCINATING.
I had to watch Beth and Gene have sex.

THE END

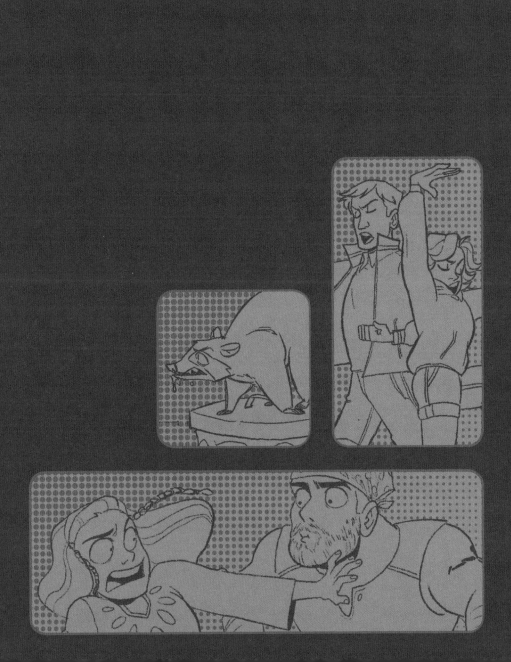

WET HOT AMERICAN SUMMER

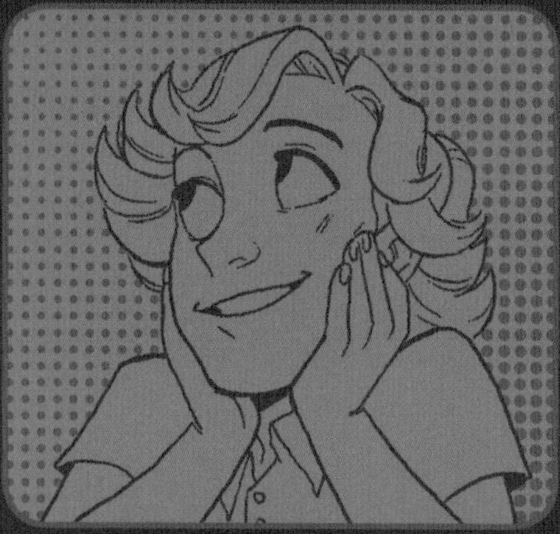

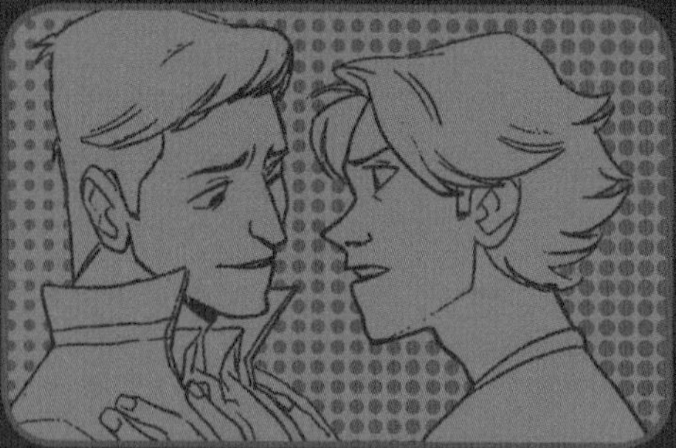

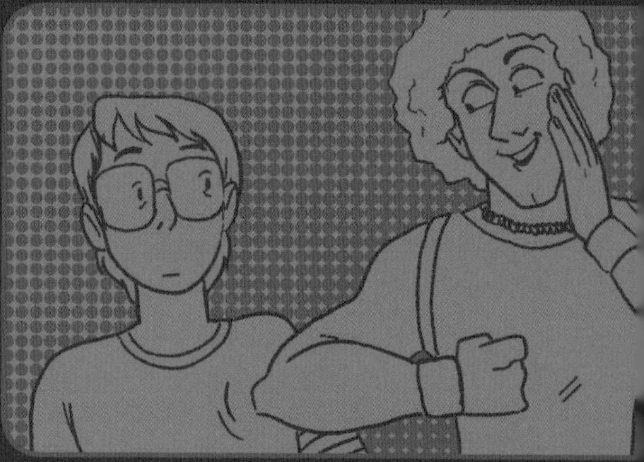

BONUS MATERIAL

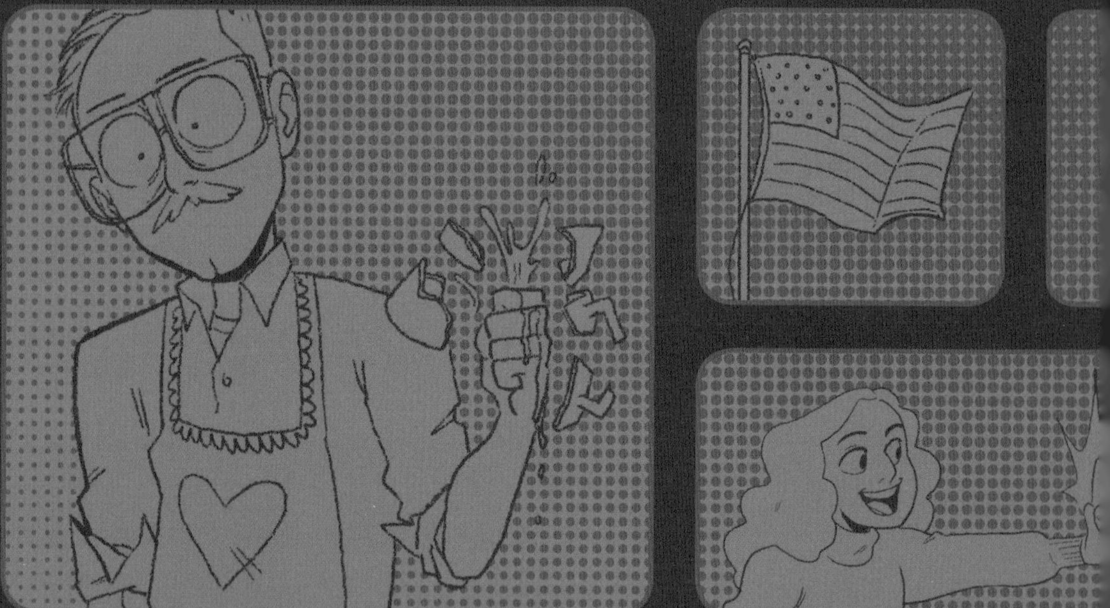

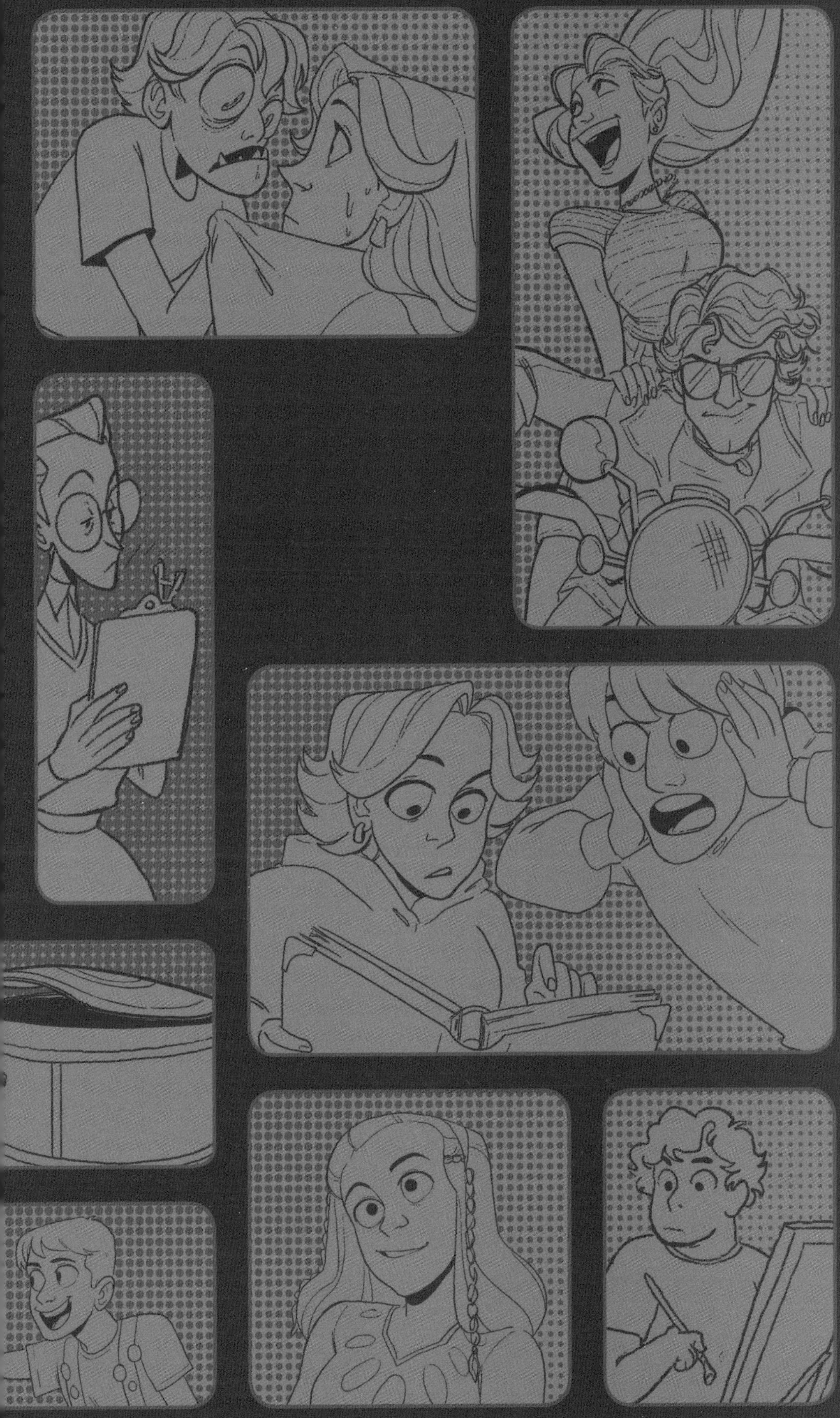

COOP

KATIE

CHARACTER DESIGNS BY NOAH HAYES

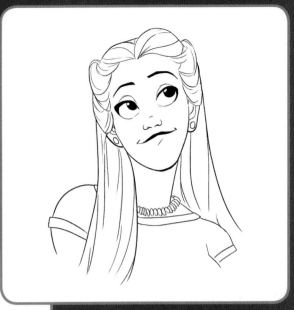

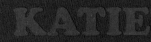

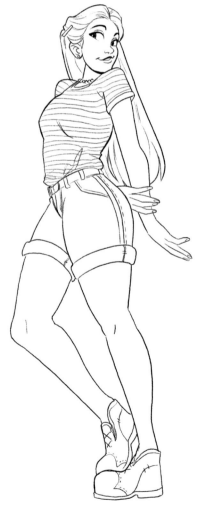

ANDY

GARY

CHARACTER DESIGNS BY NOAH HAYES

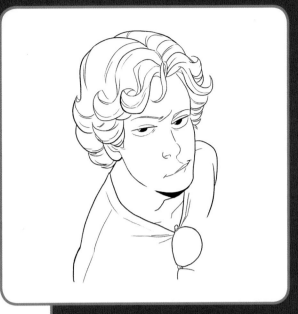

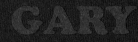

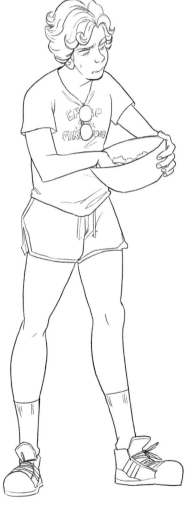

RON

WET HOT MEMORIES

When a mutual friend introduced me to "a couple of really funny guys with a really funny script" about twenty years ago, I didn't adequately prepare myself for just *how* funny and *what kind* of funny he meant (guys and script, both). I was a young New York producer with only a few credits to my name, and to find some teammates with such a similar sensibility and approach felt really right in a way it hadn't before.

Stories about the impossible conditions under which we made the movie have circulated forever; while it's true that the weather was constantly brutal, the location often inhospitable, and the money not nearly enough to do what we wanted to do, it's equally true that it was the most fun I've ever had on a shoot. On and off set, the unshakeable attitude, the depth of talent, and the fun vibe of the entire cast and crew was a constant, and I think it shines through in the karmic good will *Wet Hot* has spread in the years since.

One particular day during production really captures the *Wet Hot* experience for me. After weeks of faking beautiful weather in never-ending downpours just to stay on schedule and on budget, a day with not only rain but lightning storms was predicted. For safety we felt we had no choice but to postpone shooting—not a small deal when you're tight on time and money. So naturally we woke up to beautiful blue skies and what would've been the most perfect conditions of the whole shoot. A gamble gone wrong, a day wasted, but... Frisbee on the lawn! Beach blankets at the lake! Picnics and card games and crosswords and laughs—and maybe even some drinking and smoking. The perfect metaphor for the film overall: making something funny and weird and sweet and lasting through the talent and camaraderie of great people in difficult circumstances.

At a big awards event celebrating the best independent films of 2001, a host called *Wet Hot* "our guilty pleasure." That always stayed with me—it was said in good fun but it hinted at the idea that movies like this are inherently less valuable than the badly lit, dysfunctional family dramas which were staples of the indie film scene at the time. *Wet Hot* and the world it created are no guilty pleasures—offbeat and hilarious, yes, just like the incredible guys who walked into my office twenty years ago—but also full of goodness, heart, and wonder, same as those very people. And so it endures!

Howard Bernstein
Producer, *Wet Hot American Summer*
August 2018

CAMP FIREWOOD
1981
28 RAINY DAYS

CAMP FIREWOOD

Waterville, Maine

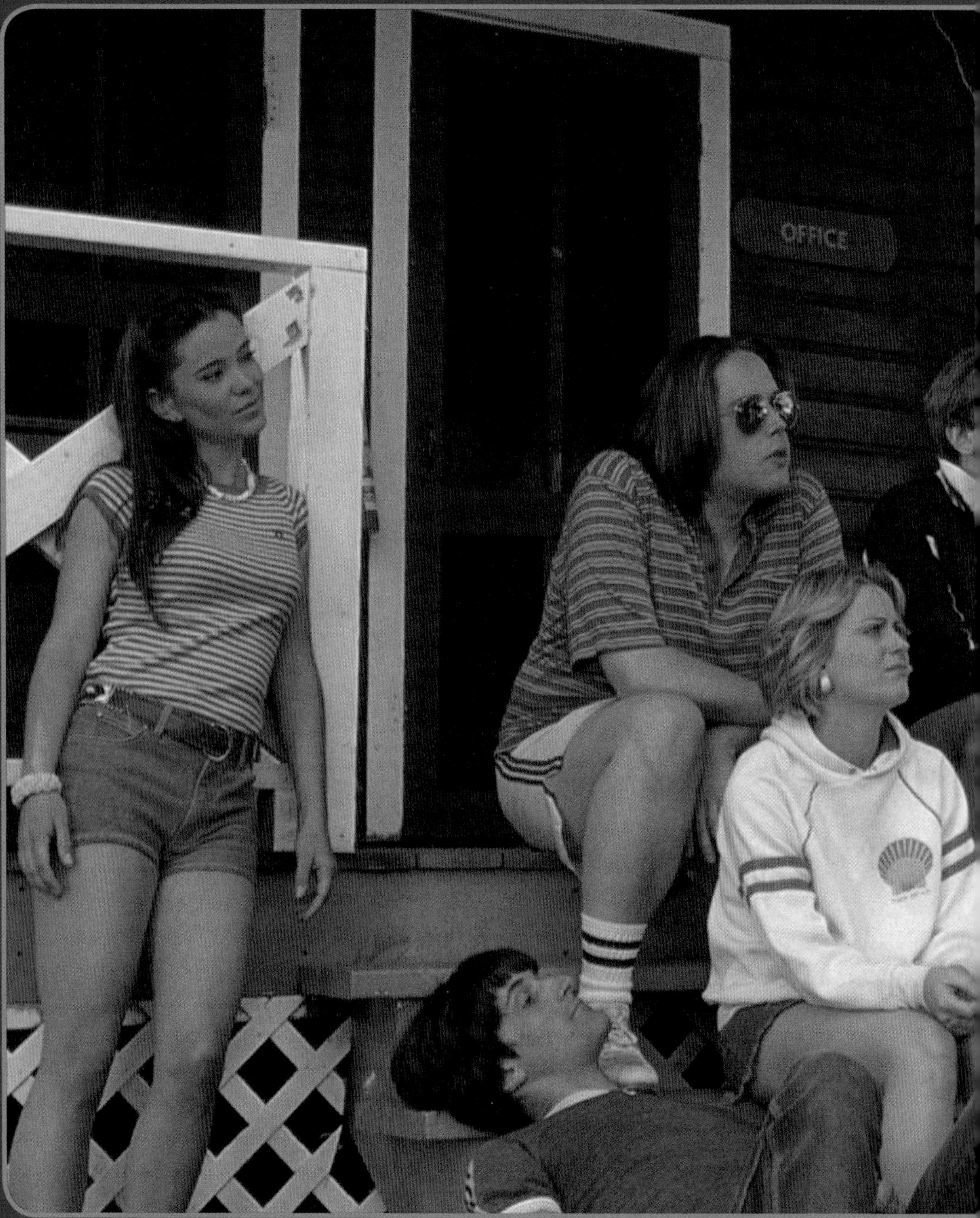
OFFICE

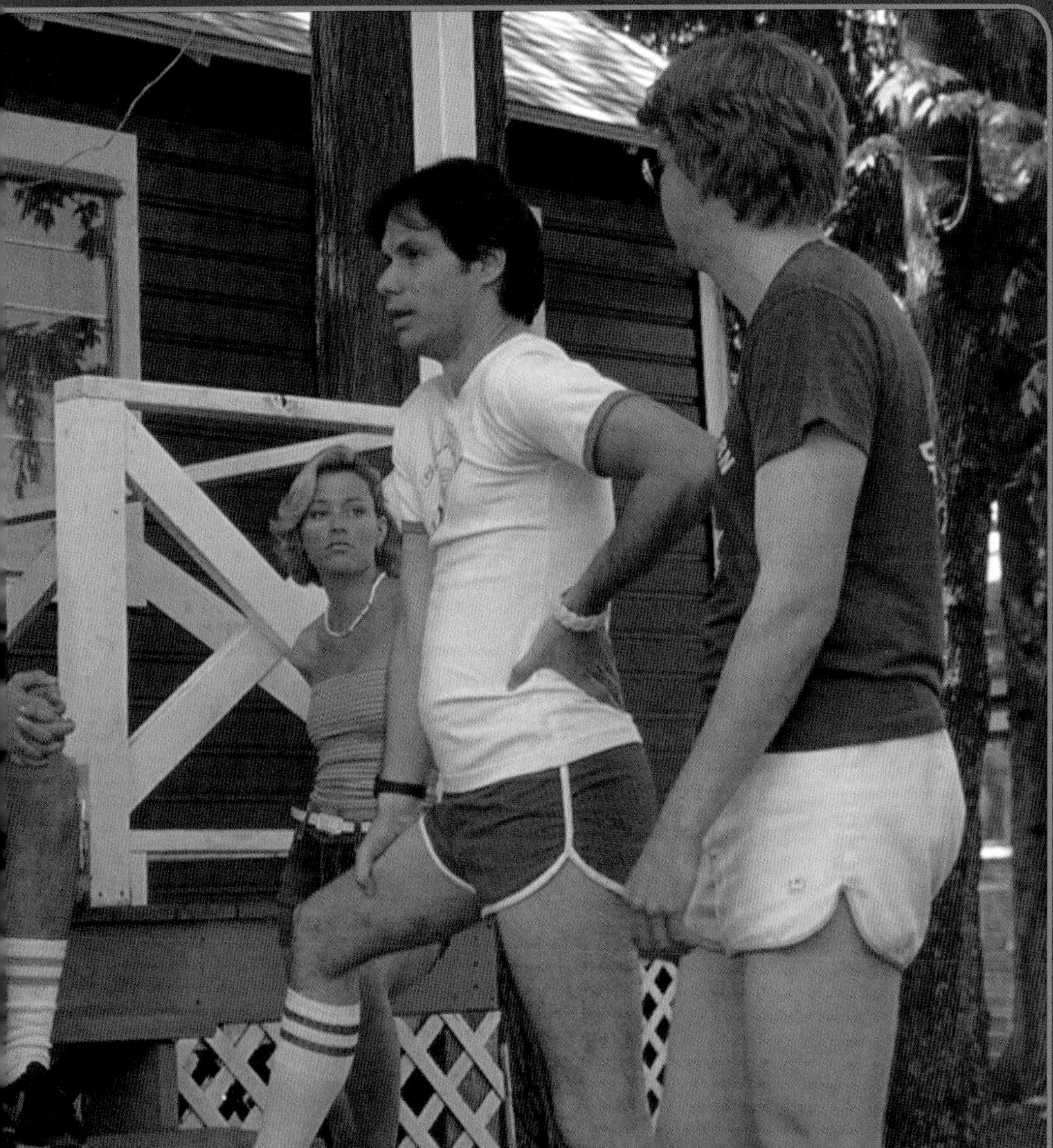

"Hey, let's all promise that in ten years from today, we'll meet again, and we'll see what kind of people we've blossomed into."

Ben

"Yeah, whatever. I guess I'm not all smart like you."

Andy

"I may regret saying this, but how dare you usurp my authority as producer...director-slash-choreographer of the talent show. I need you to know I have been busting my balls, woman!"

Susie

BONUS MATERIAL

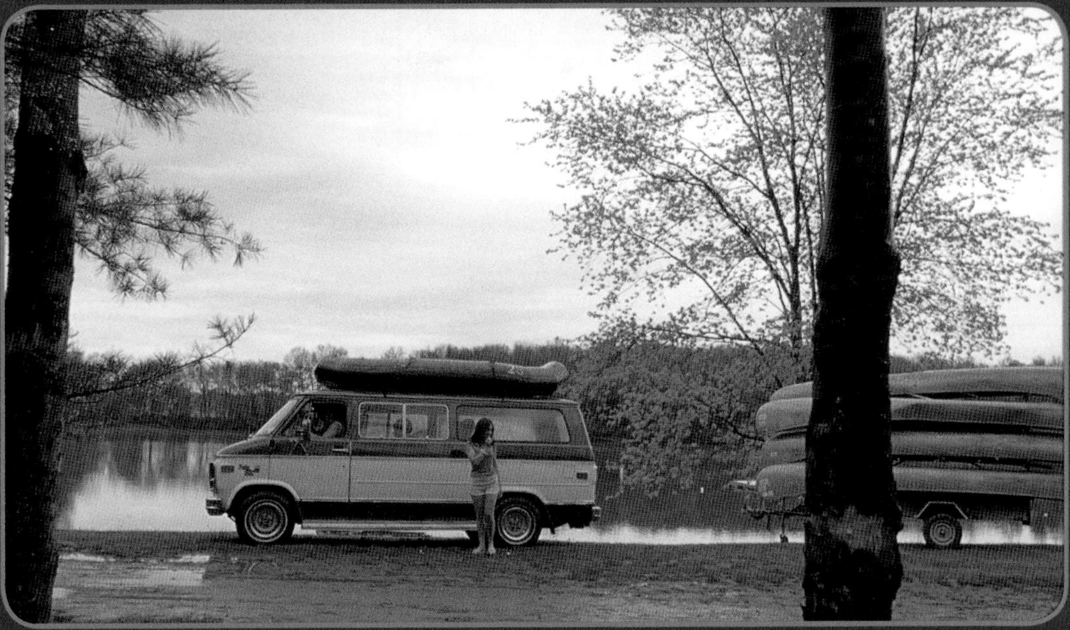

"You got a stick of gum, Victor?"
Abby

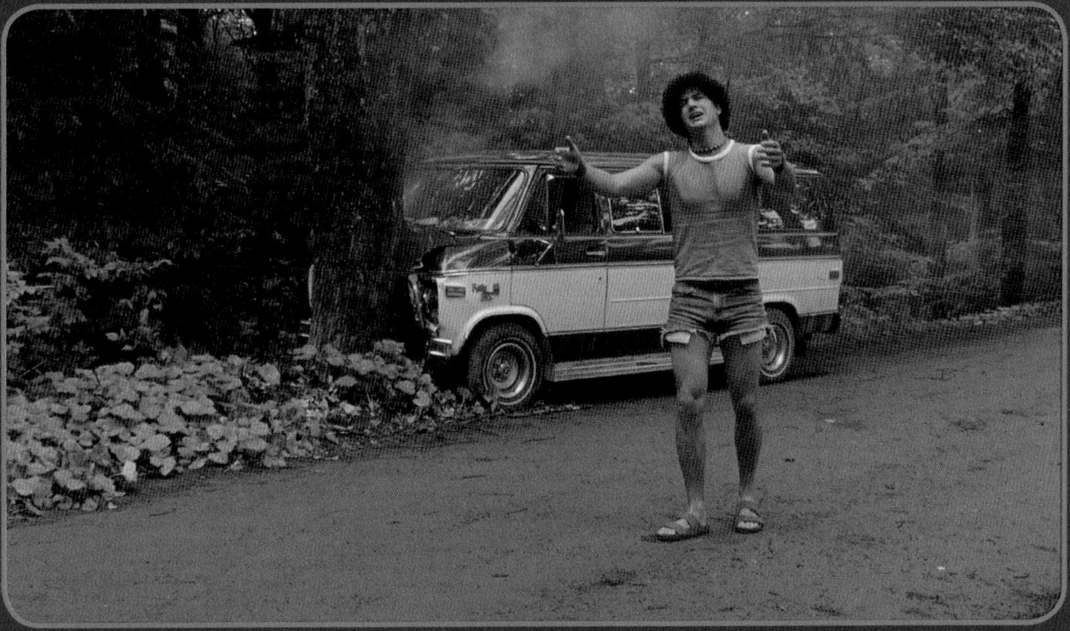

"Wait for me, Abbie Bernstein!"
Victor

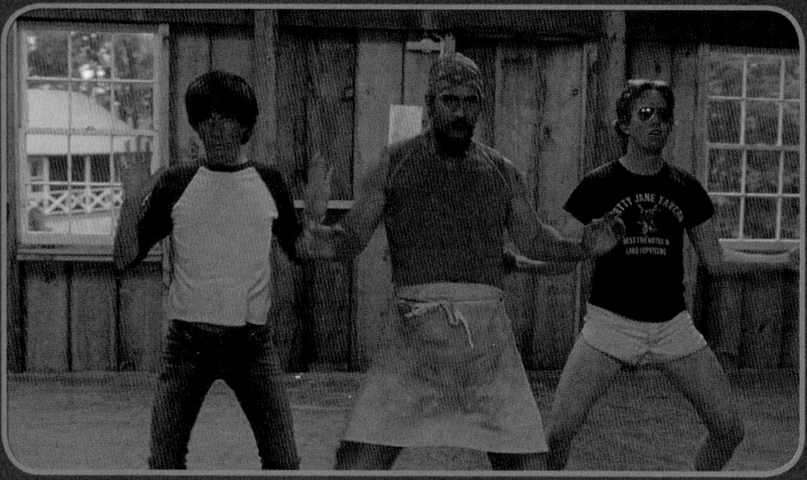

"You are ready to be taught the new way."
Gene

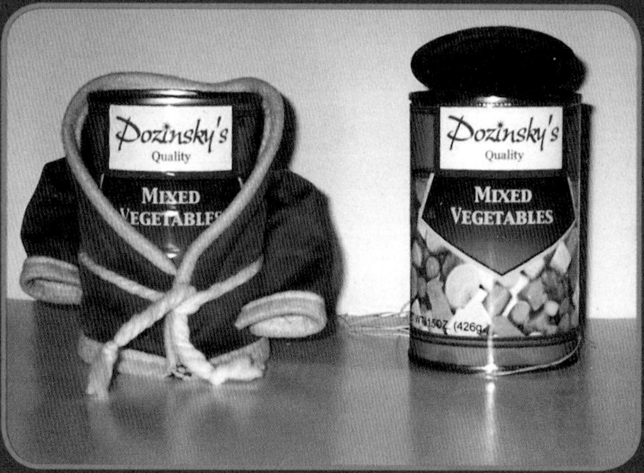
Pozinsky's
Quality
MIXED VEGETABLES
Pozinsky's
Quality
MIXED VEGETABLES

"If you wanna smear mud on your ass, smear mud on your ass—just be honest about it. Look, Gene, I've never told anyone this before, but I can suck my own dick, and I do it a lot."
Can of Vegetables

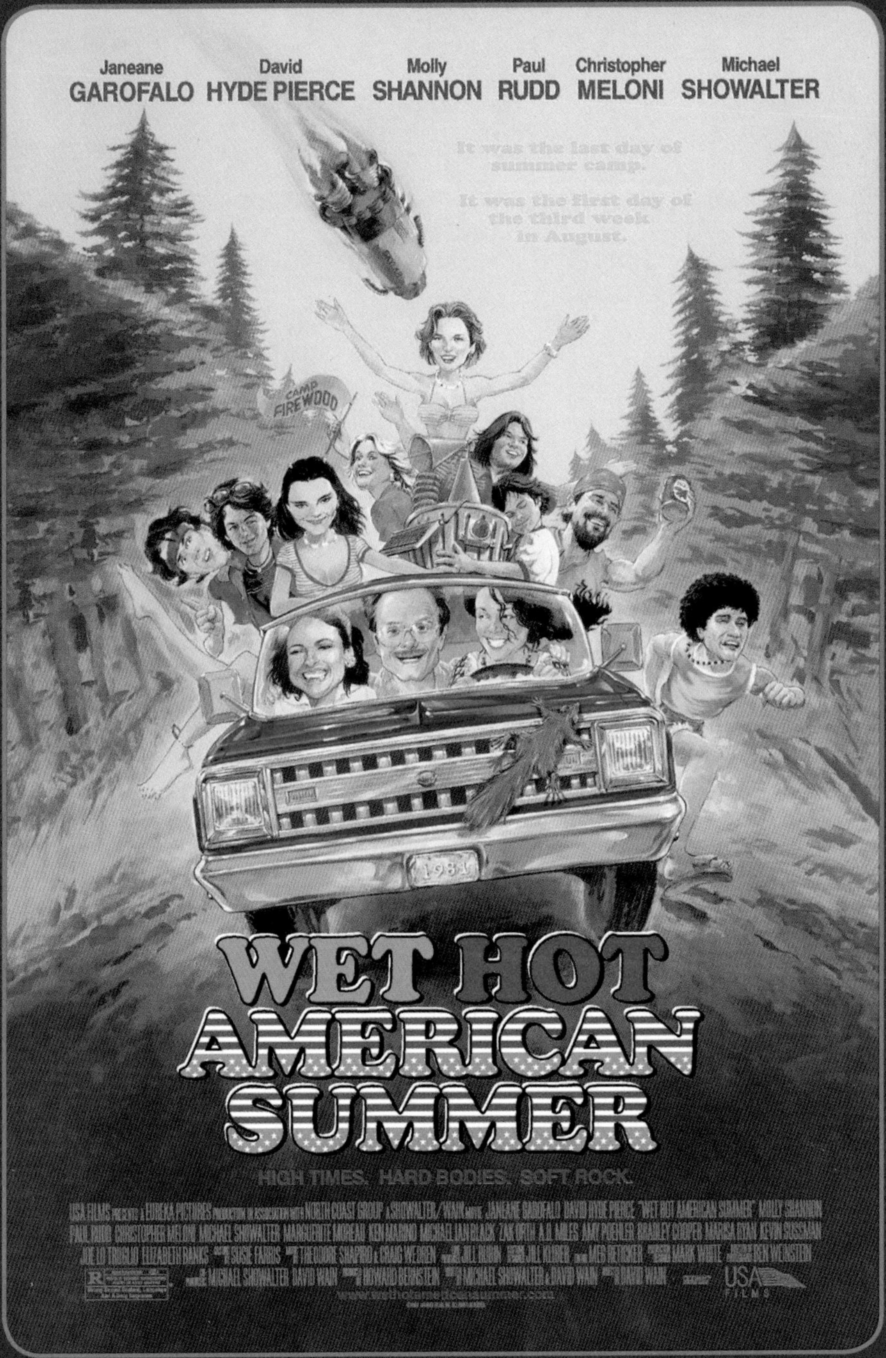
Janeane GAROFALO
David HYDE PIERCE
Molly SHANNON
Paul RUDD
Christopher MELONI
Michael SHOWALTER
It was the last day of summer camp.
It was the first day of the third week in August.
CAMP FIREWOOD
1981
WET HOT AMERICAN SUMMER
HIGH TIMES. HARD BODIES. SOFT ROCK.
USA FILMS EUREKA PICTURES NORTH COAST GROUP SHOWALTER/WAIN JANEANE GAROFALO DAVID HYDE PIERCE "WET HOT AMERICAN SUMMER" MOLLY SHANNON
PAUL RUDD CHRISTOPHER MELONI MICHAEL SHOWALTER MARGUERITE MOREAU KEN MARINO MICHAEL IAN BLACK ZAK ORTH A.D. MILES AMY POEHLER BRADLEY COOPER MARISA RYAN KEVIN SUSSMAN
JOE LO TRUGLIO ELIZABETH BANKS SUSIE FARRIS THEODORE SHAPIRO & CRAIG WEDREN JILL RUBIN JILL KLIBER MEG BETTCHER MARK WHITE KEN WEINSTEIN
MICHAEL SHOWALTER DAVID WAIN HOWARD BERNSTEIN MICHAEL SHOWALTER & DAVID WAIN DAVID WAIN
USA FILMS

DISCOVER
VISIONARY CREATORS

THE WOODS
JAMES TYNION IV • MICHAEL DIALYNAS
VOL. 1
THE ARROW

"The Spire is fantastic! My kind of genre free-for-all."
—BRIAN K. VAUGHAN (Saga)
THE SPIRE
SIMON SPURRIER
JEFF STOKELY
ANDRÉ MAY

MARK WAID · PETER KRAUSE
IRREDEEMABLE
AFTERWORD BY GRANT MORRISON

J.G. JONES
MARK WAID
STRANGE FRUIT
Foreword by
ELVIS MITCHELL

MICHAEL ALAN NELSON
DAN MORA
GABRIEL CASSATA
HEXED
THE HARLOT & THE THIEF VOLUME ONE

ABNETT & CULBARD
WILD'S END
FIRST LIGHT
"IT'S REALLY GREAT!"
JEFF LEMIRE

BOOM! STUDIOS

AVAILABLE AT YOUR LOCAL COMICS SHOP AND BOOKSTORE
WWW.**BOOM-STUDIOS**.COM

James Tynion IV

The Woods
Volume 1
ISBN: 978-1-60886-454-6 | $9.99 US
Volume 2
ISBN: 978-1-60886-495-9 | $14.99 US
Volume 3
ISBN: 978-1-60886-773-8 | $14.99 US

The Backstagers
Volume 1
ISBN: 978-1-60886-993-0 | $14.99 US

Simon Spurrier

Six-Gun Gorilla
ISBN: 978-1-60886-390-7 | $19.99 US

The Spire
ISBN: 978-1-60886-913-8 | $29.99 US

Weavers
ISBN: 978-1-60886-963-3 | $19.99 US

Mark Waid

Irredeemable
Volume 1
ISBN: 978-1-93450-690-5 | $16.99 US
Volume 2
ISBN: 978-1-60886-000-5 | $16.99 US

Incorruptible
Volume 1
ISBN: 978-1-60886-015-9 | $16.99 US
Volume 2
ISBN: 978-1-60886-028-9 | $16.99 US

Strange Fruit
ISBN: 978-1-60886-872-8 | $24.99 US

Michael Alan Nelson

Hexed The Harlot & The Thief
Volume 1
ISBN: 978-1-60886-718-9 | $14.99 US
Volume 2
ISBN: 978-1-60886-816-2 | $14.99 US

Day Men
Volume 1
ISBN: 978-1-60886-393-8 | $9.99 US
Volume 2
ISBN: 978-1-60886-852-0 | $9.99 US

Dan Abnett

Wild's End
Volume 1: First Light
ISBN: 978-1-60886-735-6 | $19.99 US
Volume 2: The Enemy Within
ISBN: 978-1-60886-877-3 | $19.99 US

Hypernaturals
Volume 1
ISBN: 978-1-60886-298-6 | $16.99 US
Volume 2
ISBN: 978-1-60886-319-8 | $19.99 US

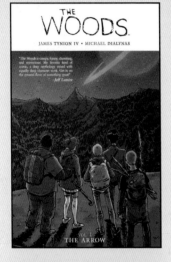

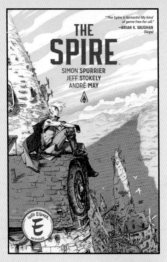

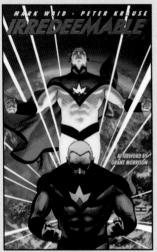

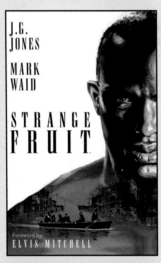

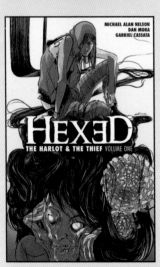

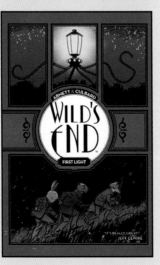

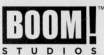